P9-CML-990

A WOMAN'S GUIDE TO RECOVERY

DISCARD

CHICAGO PUBLIC LIBRARY
SOUTH CHICAGO BRANCH
9055 S. HOUSTON AVE. 60617

DISCARD

A Woman's Guide
to Recovery

WRITTEN BY
Brenda Iliff

DIRECTOR OF THE
HAZELDEN WOMEN'S RECOVERY CENTER

HAZELDEN

CHICAGO PUBLIC LIBRARY
SOUTH CHICAGO BRANCH
9055 S. HOUSTON AVE. 60617

Hazelden
Center City, Minnesota 55012
hazelden.org

© 2008 by Hazelden Foundation
All rights reserved. Published 2008
Printed in the United States of America

No part of this publication may be reproduced, stored in a retrieval system, or transmitted in any form or by any means—electronic, mechanical, photocopying, recording, scanning, or otherwise—without the express written permission of the publisher. Failure to comply with these terms may expose you to legal action and damages for copyright infringement.

ISBN: 978-1-59285-479-0

Library of Congress Cataloging-in-Publication Data

Iliff, Brenda.
    A woman's guide to recovery / written by Brenda Iliff.
        p.   cm.
    Includes index.
    ISBN-13: 978-1-59285-479-0 (softcover)
        1. Women drug addicts—United States.   2. Women alcoholics—United States.
    3. Women alcoholics—Rehabilitation—United States.   4. Women drug addicts—
    Rehabilitation—United States.   5. Twelve-step programs—United States.   I. Title.
    HV4999.W65I53 2008
    616.86'03082—dc22

                                                        2007038959

All personal stories are used with permission. Names, dates, details, and circumstances have been changed to protect anonymity.

The views expressed herein are solely those of the author. This book is not an official publication of Alcoholics Anonymous World Services, Inc., nor does it necessarily represent the policies or practices of the AA Fellowship, a program of recovery from alcoholism.

Alcoholics Anonymous, AA, and the Big Book are registered trademarks of Alcoholics Anonymous World Services, Inc.

This book is not intended as a substitute for the advice of health care professionals.

12 11 10 09 08   6 5 4 3 2 1

Cover design by Theresa Gedig
Interior design by Ann Sudmeier
Typesetting by Prism Publishing Center

SOC

RO415612638

 To those who are about to find out that
"it never has to hurt like this again"
and to those who love them

CHICAGO PUBLIC LIBRARY
SOUTH CHICAGO BRANCH
9055 S. HOUSTON AVE. 60617

Real living begins on the far side of despair.

:: JEAN-PAUL SARTRE

Contents

Acknowledgments

I WISH TO EXPRESS MY GRATITUDE TO THOSE WHO HAVE gone before me and whose commitment to recovery makes possible so many stories like those of the women in this book as well as my own. While there are many who deserve to be named in this book, due to the anonymity of the Twelve Step fellowship they will remain nameless, but their stories and wisdom are included with a swell of gratitude. They have touched this world in a powerful way.

I wish to express thanks to Rebecca Post, a former editor at Hazelden, who suggested this book. She helped me realize the dream of a lifetime: to pass on information about the freedom of recovery to women seeking help. Karen Chernyaev, who edited the book, framed and guided the process. Her knowledge of both the publishing and addiction fields glowed as she provided guidance. The real backbone of this book was provided by the step-by-step work of Pat Samples, who took what I wrote and rewrote and kindly suggested changes. Her ability to give feedback in a kind yet helpful manner is a living example of wisdom and humility. Working with the experience and skill of these three women was a true gift.

Personally, I wish to express gratitude to my parents, family, and longtime friend Wendy, who have made the lifelong journey with me, every step of the way. Several decades, many years, one step at a time. May others be so blessed.

Introduction

THIS IS A BOOK OF GREAT HOPE. ITS PURPOSE IS TO ASSIST women in their recovery from chemical dependency.

Addiction is messy. Very messy. Like a hurricane, it leaves massive devastation in its path. The addict spins helplessly at the mercy of the storm, losing peace of mind and self-respect. She may even lose her friends, loved ones, reputation, job, health, freedom, or life. Those closest to her—family, friends, co-workers or schoolmates, community members, and others—helplessly watch her self-destruction, deeply pained over their inability to stop it. Meanwhile, they may pay dearly for her lies, failures, cruelty, and recklessness. So does society as a whole. The hurricane of addiction is no respecter of persons. It hurts those in its path and even those nearby. No one escapes unscathed.

The good news is that, despite the terrible devastation of addiction, many women have found a way out. There is a solution! Regardless of their drug of choice, lifestyle, mental and physical concerns, economic concerns, sexual orientation, race, culture, religion, or other differences, women are able to achieve freedom from the mess of addiction. If you're a woman whose use of alcohol or other drugs is creating havoc in your life—even in small ways— you'll find hope in these pages. If you're a person who cares about an addict, this book will help you understand why it's so hard for her to stop using and assure you that she can recover.

Although this book is written for women, it's not meant to be exclusive or to create a separation between women and men. In fact, the core elements of addiction and recovery are the same for every addict, male or female. For that reason, addiction is often called the great equalizer. Yet, just as we take into account many other factors in dealing with someone's addiction and recovery, so must we consider the person's gender.

Certain issues unique to women affect how they become addicted and how they recover. Women get started down the addiction path for different reasons than men do. Their addiction progresses faster, and generally their body and spirit have suffered more damage by the time they're at the door of recovery. In addition, women typically touch more lives by their addiction since they are often expected to be the central stabilizing force in their families and communities. And women work on their recovery differently than men do. Because of their innate desire for connection, many women find that recovery is a natural process for them. All of these reasons have inspired the creation of this book to offer information and support to women.

A Woman's Guide to Recovery shows how women who have been nearly destroyed by addiction find their way out of the mess. It includes many stories of women who have found recovery,* condensed from interviews with them. These stories are diverse, representing various drugs of choice, ages, cultures, ethnic backgrounds, socioeconomic situations, and living circumstances. They are breathtaking and almost unbelievable. Courageous women reveal how they moved from the despair of addiction to a life of freedom, strength, and accomplishment. Their stories are dispersed throughout the book at the ends of chapters. While a story may touch on the themes of the chapter in which it is located, it is not meant to correspond to or illustrate all points in that particular chapter. It is meant simply to illustrate one woman's way out of ad-

---

* Names have been changed to protect anonymity.

diction. Quotes from the interviews are also sprinkled throughout the book. These powerful words show that there is no one way out of addiction, just as there is no one way of becoming addicted or living with addiction. There is a way out for every woman who is willing. That's a promise. If you're struggling with addiction and hope seems way out of reach, try reading the story sections of this book first. They will open the way to hope.

This book also offers hope to those who love an addicted woman. Many women who are addicted are so lost in their chemicals that they can't recognize the pain they're in and aren't able to seek help by themselves. It may be a friend or family member who first picks up this book. For addicts and for the caring people in their lives, this book provides an important and honest perspective on addiction and, more important, the hope of recovery. After reading this book, you will have a deeper understanding of addiction as the powerful force it is, and you will know without a doubt that recovery is very possible for those willing to take one step at a time. You'll also find some direction for what your next step needs to be.

Addiction doesn't typically happen overnight, and neither does recovery. Recovery is built on knowledge and acceptance and ultimately a commitment. Learning about addiction is a good way to start this process. An addict typically thinks she's the only one who would do such crazy things, so she lives a life of secrecy. One of the first gifts for a woman in recovery is discovering that she's not alone. Women in recovery find out that many other women have gone down that dark spiral of addiction, women who also have terrible secrets and have done horrible things. Yet they have climbed out of the pit and are living a life that is beyond their wildest dreams. Learning about addiction and seeing that others have done similar things is immensely helpful in the healing process.

A Woman's Guide to Recovery offers the opportunity to learn not only about addiction, but more important, about recovery. It discusses certain basic principles that work over and over. Some key ideas about addiction and recovery will be repeated at numerous points throughout the book. The repetition not only reinforces important ideas but also assists readers who experience memory struggles, which is very common in early recovery.

One of the most basic points that bears repetition is that recovery starts when women put the chemicals down—when they stop using them. This can't be done alone. It requires the help of others. When a woman finally puts the chemicals down, she usually feels a deep emptiness inside herself. Something is needed to replace the good feelings the chemicals provided. Recovery is about filling that empty place and building a content and meaningful life without chemicals.

Although women recover in a number of ways, the emphasis in *A Woman's Guide to Recovery* will be on an approach called the Twelve Steps. Twelve Step programs such as Alcoholics Anonymous and Narcotics Anonymous are available throughout the world, and many addicts have found freedom through them. They are based on principles that are also at the heart of other ways people get sober. These principles are used in Twelve Step groups, but they are also used in some faith-based programs and in other processes and support systems that help people recover.

The Twelve Step programs use as their basic guidebooks *Alcoholics Anonymous, Narcotics Anonymous,* and other time-tested literature to help people learn about addiction and recovery. *A Woman's Guide to Recovery* is built around many of the principles taught in this literature. Because most of the older books and pamphlets on Twelve Step recovery were written by men and were based mainly on the stories of men in recovery, women have not always found it easy to identify with some of the content. Also, much of the older literature was written with language that always referred to "he" and "him" when talking about an addict. While this early literature was intended for both males and females, the authors used male pronouns to reflect the cultural custom of the time and to make the language simple. Over time, newer materials have been written that include more women's stories and perspectives, as this one does, helping women connect more strongly with the message. Because *A Woman's Guide to Recovery* is written specifically for women, the feminine pronoun is used throughout. *A Woman's Guide to Recovery* intends to draw from and to add to the entire legacy of recovery wisdom, with its attention on women's experiences with addiction and recovery.

A great many lives have been changed through Twelve Step programs. Your life can change too. Recovery from addiction comes down to one person at a time, one day at time. This book is written for one person—the woman who's desperate for hope. It's for you if you're so far down that you have to look up to see bottom. It's for you if your life is mostly okay, but your use of alcohol or other drugs is creating trouble for you that you can't seem to get on top of. It's for you if you don't think you can ever live any differently. It's for you if you feel all alone. It's for you if you feel hopeless when it comes to chemical use. It's for you if you were in recovery and quit using for a time, but then quit doing the work of recovery and returned to active addiction, feeling like a total failure. It's for you if you're sober from chemicals but want to bring more *life* to your life. It's for you if want to have your eyes come alive with the light of recovery. It's also for you if you love a woman who is an active addict and who everyone says is hopeless, and yet, because you care so much for her, you're sure there must be a solution somewhere. It's for whoever wants to understand this thing called addiction that makes messes out of lives. If you're open enough to pick up this book and read this far, it's for you.

Addiction is messy.

Recovery is possible.

It's quite a distance between those two statements—a distance that starts with one small step. Then one small step. Then one small step. Then one small step. Then one small step.

You can begin now with just one small step.

CHAPTER 1

What Does It Mean to Be an Addict?

ADDICTION IS 100 PERCENT FATAL. IT'S TRAUMATIC AND it kills. It first kills a woman's spirit, then it screws up her emotions and messes with her mental abilities. Eventually, it kills her physically. This downward spiral is sometimes a quick process, sometimes gradual, but it always moves in the same direction.

Recovery from addiction is 100 percent possible. Recovery transforms lives. Even women who have been in the most severe and devastating stages of addiction find that recovery brings them freedom, contentment, and serenity beyond their wildest dreams.

> *My climb up Mount Rainier was to show people: "Hey, I can climb a mountain even though I was a drug addict for thirty-one years." I can do this. I can change careers, which I have done. At fifty years old, I can get clean and sober.*
>
> :: JULIA

This first chapter describes the problem of addiction: what it is, what causes it, why addicts need to stop using the chemicals totally, and why most addicts can't quit on their own. It also shows how addiction is different for women. The rest of the book is a guide to the solution. Its pages are filled with hope.

For those of us caught in the killing spiral of addiction, lots of questions come up when we try to find our way out: What is this thing called addiction? What causes this out-of-control plummet into self-destruction? Why is it so hard to stop? Do we really need to quit using totally? Can't we just try to control it? Why and how is the process different for women?

Some of the answers to these questions are based on research done by scientists interested in addiction. Only recently has the research on addiction included women, yet a great deal is known about addiction and how it affects women. In addition to what researchers tell us, the millions of women who have found their way out of addiction have a lot to teach us. Their knowledge and their stories are at the heart of this book.

What Is Addiction?

In the simplest terms, addiction is continuing to do or use something compulsively without the ability to stop or stay stopped on our own, even when this activity or use causes problems. For those of us addicted to alcohol and other drugs, our chemical use *must* stop, or it will kill us. While quitting seems impossible, it's very possible in recovery.

This book is specifically about chemical addiction—addiction to alcohol and other mood-altering drugs. Its main focus is on the drugs commonly thought of as causing a "high" or intoxication, including alcohol, marijuana, methamphetamine, cocaine, narcotics, antianxiety drugs (benzodiazepines), heroin, speed, ecstasy, and acid. In these pages, you'll also learn a little about other mood-altering chemicals that are not intoxicating but can be addictive, such as nicotine, caffeine, and sugar. These nonintoxicating chemicals are discussed mainly in relation to cross-addiction and self-care.

For addiction to take hold, it doesn't matter whether the drug is legal or illegal or whether it came from the liquor store, drug dealer, or pharmacy. Addiction is addiction. Many of us with a history of addiction say that it doesn't matter which chemical we use, because we're addicted to "more."

Women and Addiction Historically

A huge stigma has long surrounded women and addiction. While women have always experienced addiction, for the most part they were "invisible" addicts. Their families were ashamed of them. No one talked about their problem, and in many cases they were kept hidden away in their homes. This is still true for some women, particularly in some cultures.

The perception of the "invisible" addict has changed somewhat over time to being "visible with stigma." *Stigma* can be defined as severe social disapproval. Addiction carries a stigma for both men and women, but the stigma is even greater for women. We can up the ante regarding stigma if the addicted woman is a mother. Dr. Benjamin Rush, who founded American psychiatry in the 1700s, referred to addiction as an illness, but when it came to addiction among women, he referred to it as part of a "breeding sickness." Society seems to have a harder time accepting a mom on meth than a dad using drugs. Since women in most cultures are the primary caregivers for children, the welfare of their children is an added concern because of the betrayal of the parent-child bond that comes with addiction. Since some cultures now encourage dads to play a larger role in caring for their children, the stigma concerning women may eventually become less severe.

As women started to get into recovery from addiction, they still faced stigma. Years ago, it was assumed that if a woman was an alcoholic, she was also a "loose lady." Words such as *lush, fallen woman,* and *slut* have long been associated with women who were "falling down drunk." This stigma was present even for women in early Alcoholics Anonymous groups. Many of the wives of alcoholics did not want their alcoholic husbands to be around alcoholic women in recovery, because they assumed these women were "loose." In fact, early on, it was the wives of the alcoholic men who would help the alcoholic women. While women have since grown to be a large part of the Twelve Step fellowship, society still applies more stigma to women who are addicted than to men with the disease. Stigma can block women from getting help and getting into recovery. Learning about addiction and recovery can help to break through the stigma of addiction and make it easier for women to break free of its chains.

What Causes Addiction?

Many factors affect whether a person becomes an addict. Typically, multiple factors come together to bring about someone's addiction. Knowing these causes doesn't help us personally solve our problem with addiction, but it does help us understand this condition better and realize why some people are more likely than others to become addicted.

Genetic Predisposition

Some of us are genetically predisposed for addiction, meaning we're more likely than others to become addicted because of our physical makeup. If our parents and grandparents or other biological relatives were addicts, we may carry the genes that can cause addiction. We may be born with that risk. If we never use chemicals, we won't become addicted. However, most people at some time or other in their lives try chemicals. Some become addicted, others don't. Even some children or grandchildren of alcoholics and addicts can drink or use other drugs without becoming addicted. The family's addictive genes may not have been passed along to them when they were born, or they may not have been affected by other factors that cause addiction. Genes can set us up for addiction, but other factors may help push us over the line. Much research is being done about the link between genetics and addiction. Someday scientists may locate the specific gene or other physical factors that make people vulnerable to addiction, which may help eventually stamp out addiction. At this point, however, science has not done this. It *does* tell us, though, that certain women are more vulnerable to addiction.

Developmental Factors

Developmental factors also play into who gets addicted. The younger we are when we start using, the more likely we'll become addicted. The writers of the Big Book of *Alcoholics Anonymous* in the 1930s noted that young people progress faster in addiction than older people. Since that time, scientists have helped to explain why. A child's environment and personality can contribute to this early addiction, but the main influence is brain development. The brain of a young person is not fully developed. It's like the shell of the house, but the rooms aren't finished until around age twenty-one or twenty-two. Therefore, the brains of young people are more vulnerable to the effects of drugs.

Type and Use of Drug

The type of drug we use, as well as its purity, its availability, and the way it's administered all can influence whether we get addicted. Some drugs are more potent than others, and some ways of using drugs are more potent. The speed and intensity of the high depend on the drug and how the drug is taken in. For instance, shooting or smoking a drug can produce a faster high than drinking or swallowing one. It takes longer when the drug has to go through the digestive system to get to the brain, and some of the effect is diluted by the time it gets there.

Addictive Personality

Some people are said to have an "addictive personality." While this is not a medical or mental health diagnosis, experience shows that some people are more likely to get addicted to something—*anything!* Many of us as addicts say that we knew we were in trouble the first time we used, because we loved the addictive substance or activity so much that we had an exceptionally strong desire for more of it. Some of us say that we are addicted to "more." No matter what we get our hands on, we think we have to have more of it. Our addictive personality makes us more likely to become addicted to something else after we stop using chemicals. That's why some people go from craving alcohol to craving food or gambling or sex or relationships or other addictive substances or behaviors. Chapter 7, on cross-addiction, talks more about this tendency.

The Good Feeling

Why do we keep using when we know how bad things will get for us? Many of us just started out using to feel good. Let's face it: Chemicals do make us feel good. Ecstatically good. If they didn't work that way, we wouldn't keep going back to them. We wouldn't get addicted. Some of us describe our first use as "feeling like I belonged." Others say, "This is what I've been waiting for!" or "This is it!" or "Where has this been all my life?" Another common description of the experience is "love at first sight." Not all of us had such a dramatic first experience with drug use; our attraction to a chemical built over time. But in all cases, using the chemical makes us feel good or does something for us that we like, or we wouldn't keep going back to it. In fact, it does something powerful for us. Electric! But that electric feeling doesn't last forever.

While originally we may have used to feel good, eventually we begin using just to feel normal, and sometimes to try to get out of despair. We get to the point where we *need* to use just to cope with life, and the thing that was so electric early on becomes our death sentence.

> *From the time I was fourteen years old until the time I was twenty-six, when I got sober, I did not draw a sober breath. Every single day I used something to take away the pain. Eventually, it got to a point where I didn't have the choice anymore as to whether I wanted to do it.*
>
> :: FANNIE MAE

Other Influences

Many other influences affect whether we get addicted or not. These include how much and how often we use, which specific chemicals we use and how they impact the brain, how we take in the chemicals—orally or by smoking or injection—the degree of emotional and physical pain we're in, any mental health and emotional issues we have, and influences in our environment such as our living situation and socioeconomic and cultural issues. While none of these alone causes addiction, a mixture of them can be a recipe for addiction.

Reasons Don't Matter

Addiction has many possible causes. Once we're addicted, the reason we're addicted doesn't really matter. If we get caught up in trying to figure out what caused our addiction, we may never find our way out. We may just keep on using and delay living in the fullness of recovery. Addiction is trauma to any woman experiencing it and to those who love her. There is no need to prolong the agony by focusing on why. What matters is learning how addiction works and how to get out from under its tyranny.

What's So Different about Women and Addiction?

Some people mistakenly believe that addiction doesn't happen to women, but addiction is an equal opportunity disease. Women may get addicted in different ways and for different reasons than men do, but they still get addicted. In fact, addiction takes down women faster than it takes down men. It affects women's bodies differently. Drink for drink, drug for drug, women are in much worse shape than men physically and emotionally by the time they quit using. The Big Book told us in 1939 that women progress faster than men in addiction. Science is now telling us why.

Getting Addicted

Women typically start using chemicals—and eventually become addicted—for different reasons than men do. Men usually start using for recreational use or because they like the effect of the drug. Women, on the other hand, start using for a variety of reasons. They may start using to lose weight, reduce sexual inhibition, relieve stress, improve their mood, increase their self-confidence, belong to their group, or even avoid hurting someone else's feelings by saying no to a drug or drink.

Physical Differences

Women may experience more physical effects from chemical use than men do. This is particularly true with alcohol but also with other chemicals to varying degrees. One drink of alcohol, for example, has twice the impact on a woman's body than on a man's because of differences in the bodily makeup of the two sexes—*twice the impact!* Women's bodies absorb and make use of chemicals differently. Our bodies contain more fatty tissue proportionally than men's bodies, and alcohol gets absorbed more slowly in fat than in water. The fatty tissue keeps alcohol in the bloodstream longer, so our brains and other organs are exposed to higher concentrations of alcohol. The bottom line is that women absorb more of the alcohol because it sits in the organs longer.

Women also produce less alcohol dehydrogenase, the stomach enzyme that breaks down alcohol. Less breakdown of alcohol in the digestive system leads to greater blood alcohol concentration. Again, this higher level of alcohol creates more damage in the body, including the brain.

All addicts, women and men, are more likely than other people to have accidents, malnourishment, respiratory and circulatory diseases, cancers (throat and stomach), sexually transmitted diseases, liver damage, and gastrointestinal problems such as ulcers. Women are at more risk for certain conditions, such as liver damage, because the chemicals take longer to pass through the higher amounts of fatty tissue present in a woman's liver.

In addition to the diseases common for men and women with addiction, women with addiction have a greater risk than other women of having breast cancer (due to increased estrogen production), osteoporosis, ob-gyn problems, pregnancy problems, negative effects on newborn children, and developing other medical disorders. Brain atrophy—the starvation and shriveling up of the brain—and the loss of brain volume happen more quickly in women, due to the high concentration of drugs in the system. Women also report more disabilities from using, such as difficulty climbing stairs and walking long distances. Our bodies hold drugs longer and deteriorate faster.

Every year, tens of thousands of women die from causes related to addiction, such as homicide, overdose, suicide, physiological deterioration, and accidents. The exact number is unknown, because even when addiction is a direct or contributing cause to a death, that link may not be reported by those who keep the statistics on mortality. Statistics do show that the death rate among female alcoholics is higher than male alcoholics' because of their increased risk for suicide, alcohol-related accidents, cirrhosis, and hepatitis. Four times as many addicted women attempt suicide as does the general population, and in some parts of the world, more women than men kill themselves due to addiction. That's the ultimate payment to addiction. The hopelessness becomes too great. The despair and loneliness are devastating. There is a way out, but some women never find it or lose sight of it momentarily, and it costs them their lives. In one way or another, unchecked addiction is 100 percent fatal.

> *The lowest point was I just wanted to die. I wanted to kill the outside so I wouldn't feel no more pain on the inside.*
>
> :: GLORIA

Mental Health Concerns

Women who are addicted also tend to have different emotional or mental health issues than men do. While addicts generally have high rates of depression and anxiety, women tend to report greater discomfort in these areas. Women are more likely to have a history of trauma; eating disorders are also more likely. These mental health issues will be explored in later chapters.

Social Concerns

All of us with addiction have concerns about how our disease affects others around us. We may have made a mess of our lives financially and legally and in our relationships and careers. Our families, in particular, may be deeply affected by our addiction. As women, we're often the central stabilizing factor in our families. Addiction erodes that role, and the chaos we feel inside seeps out and throws entire families into a spin.

Addiction Is a Disease

Addiction is often described as a disease. In fact, in 1955, the American Medical Association, the largest organization of doctors in the United States, formally decided to call alcoholism a disease. Two centuries before that, Dr. Benjamin Rush talked about alcoholism as an illness. He compared it to other hereditary illnesses. Today, most chemical dependency treatment programs regard addiction as a disease. So, what is a disease? In general, a disease is primary in nature, has specific symptoms, is chronic, and can be fatal.

A Primary Condition

A disease is a health problem that is primary in nature. That means it wasn't caused by something else, and it's not a symptom of another disorder. It stands on its own. Though addiction has a genetic component and may be affected by other conditions in a person's life, it's not solely the result of any of these factors. Addiction is a *primary* condition. It stands on its own, and it needs to be treated on its own.

We Didn't Cause It

A disease is not caused by the person who has it. For instance, women with cancer, cardiac problems, diabetes, or hypertension may have a biological predisposition to these diseases, and their environment and behavior may also have a bearing on their illness. But, no matter what the influences on these diseases, the people who have them didn't choose to get them. Certain behaviors may have made them more vulnerable to the disease, but they're not weak-willed or bad people because they have them. We don't blame people for having a disease they didn't choose to get. We addicts didn't choose to get our disease, either. We're not, as people sometimes say, immoral or lacking willpower. We may feel like the lowest of the low. We may have done some bad things, even some terrible things, but that doesn't mean we chose to cross the line into the disease of addiction.

Because addiction is a disease, which is primary in nature, trying to find out what caused our addiction is a waste of time. Some of us spent years in therapy trying to figure out why we were using. We thought that if we could just learn why, we'd be able to cut back or quit our using. We eventually found we were just spinning our wheels. We'd try to figure out why and continued to use.

Some of us have coexisting mental health issues along with our addiction. We may want to find out which came first, and why. It really doesn't matter. It's like trying to answer the question "Which came first: the chicken or the egg?" It's pointless. What matters is that we have both the chicken and egg. Both need to be treated. It doesn't matter why.

Some therapists won't work on emotional issues with someone who is active in addiction if she isn't working on getting sober. They feel it's a waste of time and money. One reason is that the first thing active addicts do when they encounter pain in therapy is use! It's important to get into recovery if we expect to get good results from therapy. It's not a question of why. It's a question of what. What do I have? What do I need to do?

Although addiction is a disease and we're not the cause of it, that doesn't mean that we can sit back and do nothing about our condition. Just as a diabetic must control sugar intake and use insulin, we addicts have a daily recovery plan to follow to maintain our well-being. That plan allows us to put down the chemicals and not use them. Though we're not responsible for getting the disease of addiction, we're responsible for doing the work of our recovery. We may not have chosen to have the disease of addiction, but we do have to clean up the mess. With the help of others in recovery, this is very possible.

It's Chronic

A disease is not only primary in nature; it's also chronic, meaning it's long-term. That's especially important to remember after we've been in recovery for a while. Just because we've stopped using chemicals doesn't mean we can stop paying attention to our disease. It needs our constant vigilance. A chronic disease needs long-term intervention, not just a couple of weeks of antibiotics or other interventions. It's a long-term, chronic condition.

It's Progressive

Diseases are also progressive. They have a describable, predictable pattern of getting worse. Without intervention, addiction will get worse over time. It's ultimately fatal. In the meantime, it will get messier and messier. *That's a guarantee!* It may get worse quickly, it may get worse slowly, but unless we make some sort of huge change through serious recovery work, our lives will only get worse.

Many of us slid gradually into addiction without even noticing this happening. We are like the frog in the old frog-on-the-stove story. As the story goes, if you throw a frog into a pot of boiling water, it will jump out quickly. However, if you put the frog into a pot of water at room temperature, the frog will like being in the water at first. If you heat the water slowly, the frog will stay in the pot and gradually adapt to the temperature change. Eventually, though, when the water boils, the frog will die.

The frog story illustrates what can happen with addiction. Using chemicals—and the mess that our using creates—becomes familiar. We simply adjust. We adapt to the addiction and fail to see how it's heating up, getting worse, killing us. We think that's the way life is—how could it be any different? Even if we recognize that our addiction is killing us, most of us don't at first believe we can get out.

The progression of the disease can also be thought of as a downward spiral. Somewhere in the process of our using, things start to go downhill. Then, as we use more and more, we lose more and more. After a while, along comes something that gets our attention or the attention of someone else in our lives. Maybe we get in trouble because of our using, or someone questions our use, so we pull it together for a while. We move back up the spiral. We're on good behavior. As addicts, we're not dumb. We know when the heat is on, and many of us can clean up our act somewhat for a while. We may quit using for a period, cut back, swear off, switch chemicals, go to treatment, or try an AA meeting. We need to get the heat off, so we try to look good. This "good behavior" may last for some time, but eventually, without recovery, we spiral down again. This up and down spiraling can happen over and over throughout our lifespan. With certain drugs, these changes can happen fairly often and quickly. Each time, we move further down the spiral toward destruction.

The Downward Spiral

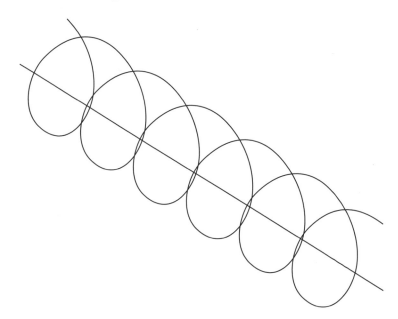

Addiction is a brain disease. Medical researchers are helping us learn more and more about the brain all the time. Drugs change our brain chemistry. The high, or feeling of relief, we experience when using chemicals makes it obvious that the drugs are altering the chemistry in our brains. The change in our brain chemistry can be long-term, but in most cases a return to normal brain functioning begins with abstinence.

Addiction happens in the limbic system in the brain. This is the brain's reward system, the pleasure system. The limbic system is deep inside the brain. It's the part of the brain that triggers us to feel pleasure, and it's also where some of the automatic responses that keep us functioning, such as breathing, come from. When we overload this system with an onslaught of chemicals, two things can happen. First, our brain stops producing its own essential feel-good chemicals over time, and second, it gets busy adding "receptor" sites to absorb the extra feel-good chemicals. When we stop feeding our body drugs, our brain tells us we need more. It's left with extra receptor sites eager to take in more feel-good chemicals, and yet it can produce few of these chemicals naturally.

Some researchers say that addiction "hijacks" the brain. It changes the structure, anatomy, and chemistry of the brain, including the activity of hormones and of the brain's chemical messengers, called neurotransmitters. After our brains adapt this way to the long-term onslaught of outside chemicals, we start craving these chemicals. We actually need them to feel normal, because our brains have been altered.

The good news is that the brain can be changed back to its normal state. But this change takes time. Even after we've gone through detox and no longer have the extra chemicals in our system, the brain will crave the feelings of pleasure it's used to experiencing from these chemicals. Fortunately, recovery changes the brain. Over time, the cravings disappear.

What Are the Symptoms of Addiction?

Like all diseases, addiction has specific symptoms. A symptom is an indication of a certain condition. It's not the condition itself, but one sign of it. If a person has several symptoms that point to a particular condition, the person most likely has that disease.

Withdrawal

Withdrawal is one symptom of addiction. Withdrawal is a physical reaction to quitting or cutting back on the use of chemicals. (Of course, any attempt to cut back or control the use never works for long. The chemical use has to stop completely. But, if an addict does try to cut back, there may still be an experience of withdrawal.) Withdrawal is generally uncomfortable, sometimes quite painful, and may be life threatening. Some addicts have this symptom and some don't. Withdrawal is the body's attempt to adapt to the absence of the chemicals it has come to depend on. It overcompensates in some way, depending on the drugs used and other factors, trying to get back in balance. Sometimes this overcompensation can be fatal.

For instance, alcohol is a depressant. It slows down the body's functioning. In withdrawal from alcohol, the body overcompensates by speeding everything up. The person may experience shaking, trembling, even seizures and delirium. More people die while withdrawing from alcohol than while withdrawing from any other drug.

The withdrawal process is different with other drugs. Methamphetamine is a stimulant. When using it, people go faster. When they're withdrawing from it, they "crash," or sleep. Everything in their physical system slows down. Heroin numbs people out. When heroin addicts go into withdrawal, they may feel like they're dying—

everything hurts. Even their bones may hurt. The nerves that were numb are coming back to life and overcompensating.

With some chemicals, such as narcotics, people may experience withdrawal when stopping after using for as little as a week. People who've had surgery and have been on narcotics short-term, for example, may have mild withdrawal symptoms. Other chemicals take longer to create the type of changes in a person's body that result in withdrawal when quitting.

Withdrawal can be life threatening, depending on the chemical. Alcohol can create serious medical complications, such as seizures, delirium tremens (DTs), or even death. It can also have some less serious but still very uncomfortable symptoms, such as nausea, vomiting, sweating, shakes, insomnia, and anxiety. Narcotics withdrawal may produce muscle aches, fever, insomnia, feeling down, vomiting and diarrhea, and other symptoms. Benzodiazepine withdrawal is generally a longer withdrawal, with possible hand tremors, anxiety, seizures, twitching, hallucinations, nausea, vomiting, sweating, and insomnia. When someone is in withdrawal from alcohol, narcotics, or benzodiazepines, medical intervention is critically important. Medical help or advice should be sought for withdrawal from *all* chemicals.

Experiencing withdrawal doesn't always indicate that the person is an addict. A woman who is only using narcotics short-term following surgery may have withdrawal symptoms. Her body has become physically dependent on the chemical and needs to adjust when the chemical is no longer there, but that doesn't make her an addict. Withdrawal alone is not enough to warrant a diagnosis of addiction. It's just one symptom.

Many addicts don't even experience physical withdrawal. The effects of withdrawal depend on the chemical they're using, how frequently they're using it, over what period of time, and other factors. Some people mistakenly think they're not addicts because they never have physical withdrawal symptoms when they stop using. The truth is, even if someone doesn't experience withdrawal, she may be an addict. The other symptoms are more common.

Tolerance

Another symptom of addiction is physical tolerance for a chemical. Again, people with this symptom are not necessarily addicts, nor do all addicts have this symptom. Tolerance is the condition of getting so used to a drug that the body needs more of it to have the same pleasurable effect.

The first time we took a drink, we may have felt "woozy" on one drink. After three drinks, we may have felt drunk. Over time, if we continued to drink again and again, our bodies got used to the chemical and felt little or no effect from one drink. It now takes three drinks for us to feel a little off-center and six to eight to get drunk. Our bodies "tolerate" more of the drug. This tolerance increases as our bodies adapt to the chemical, and we need more of it to have the desired effect.

Tolerance is particularly noticeable with nicotine. The first time most people smoke a cigarette, they get dizzy or nauseated. Some people even vomit the first time they smoke. Soon, the body adapts to the nicotine, and the cigarette gives them what they are seeking: some sort of relief or mini-high. With nicotine, the body adapts fairly quickly, and while at first one cigarette leaves the person feeling dizzy or nauseated, soon one cigarette produces relief. That's a part of tolerance; the body adapts to the use of the chemical. Over time, the body needs more cigarettes, or needs to have them smoked closer together, to have the relief or the mini-high that at one time one cigarette alone provided. That's tolerance—needing to have more in order to have the desired effect. Tolerance is what allows some smokers to smoke three packs a day. They didn't start out with that tolerance when they smoked their first cigarette.

Preoccupation

A major symptom of addiction is preoccupation with using. Preoccupation is thinking a great deal about doing something even when we're not doing it. It's looking forward to it, planning it, thinking about it. As addicts, our attention is almost constantly on the chemical or the next high or the next comfort from the drug. Our life is centered around the chemical and using it, thinking about using it, recovering from using it, planning to use it, obtaining it, hiding it, hiding our behavior around it, and trying to clean up our messes. Sometimes the anticipation of using our chemical brings a high in itself. Eventually everything gets focused on the chemical and its effects. Granted, we may not be *using* the chemical 24/7, but we're thinking about it, planning on getting it, planning on how to get out of the bind it got us in, and recovering from our use. It occupies much of our thinking. This "monkey chatter" goes on and on in our thoughts. Our whole life eventually focuses on the addiction.

Loss of Control

Another overarching symptom of addiction is the loss of control around using the chemical. We may not lose control every single time, but we can't trust our own good intentions. We may say we'll just have two drinks, but that doesn't mean we can stop at two. Sometimes we're able to follow through on our promise, but a more likely result is that we end up waking up next to a stranger or we're unable to remember where we left our car or whom we left our young children with.

When we or others start to have concerns about our using, we may attempt to control it. *Attempt* is the key word here. Normal people *do* control their using; they don't *attempt* to control it. We may quit for a specific period, not use on weekdays, not use before 4 p.m., cut back, switch the chemicals we use, swear off, not have the chemicals in the house, not use alone, limit how much we use, never use in the morning, read self-help books, go to our church/

mosque/synagogue, change jobs, move to get away from stress, or leave a relationship. Do some of these seem absurd? They may to the person who has never made an attempt to control use, but the addict who's trying to figure out how to stop or limit her using will try such measures countless times. Some of these methods may appear to work for a time, but in the long run these efforts to control addiction are fruitless.

Using Despite Negative Consequences

Another strong symptom or indication of addiction is continuing to use despite negative consequences. Normal users change their use when they experience problems with their using. They may quit altogether or cut back. Many teenagers and young adults experiment with drinking and other chemicals, but it's not normal for a forty- or fifty-year-old to be smoking pot daily or heavily partying all weekend long. Normal users discover unpleasant or dangerous consequences, and they cut back or quit. Addicts just keep going and going. They tell themselves, *This time it will be different! It was bad luck in the past, It's so-and-so's fault,* or *The judge has it in for me.* Is it maybe just easier to deny we have this problem? Maybe we're really not an addict? Maybe it's not that bad?

> *Well, if it's causing problems in your life, big or small, something's wrong. You need to look at what's going on.*
>
> :: KAREN

Denial

Denial is a key symptom of addiction. It comes glommed on to this disease, no matter how smart we are or how honest we think we are. Psychologists tell us that denial is a conscious or unconscious defense that humans use to block anxiety when they feel threatened. It's a normal human response when people expect to lose something they value greatly.

With addiction, denial runs deep, like the bone marrow in our bodies. It's a lot like being in a fog that keeps us from seeing things clearly. For some of us, it can be so powerful that it blinds us totally to reality. We not only deny that there is a problem at all, but even when we acknowledge it, we deny how severe it is. Addiction is the one disease that tells us we don't have it.

It's a kind of insanity—telling ourselves we don't have it. We look it right in the face and say it isn't so. We may use various forms of denial, such as lying, telling half-truths, blaming others, concealing our use, getting angry, trying to be funny, bargaining, rationalizing, judging others, switching the focus, intellectualizing, minimizing, agreeing superficially to get people off our case, retreating—the list is endless. We deny our using and the severity of its consequences. We deny the need for change, the need to put down the chemicals. Some of our denial, such as telling lies, is blatant, but mostly we don't think we have a problem, so why would we say anything about it?

Most of us don't see our addiction or the full extent of the damage it's causing. Others usually see the state we're in before we do. We're using and our situation is worsening, but because our brains are chemically altered, we don't see our life the way it really is. Many of us, as we sober up, are in horror when we realize what our life was like when we were using. Some of us describe it as slowly coming out of the fog of denial.

In active addiction, you don't respect yourself from the time you put that pipe in your mouth. You have no morals, no values. You have no dignity. You have nothing. Then when the high comes down, and you start to think about what you've done, the shame and the guilt are so strong that you pick that pipe up again.

:: GLENDA

Denial not only tries to keep us from looking at addiction, it also tries to keep us thinking of ourselves as different and separate from other addicts. Denial tells us that we're not addicts or that we're not "like those other people" or that our addiction isn't that bad. Granted, our stories may have different twists and turns, different drugs of choice, different progression and life circumstances, but the common denominator is that we need to put down the chemicals. Totally. Facing this truth is one of the scariest things we'll go through. Many of us, in the beginning, are petrified to think of not having our chemical in our life. Purely petrified. That may be the main reason we keep ourselves in denial. If we admit we're an addict, if we come out and say we can relate to other addicts, we need to do something about it. We will have to put down the chemicals even though we're sure we can't do it. That's a terrifying thought.

> *Something important I've heard people in recovery say is "Connect, don't compare." Like when someone's talking, we should try to relate to what they're saying, versus "I didn't do that," "I wasn't that bad," or "I never drank like that."*
>
> :: BONNIE

As we look at the various symptoms of the disease, we might not relate to some of the symptoms at all. We might try to take ourselves off the hook by saying, "Not me!" "I don't do that," "I don't have that one," or "I'm not that bad." We may even feel superior to others who have symptoms we don't have: "I'd never do that!" or "I'm not like her." But we don't need to have all the symptoms to be an addict. We need to pay attention to the symptoms that we have versus the ones we don't. And we need to understand that as the disease progresses, it brings with it more symptoms. Those of us who haven't experienced all the symptoms of addiction or who function fairly well despite having a history of addiction have learned that even if we haven't experienced a particular symptom *yet*, it may show up tomorrow. YET stands for *you're eligible too!*

This disease of addiction is no respecter of persons. We may have the gifts of intelligence, personality, kindness, wealth, good looks, humor, or talent, but addiction will twist and turn and use these gifts to keep us from getting sober. We addicts think our strengths will keep us from getting worse or will get us out of jams, but addiction strangles our strength in order to keep itself alive and well. In addiction, our greatest strength can become our Achilles' heel, reinforcing our denial.

> *I was in denial. I just felt like I had no problem.*
> *I thought to myself,* How can an Iowa girl become a drug addict? How can that happen? Being raised in the Bible belt of America?
>
> :: JULIA

Hiding and Sneaking

In addiction, many of us live a double life. We may hide how much or how often or when we use. Hiding and sneaking help keep us in denial. We don't see the whole picture ourselves and try to keep it from others. We conceal the amount of our use, and we may even keep secret the fact that we're using any chemical at all. A working mom with three kids who uses meth to keep up with her busy life may hide from her family, friends, and employer the fact that she's even using a chemical, let alone what she does to obtain it.

Many of us who are now in recovery admit that we kept secrets about what we did when we were using the chemicals. We kept secrets about how we got them, whom we hung out with, how we behaved, how much we used, how often we used, how many times we tried to quit and couldn't—just lots of secrets around the addiction. Put simply, addiction is about sneaking and hiding. Anytime we're sneaking and hiding, we're in trouble. We know we're not being

honest with ourselves or others. We're back into denial and covering up from ourselves and others. Our ego is doing the denying,
but there's a part of us that knows what the ego's up to, and we feel
the need to hide and conceal it. We're full of shame and guilt about
our behavior, and hiding and sneaking and denial are ways to keep
from looking at what's really going on.

As addicts, we feel tons of shame about all these secrets. We
think to ourselves, *If anyone ever knew . . .* or *I must be the only
person who's this bad.* Living a double life and then keeping the
secrets fills us with shame. A huge part of the healing in recovery
is hearing the so-familiar secrets of others and realizing, *I am not
a bad woman. I'm a woman with an addiction, just like these other
women.* Hearing other women's stories starts to normalize what
we've done as an addict. We recognize that we're not alone in our
addiction. We start paying attention to how similar we are rather
than focusing on how different we think we are.

Universal Symptoms of Addiction

All addicts who are being honest with themselves can identify with
the following statement: "I can't use, and I can't quit."

In "The Doctor's Opinion" in the Big Book of *Alcoholics Anonymous,* Dr. William Silkworth speaks about an allergy of the body
and an obsession of the mind. He states that some people are genetically different, and their bodies react allergically to alcohol.
Allergically? At first take, that statement can seem absurd. *Come
on, we love the feeling that comes from using. We don't break out in
a rash or swell up or experience anything like that. In fact, quite the
opposite. We feel good when using, or at least we feel some relief.*

What's an allergy? An allergy is an abnormal reaction to a common substance. Some people are allergic to shellfish, and when they
eat it, their throats swell and they can't breathe. They go to great
lengths to avoid shellfish. Their reaction to shellfish is an abnormal
reaction. Most of us can have shellfish without any concerns. To

be able to eat and enjoy shellfish is a normal reaction to a common substance.

Alcohol is also a common substance. Most people can drink it without any real problems. When we addicts start drinking, we don't know for sure when we'll stop. Sometimes we may have the amount we planned on having, and other times it's another ten years of using and lots of losses and possible death before we stop. We just don't know. That's not normal. It's an abnormal reaction to a common substance. Normal people stop when they say they are going to stop. We can't always depend on stopping as we planned. So what's the conclusion? We have to stop using chemicals completely.

Unlike normal people with an allergy, who accept that they have to stay away from substances causing allergic reactions, we can't seem to fathom living without our chemicals. We think this normal process of avoiding the allergy-inducing substance doesn't apply to us. *What do you mean, the only relief is entire abstinence? Entire? No chemical use? Come on!* Of course, we've heard this all before in various forms: "Don't use," "Just say no," "Don't start." Doesn't it indeed make sense to stay away from something that's causing us problems?

Just like the people who are allergic to shellfish, we have to stay away from what we're allergic to. These people no longer eat shellfish. They don't seek it out to have "just one" or say, "Let me try *this* kind of shellfish instead." They know they can't "use"—and they don't. How many of us have heard the people who love us say to us, "Just don't use"? Of course they're right that we need to stop using. We need to put the chemicals down completely. We know that we can't use. So, why do we?

Well, that's the second part of the problem that Dr. Silkworth describes. Members of Twelve Step programs refer to it as the "obsession of the mind." It's similar to the preoccupation symptom referred to earlier—the monkey chatter. Not only are our bodies abnormal in that we can't use chemicals responsibly, but our minds also tell us that we don't have a problem, that we aren't really different. Our minds tell us things like *Now that you haven't used for two weeks, you could probably have just a little,* or *Just switch to marijuana instead of the cocaine,* or *If you use pills, you'll use them responsibly,* or *How about some wine instead of the hard liquor?* or *Now you know something about women's addiction after reading this book, so you can use responsibly,* or *You worked on your issues in therapy, so now you should be able to drink,* or *No one will know,* or . . . fill in the blank.

The obsession of the mind keeps us from staying quit. It's a form of denial. It tells us that things weren't all that bad when we were using or possibly even that we're not addicts. Even though we've stopped using chemicals, our mental obsession brings us into denial, creating lies in our mind such as *Just one won't hurt,* or *It really wasn't that bad,* or *You can drink alcohol as long as you don't pick up that crack.* It talks us into trying our chemicals once again. The Big Book tells us that we are "restless, irritable and discontented" (p. xxviii) until we can find the "ease and comfort" (p. xxix) that come from taking a few drinks. The mental obsession makes us remember the good times and forget the despair. It talks us into trying one more round by filtering out all the negative experiences we've had because of using. We think that somehow we'll be able to control our using, that this time will be different.

> CO *Because we all have the underlying thing of alcoholism—once we start, we can't stop, and then the mental obsession—there are a lot of parts of the Big Book that I now realize are totally my story, just like it was for the people in 1939.*
>
> :: BONNIE

Powerlessness: The Most Powerful Place

This "can't use/can't quit" problem is what the First Step of the Twelve Steps of Alcoholics Anonymous is all about. "We admitted we were powerless over [drugs]—that our lives had become unmanageable" (*Alcoholics Anonymous,* p. 59). Many of us know that once we start using, we're in trouble because we can't stop. We know that when we use, our life becomes a mess—unmanageable, as the First Step says. What's harder to understand and even harder to believe is that even when we're totally sober, totally straight, and totally clean, we're still powerless over chemicals. Even without a single drug in our system, the addiction still has power over us. Something in us keeps telling us that we can try it one more time and it will be different. How many times have we said, "This time it will be different"? A driving force within us seeks the "ease and comfort" that come from a few drinks. The word *powerless* in the First Step means this: *Whether using or not using, I'm in trouble. I can't use but I can't quit but I can't use but I can't quit but I can't use but I can't quit.* How hopeless can it get? We're powerless. That's why many of us stay in denial. It's all too overwhelming. We can't use and yet can't quit.

When we first start to comprehend the wreckage of our lives and realize that our chemicals are creating the mess we're in, we get scared. Actually, we get terrified. When we admit that we're addicts and recognize with our innermost knowing that we need to change, we experience some of the most terrifying moments in our lives. At the same time, we feel some sense of relief when we learn about addiction and realize we're not alone. Mostly, though, intense fear and confusion set in. *How can it be that I have to put down my chemicals to get out of addiction? I'm an addict—and the solution is not to use?* Not using seems totally impossible. *Aren't addicts powerless over their drugs?*

Yes, they are, and when we get this, when it sinks deeply into our hearts and minds, we're at the First Step of the Twelve Steps. We admit we're powerless over alcohol or meth or cocaine or heroin or pills or whatever our enslaving chemical is. Powerless. Unable to stop once we start *and* unable to quit or stay quit. Can't use but can't quit but can't use but can't quit but can't use but can't quit, and the circle continues. No wonder we feel hopeless, powerless.

This "gift of desperation" is right where recovery begins. It's the gift that turns our life around. The pain of desperation makes us willing to change. When we become completely convinced that we can't use and can't quit, we're right where we need to be. Somewhere inside us, we realize that our situation is hopeless.

> *I remember hearing a woman at a meeting saying, one time, and I couldn't believe she said this: "I wish you desperation." And I thought,* what a horrible thing to say! *But it wasn't until I reached desperation, when I lost all my money, and had my car stolen, and lost my place to live, I had no friends, I basically had lost everything except my mind, and that of course was questionable— that I finally surrendered to say that I needed help.*
>
> :: JULIA

CHAPTER 2

A Way Out

⤳ *Never think,* I can't do this, *because your addict
wants to keep you in that lifestyle. But your Higher
Power wants you to live free, to fly above it, to climb
a mountain, to get out of your addiction. He wants you
to stand up and say, "There's no more stigma of being a
drug addict or an alcoholic." You have a whole new door
opening up to you when you humble yourself and say, "I
need help." That's the first step. There is always hope for
people. And hope opens the door to a whole new life.*

:: JULIA

THERE IS A WAY OUT OF ADDICTION. IT'S CALLED RECOV-
ery. Addiction does indeed seem hopeless. Yet, every single one
of us can make her way out. That doesn't seem possible at first,
when all we experience is a state of hopelessness and desperation.
Ironically, that is the place from which our recovery can spring.
The gift of desperation leads to a way out.

For some of us, this hopelessness—this sense of desperation—
develops over time. As we put down the chemicals, the fog starts
to lift, and we see our life more clearly. For others, this awareness happens quickly. All of a sudden, we realize that chemicals
have caused pain and havoc in our life and that we can't quit.
It could just be a gentle tap on the shoulder by a friend that gets
our attention. Or our wake-up call could be as dramatic as the

29

welfare agency coming to take away our children as we realize this is the end of the line for us. In some way, we fall flat on our face and "kiss the concrete." Any number of things could prompt this type of abrupt shift in how we see our life. Another way we may get to the state of hopelessness is by learning about addiction. We start relating to familiar experiences in the stories of other addicts. However it happens, we have what's often referred to as an "aha" moment, a "moment of truth" or a mini "spiritual awakening."

When I was in prison, I had what I call a moment of clarity. When I was going in and out of county jails, I used to see the new women that would come in, and the other women would rush out to greet them like they were great friends. I guess you'd say they were jail friends. I know the first few times I was in jail, it used to freak me out. Like, oh my God, I can't believe these people are happy to see other people back in jail. Then, the last couple times I went to county jail, I was that familiar face. People would say, "Hey, Karen, it's good to see you!" When I was in federal prison, the same thing would happen when the flights with the new women would come into the facility every couple weeks. I remember one night sitting out in the yard on this bench by myself, and I was watching these new women come in on the flight, and all these other women were running to see if their friends were there. I had this moment where I realized that if I didn't knock it off and I didn't do something different, I was going to continue to be that familiar face in prison for the rest of my life. That was a really big turning point for me. It was like a lightning bolt hit me, or I had a spiritual awakening, or however you want to phrase it. I can tell you how warm it was outside at that moment. I can tell you what the colors were in the sky

when the sun was setting. I can tell you what the grass
smelled like, even to this day. That's how clear that mo-
ment was for me.

:: **KAREN**

When we get the first clear glimpse of how deep the hole is that
we've fallen into, any notion of having a life without our chemicals is difficult to fathom—even when we want desperately to stop
using them. We know we need to put the chemicals down totally,
but how can we? The patterns of our addiction have become so
familiar, how else is there to live?

There is a way out—a "solution," as the Big Book calls it. It's not
a way many of us would have chosen. We may think it's ridiculous
that we need to stop using. We may dislike the so-called solution.
We even hate some of the things it requires, and yet we see it working for others, and we think maybe it could work for us too. Other
people's stories of addiction and recovery give us that hope.

I had to get sober, beyond anything else. I had to
stop doing the thing that was killing me. Once I put
down the drugs and the alcohol, there was a clarity that
I was to experience that I hadn't experienced before.

:: **FANNIE MAE**

Connection

Just as the problem has two parts—can't use/can't quit—the solution also has two parts. The first part of the solution is about making connections—connections with others, ourselves, and a Higher
Power. Women tend to connect with others most powerfully
through stories. We learn about addiction and about ourselves
from the experiences of other addicts. Hearing about someone

who did the same awful, unspeakable things as we did, who is no longer doing them, can be life changing. To hear of the hurt, the isolation, and the secrets—all so familiar to us—is healing. No fluff comes through in these stories from other women, just the raw truth. Hearing this nitty-gritty honesty is what helps us to identify with others. Then, we start to share our pieces of our own story with others, and that's even more healing. Eventually, we learn to tell the whole truth about ourselves—as we hear the full truth about others—and the connection comes full circle.

Connection breaks the isolation of addiction, and it's one of the most powerful aspects of recovery for women. As we connect with other people who share our experience, we start to feel as if we belong to the human race. We belong to a community of other recovering people. In Alcoholics Anonymous and other Twelve Step programs, this belonging is called "the fellowship." While this term is in the masculine form, it refers to a connection with all recovering addicts in the program, women and men. Other phrases for addicts in recovery as a group are "people in the program," "recovering community," and "community of recovering people." Regardless of the label used, it's all about the connection of one person with another to overcome addiction.

The Big Book talks about this connection and compares it to what happens when people are rescued from a shipwreck. Regardless of their individual nationality, wealth, religion, race, sexual orientation, intelligence level, social status, or other differences, shipwreck survivors feel a closeness, a bonding, with the other people who were saved from their common peril. The same is true with recovery. No matter what usually separates us from other people, when we're "rescued" from addiction, we connect with those who are in the same boat with us. We connect with people we may not have even considered connecting with in the past. Many of us describe our first chemical use as "finally belonging." In recovery, we come to describe ourselves as "finally belonging" in a much more meaningful way.

Addiction can be the block that stands between us and others. Like a wall that surrounds us, it prevents heart connections from getting through. As we hear stories of addiction and share our story with other recovering addicts, the wall comes down slowly, brick by brick. Or, it may collapse quickly. We may feel the power of connection with another person heart to heart—for maybe just twenty seconds at first, and then, before long, a minute and even five minutes. When we first make such connections, we can feel indescribably wonderful. Sometimes this connection comes from just listening and not feeling alone anymore, and sometimes it comes from sharing something of ourselves. Either way, we find a feeling of belonging that many of us have been seeking all our lives.

> *Part of what had me pick up in the first place was those feelings of feeling different, of not fitting in. So, it wasn't a surprise, I'm sure, in anybody who was paying attention to me as a kid, that eventually I would find a way out of that gnawing pain. For years I did. For years I was a human garbage can.*
>
> :: FANNIE MAE

The Program

You may be thinking, *It's fine to hear other people's stories and make connections with others. Sure, they may inspire me to put the chemicals down, but then what? What do I do to stay clean, to stay sober? How do I manage when I'm hurting, when I'm happy, when life's ups and downs come?*

Here's where the second part of the solution comes in: doing the work of recovery, also called "working the program." Working the program of recovery means developing a new way of living based on a set of recovery principles. A program of recovery teaches us how to live without chemicals. It also offers so much more. The basic guide to this way of living and to these principles is the book *Alcoholics Anonymous* (also known as the Big Book). There are several short quotes from the fourth edition of the Big Book in *A Woman's Guide to Recovery*. Many other books have also been written that are based on the principles in the Big Book. These are principles commonly accepted across many cultures, religions, and other belief systems. They are strong, universal principles.

Because of the strength of addiction, we find we need a strong way of living. We can't be messing around. We don't need information that tickles our ears or appeals to us emotionally. We need something that works. We need to read whatever Twelve Step literature helps us the most in moving forward in our recovery. We also need personal direction and support to follow this program and to live by these principles. This personal help comes from other people in recovery who are working the same solution. Others who've gone on before us can help show us the way. Alcoholics Anonymous started when one man reached out to another, and

The fellowship of Alcoholics Anonymous would not exist without a woman. Henrietta Seiberling was responsible for bringing together the two people who founded the organization. This woman, by literally practicing "connection," changed the course of the lives of millions of people in the world today. Other women in AA's early days also helped to build the connections that contributed to its successful growth. Their stories can be found in a number of AA's publications.

then together they reached out to one more, and then the three of them reached out to more addicts, one at a time. That's how the fellowship grew, soon including women.

In our recovery community today, one woman reaches out to another woman, and together they reach out to one more, and the growing fellowship keeps reaching out to more addicts, one at a time. That's the fellowship in action. What provides the real bonding is not only being saved from a common peril like the people in a shipwreck, but building life on the stable foundation of the principles of recovery. We're learning to live life in a whole new way, on a whole new foundation.

For many of us, this solution doesn't sound appealing. In fact, at this point many of us may be questioning whether we're really an addict. *Put the chemicals down? Totally? A whole new way of living? Do I really need all this?* Most of us ask these question when we hear the solution, and it's a good thing we do. If we're not an addict, then we don't need the solution. If we are an addict, life has become pretty raw, and we need to do something to change. Our way isn't working. Many of us have the experience of trying to get sober on our own. We may succeed for a while, but that success doesn't last too long. To finally be free of the chemicals that enslave us, we need to make a big change.

We need something that will help us to live life as it comes to us instead of substituting chemicals for living. As an addict, when we feel pain, we want to use. When we feel happy, we want to feel happier, so we use. When we're lonely, we get out our best friend: pot or wine or heroin. We may use to add some excitement to our lives or to calm ourselves. The sun is shining; the sun is not shining. We always have a reason why we "need" to use. At the same time, we know the hell that using will lead to, but we come up with more reasons—reasons why it's okay anyway. "This time" it will be different. "Somehow" I'll be able to control myself. "I'm only going to have a little." There's always a reason. In the end, there's always hell to pay.

When we see the changed lives of others and compare them to our hopeless situation, we have two choices. We can continue to use and end up in a psychiatric hospital, a jail, or an early grave, or we can pursue recovery. The Alcoholics Anonymous literature talks about pursuing recovery with the "desperation" of a drowning person. There is no middle-of-the-road solution. There are no half-measures that work. Sure, most of us try shortcuts, and a few people have some measure of success with staying off chemicals for a while. What half-measures clearly don't do is help us develop a foundation for life that is stable and worth living. When we see freedom in others in the fellowship, when we see their happiness and serenity, why would we want to stop short of getting it all?

> *I've had friends who have died from overdoses, and I always think when that happens that if they'd just given recovery a chance, maybe they'd have been able to experience even half the joy that I feel now. And it makes me so sad.*
>
> :: KAREN

As you read this, be assured that if you pursue recovery with even half the vigor you used to pursue your chemicals, recovery is possible. Consider all the time, money, and effort you put into using, recovering from using, thinking about using, hiding and sneaking your using, and the list goes on. Recovery is about freedom. Freedom from the craziness of all this waste and misery. Freedom to live in today, just for today. Freedom to learn to love yourself, others, and a Higher Power. Freedom. How free do you want to be?

The one thing that can get in the way of true freedom for any of us addicts is not looking fully into the solution. It certainly won't work if we don't try it. Sometimes in early recovery, we are told to "act as if." Act as if we care. Act as if we matter. Act as if we want to do something. At first, we may wonder, *Isn't it dishonest to "act as if"?* That's an interesting question coming from addicts who haven't been truly honest in a long time. Actually, it's not dishonest. It's starting to act our way into right thinking. The feelings will come later. This topic will be discussed more in chapter 6, on feelings. For now, "acting as if" is the way to begin.

We're given many suggestions early in recovery, and we need to put the suggestions into action. We're at the point where it's clearly time to "do it." This is our life we're messing around with. In early recovery, getting and staying clean is about doing what works, not doing what *we think* works. Our way hasn't worked so far. Why would it start working now?

"Willingness, honesty and open mindedness are the essentials of recovery" (*Alcoholics Anonymous*, p. 568). *Essentials.* The acronym WHO helps us to remember *willingness, honesty,* and *open-mindedness.* Willingness comes first and naturally leads to the other two—willingness to be open to another way of doing things, willingness to be honest, willingness to show up, willingness to learn, willingness to listen, willingness. When we're willing, a lot starts to fall into place. It's like we're giving ourselves a gift that keeps circling back to help us. A little bit of willingness gets us to take one small action to move us forward in the right direction. Then, by taking that action, we become a little more willing. We're

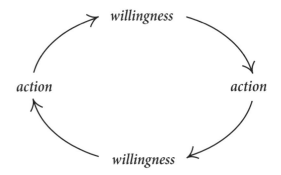

ready to take another action. That action, in turn, creates more willingness, and this ongoing cycle of willingness and small actions is how we keep moving forward in our recovery. Willingness quickly changes our lives for the better. This change has happened to millions of women, and it can happen to you too.

Principles

We move out of addiction into recovery in a variety of ways. Yet, the stories of recovery have something in common: the principles of recovery. These principles are solid truths or qualities that are essential to our recovery no matter our culture, religion, intelligence, sexual orientation, socioeconomic status, ethnic heritage, parental status, employment status, educational level, or even our gender. They are working for millions of us. Living by these principles changes lives radically, leading us from the isolation and despair of addiction to the freedom of recovery.

Some of the principles have already been introduced earlier in this chapter. Willingness, honesty, and open-mindedness are three essential principles. Connection with other addicts (fellowship) is another one. The Twelve Steps offer a set of core principles. The program is based on working the Twelve Steps, and a core principle is reflected in each Step. As we work these Steps and live by these principles, our lives change. The Twelve Steps and their related principles are listed below. They will be discussed in more depth in later chapters.

The Twelve Steps
These are the Twelve Steps as they appear in *Alcoholics Anonymous* (pp. 59–60):

> 1. We admitted we were powerless over alcohol—that our lives had become unmanageable.

2. Came to believe that a Power greater than ourselves could restore us to sanity.

3. Made a decision to turn our will and our lives to the care of God *as we understood Him.*

4. Made a searching and fearless moral inventory of ourselves.

5. Admitted to God, to ourselves, and to another human being the exact nature of our wrongs.

6. Were entirely ready to have God remove all these defects of character.

7. Humbly asked Him to remove our shortcomings.

8. Made a list of all persons we had harmed, and became willing to make amends to them all.

9. Made direct amends to such people wherever possible, except when to do so would injure them or others.

10. Continued to take personal inventory and when we were wrong promptly admitted it.

11. Sought through prayer and meditation to improve our conscious contact with God *as we understood Him,* praying only for knowledge of His will for us and the power to carry that out.

12. Having had a spiritual awakening as the result of these steps, we tried to carry this message to alcoholics, and to practice these principles in all our affairs.

The Twelve Principles

Here is a list of the spiritual principles reflected in each Step.

Step One: Honesty
Step Two: Hope
Step Three: Faith
Step Four: Courage
Step Five: Integrity
Step Six: Willingness
Step Seven: Humility
Step Eight: Compassion
Step Nine: Justice

Step Ten: Perseverance

Step Eleven: Spiritual Awareness

Step Twelve: Service

Sound like a lot to work on? Yes, recovery asks a lot of us, but the program helps us to learn how to use these principles, and the principles themselves are pretty simple. We practice them one step at a time, one day at a time.

Simple, but not easy. As you read these first few chapters, if you're becoming open to looking at your addiction and the solution, you've already started. You're beginning to look squarely at the addiction and the mess it is making of your life. No more excuses, rationalization, or blaming. It's time to get honest. Scampering around the issue doesn't work with addiction. Honesty is one of the key principles. It's the basis for the First Step. By being honest, you've already begun making your way out.

What's Different for Women in Recovery?

Addiction is addiction. All addicts, both men and women, need to put down the chemicals. The principles of recovery work equally well for both men and women. Women's experiences may differ somewhat from men's as they find their way out of addiction and into recovery. Some of these differences are common to many women.

Cringing at the Thought of Powerlessness

Some of us struggle with the term *powerless* in the First Step. As women, we may feel like we've been powerless victims most of our lives, and we feel rebellious when we're told we're powerless and that's just the way it is. Why would we give ourselves up completely? That's not the gist of the First Step, though. In fact, it's one of the first paradoxes of the program of recovery that women experience. We find that if we want to see women with power, we need look no further than some of the women in recovery. These women are on fire.

A paradox is something that doesn't make sense. It's the opposite of what we think is true, but it *is* true. The paradox in Step One is that when we admit powerlessness over chemicals, we start to *get* power. When we take a deep and honest look at the fact that we can't use responsibly, can't stay quit on our own, and have made a mess of our lives, well, that's when we're on our way. For the first time in a long time, we—not the addiction—are in the driver's seat. Admitting our powerlessness over chemicals allows us the opportunity to discover the true power that comes through the program of recovery.

> *I remember going to speak at a meeting at a treatment center where the director was a friend of mine. When he introduced me to the group, he said to them, "I'd like to introduce you to a friend of mine. We've pretty much known each other for all of our lives. And this is one person that I didn't think ever would sober up." When he said that, my jaw dropped. I was shocked that this was the opinion he had of me. That brought home to me the miracle of sobriety. I believe I am a miracle.*
>
> :: JOANNE

Basking in the Feeling of Connection

The program of recovery is a natural for women. Most of us like to feel connected. Many of us enjoy looking out for each other and talking to each other. In fact, many of us find that our self-esteem rises as we connect with others. Addiction blocks these meaningful connections. Recovery removes the blockages and builds or renews the connections.

Some of our tendency to connect and communicate has a physical cause. In fact, it could be said that we are "wired for connection." Scientists who study the brain have learned that the female brain has more connection and communication activity than the male brain. For instance, the average woman uses 20,000 words a day, while men average 7,000 words. This gender difference is apparent even in young children. Young female babies study faces much more than baby boys do. A young girl's day can be made or ruined based on what's happening with her friendships. Teen girls spend hours on the phone communicating. Having a fight with a best friend becomes a major crisis. Throughout our lives, we women tend to focus more than men do on communication and relationships. Generally, women remember details of emotional connections and fights much more clearly than men. While some of these gender differences can be attributed to society's expectations and to upbringing, women's focus on connection has a lot to do with the female brain structure.

Women also have a history of gathering in groups to talk about their lives and to help each other. Quilting bees were a time not only to make quilts to provide warmth for the family but also to share stories and get advice and support. Men usually do things alone or side by side, but most women feel natural when they gather together to do things, to share, and to care for one another. Sharing and caring are natural for most women, but addiction robs us of that. In addiction, we become separated from others. We do things that hurt people. People learn not to trust us, not to count on us. Some of them may even leave our lives. Recovery is the opposite. It's about caring, communicating, connecting again— reclaiming the gift of being a woman.

Feeling Equal, Sharing Power

Recovery groups are also natural for women because, as with addiction, recovery is the great equalizer. Women typically prefer to share power, and Alcoholics Anonymous and other Twelve Step groups do just that. They are nonhierarchical. The ground is level in these groups. No one is considered better or worse, higher or lower than another. In fact, many of us may not know where others in the fellowship work, where they shop, or much about their family lives, but we know their deepest secrets and their pain. The level ground of recovery is the one and only level in the Twelve Step fellowship.

Recovery is natural for women. When we're new to recovery, this may seem hard to swallow. We may despise the thought of being a part of a group. We may think it's not so for us, that we're a hopeless case. Be assured, this isn't true!

No one is too hopeless for recovery, but it will take some work. You may say, "I'm not an addict, so I don't need to do this," or "I know I'm an addict, but I can't put down the chemicals, so I'll just try to control my use again," or "I know I'm an addict, but this won't work for me." These ways of thinking seem like the only way out, but they're just a ticket to more misery and loneliness. Recovery is possible! It's possible to put down the chemicals and live a full life. It works and it takes work. Other women who have experienced recovery can show you how they've done it. You'll learn from them how to make the program work in your life, in your own way. The important thing is to *do it.*

You *can* do it. With the help of others in recovery, you *will.*

FANNIE MAE'S STORY

I got sober when I was twenty-six years old, and I've been sober twenty-seven years. I picked up my very first drink when I was fourteen. Between fourteen and twenty-six, I did not draw a sober breath. When I was about six years old, I was like a country bumpkin, having moved from the South to a sophisticated part of New York. We were really poor. We wore hand-me-downs, my sister and I. We had a strong

Southern drawl. I just didn't fit in. The kids made sure I knew that, and they ripped me apart. They made such horrible fun of me.

At that stage of my life, I didn't have the kind of program for living that says, "You don't have to take that." I just internalized everything. From a very early age, I discovered that the way around those horrible feelings was to escape. My earliest escape came through books and movies. When they stopped working for me, I discovered the wonderful world of drugs and alcohol. Picking up my first drink and drugs started as a way to feel okay in my own skin. I just hated myself as a child, being black, being a girl, being poor, being a Southerner. It was just a way to not have to feel.

When I was fourteen years old, I was strung out on heroin. When I was eighteen, I dropped out of school, and I was living as a homeless teen on the streets of New York. I didn't have a place to go. I went from bed to bed, whoever would take me in. I lived on the streets for a good deal of time when I was a young person. By the time I was twenty-one, I was selling my body. I was a prostitute to pay for my drugs and my alcohol. I was a teenager in the sixties, and everything was about better living through chemistry. My whole life during those early years was either about taking care of the addiction or feeding into the sickness that prompted me to be addicted in the first place.

I was introduced to a community of people who were not drinking and using, and I wasn't ready to join them, to stop drinking. So, I did a "geographic." I moved from New York City to Las Vegas, Nevada, thinking that life was going to be different. I failed to realize that when I physically moved from one place, I took me with me. My addiction, my bad habits, my bad attitude—they all trailed along to Vegas with me.

About nine months later, I got hit by a car in a blackout. When they found my limp body lying in the middle of the street, my left leg had come up behind my head, with the bone sticking straight out. They didn't think I was going to live, or walk again. I was on crutches and in a cast for almost my entire first year of sobriety. Today I walk with a limp. I have the scar on my leg, the battle scar. Every time I look at my leg and the ugliness of the scar, I'm reminded of every drink I took, of every drug I took, and of every inappropriate act as a woman I ever performed. I need to look at my leg and be reminded that if I choose to pick up today, I could easily be back in that place. So that's how I got sober. That was the wake-up call. Even then, I didn't get sober right away. That's how sick the disease is. It took me another month and a half until I actually put down the drinks. I had to stop doing the thing that was killing me.

I quit cold turkey. I quit on my own. It was very hard. Everything I've ever been strung out on, I've kicked cold turkey. I kicked heroin cold turkey. I kicked cigarettes later cold turkey. I kicked alcohol cold turkey. It was very hard going through the DTs when you're only twenty-six years old, not knowing what's happening. I found a community of people who were trying to stay sober like I was. Thank God, because I don't think I could have done it on my own.

One of the hardest things for me after I got sober was dealing with the shame of who I had become when I was drinking and using drugs. I found myself standing in the shower, trying to take off what I thought was the surface dirt. I would scrub and I'd scrub—so hard I ripped my skin open. I kept thinking, if I cleaned my body, I would clean who I am on the inside. And I couldn't. No amount of soap and water, no amount of pretty clothes, no amount of perfume would ever take away the stench of who I had become as a woman alcoholic.

Yet I can tell you today, twenty-seven years later, I'm in a place where I have forgiven myself. The primary reason that I have forgiven myself is that I no longer behave that way. But it's taken all the years that I'm sober to get to the place where I no longer hate who I am. I mean, there were days when I'd look at myself in the mirror, and I couldn't stand the image that looked back at me. Like when I was little, I used to use razor blades to try to scrape off my skin. I'd used bleaching cream to try to take off my color. Because again, as a child, I hated who I was so much.

What has been really amazing for me is that after the initial first few years of just learning how not to drink and use drugs (and that's what it was—a learning process), I started to open to the endless possibilities that were really available to me in my life. I had never felt hopeful. I had never believed that I could have a life like the people I read about or saw in the movies or on television. I was about two years sober when I started to get a glimmer that, you know what? I could create any kind of life I wanted. It was then that I decided to go back to school.

I decided to become a lawyer. There were many people who told me I was out of my mind—dream busters. They would say to me, "Who do you think you are? You're an ex-hooker with a criminal record." And I was a high school dropout. So much of my recovery has been about having the courage to go for my dream, despite the naysayers—despite the people around me who didn't think I could do it, and despite my own old beliefs that said I couldn't do it. At this stage of my life, I stopped giving these people and these beliefs power, and I started to just take baby steps to move in the direction where I wanted to be.

Becoming a lawyer was the first major goal I'd ever had in my whole life, and it was the first accomplishment I had ever experienced other than staying sober. It took me ten years. First I got my GED, then I put myself through college, and then I worked my way through law school. I ended up going to a great law school, where it was hard to get in. It was even harder to get out. Much of the time I felt like a failure. The insecurities in my brain kept saying, *You can't do it. You can't do it. You can't do it.*

What kept me going was God and the support system that I had built up around me. I had a mentor as well, who was just an amazing woman. She just kept saying to me, "You can do anything you want if you are willing to do the work. You've got the tools today to do it." She just kept encouraging me to go to that God, go to that source.

A lot of people say you have to have confidence in yourself, and then the good life will follow. I believe that's garbage. See, had I waited to feel confident, had I waited to feel like I could do something, I'd still be sitting, waiting. I had to be willing to take an action, even though I didn't believe I was going to get there. That's how I got through school. I became willing to move my feet. I was willing to just keep showing up. I didn't believe I was going to become a lawyer, actually, until the day I was confirmed and given my license to practice.

Even today, I don't always believe in myself. There are times when I feel a little doubtful, but I'm willing to do the work, no matter what. God bless that woman who was my mentor. She just kept saying to me, "Life is not always easy. If you sit and wait for it to be easy, you'll be waiting forever." If I was feeling anxious or something, I was told, "Go do service." I was told, "Well, you just gotta sit with it. You feel the feelings, and you won't die from them, but you just feel them." As a result, today, hard work doesn't bother me. If I'm a little depressed at times, it doesn't destroy me.

Eventually, I stopped practicing law and went for another dream: I wanted to be a writer. I've published two books. I never thought I could do anything like that. I also ran two 26.2-mile marathons in my forties. Those were major accomplishments because, physically, I had destroyed my body.

In sobriety, I've learned how to take care of myself. I actually have osteoporosis in certain parts of my body because of not taking care of myself early in life. Well, I can't change that, but there are some things I can do today to prevent it from spreading even more so. So I exercise. I use weights. I'm careful about what I put in my mouth today. I take vitamins. I'm in a weight-loss program, and I just took off twenty-six pounds. I'm mindful of what I eat. I take care of my skin. I get screenings annually. I see my general practitioner. I also have my gynecological exam, and I have a mammogram every year. I had my bone density exam done last year. I have an eye exam every year. I'm willing to do the things I need to do to take care of myself.

I've learned to take care of myself around men. I used to put myself in a position to be beat up by men. I was always being physically assaulted. I remember once, a pimp I was with stabbed me in my foot with a pair of scissors. Never again. No more. I will not allow another man to put his hands on me. One of the hardest things that I had to come to terms with, particularly in early sobriety, was that I was not going to die without a man. I'm an ex-hooker, so my whole life was about being kept, having somebody there. So, there were days when I'd cry myself to sleep on a holiday when I was getting sober, when I was alone. At the same time, I had to just deal with it. Part of how I dealt with it was that I got involved in service, I made friends with women, and I found activities that were of interest to me.

Over time, I did date lots of guys, but I waited until I was forty-five before I got married, and I was interviewing him! It wasn't just matter of whether he liked me, it was whether I liked this guy. By then I had spent enough time focusing on my own self that I could set conditions in the relationship, and if the guy didn't want to meet them, fine. But then he was gone. I didn't feel torn apart and like I had to settle because he didn't like it. In my case, he had to like my cats. My husband laughs about that today, because he knew that the way to my heart was to like my cats.

Where I am today has happened over time. In the very beginning, even when I was early in sobriety, I was still sleeping with other people's husbands. I was still being kept. I was still being paid to sleep with guys. So, it was gradual. I was about three or four years sober maybe when I actually became self-supporting through my own contributions. That was a big highlight for me—the day that I stopped taking money from men.

The other lesson I learned was to stop using excuses for how I was behaving. When I wanted to go back to school, I remember complaining to my mentor how, you know, "Poor me, poor me. I can't do anything. Because of my race, they won't let me." I would also use the fact that I was a woman. I would say, "I'm only a girl. I might as well just get married and have babies." And while getting married and having babies is great, if that's what you want to do, it's not the road for many of us. So, I had to stop using my race, my gender, and my history as excuses for either not doing something that I really wanted to do, or as an excuse for my bad behavior.

CHAPTER 3

Getting Started

TO GET FULLY INTO RECOVERY AND TO STAY IN RECOV-ery, we may have to deal with several immediate concerns, and fairly quickly. However, working on them isn't as simple as one, two, three, and then four. Several of them may need to be handled at once. We may need to make sure one thing is getting set up while we start work on another and begin plans for yet another. The good news is that many women have gone through this journey ahead of us, so they can help us sort out what to do when.

Safety

The most pressing concern for all of us as soon as we enter recovery is *safety*. Beyond such physical needs as food, air, and water, safety is the most critical need we have as human beings, according to the hierarchy of needs described by the famous psychologist Abraham Maslow. While we were using, our drugs alone were enough to put us in danger, but we may have also spent time in dangerous places and gotten into some unhealthy relationships. Recovery is a time to begin taking care of and valuing ourselves physically, emotionally, mentally, and spiritually. Following are some safety issues to consider right from the start.

Detox

When getting off chemicals, physical withdrawal can pose a danger. As mentioned in chapter 1, when the chemicals are leaving the body, the body experiences a shock to the system. It's used to the chemicals. It depends on having them. So, when they're removed, the body overcompensates.

A simple way to think about physical withdrawal is this: it creates the opposite effect from what the chemical creates. If a drug, such as methamphetamine, gives us energy and the ability to stay up for days, withdrawal makes us crash. By contrast, alcohol is a depressant that slows down the body. During withdrawal, the body speeds up, overcompensating for the slowness that happens during the alcohol use. That's why people in alcohol withdrawal shake, have tremors, and may even have seizures or delirium tremens. The effects of alcohol withdrawal are so potent that more people die in withdrawal from alcohol than from any other drug. For this reason, medical attention is always needed for alcohol withdrawal.

With all drugs, seeking medical advice for withdrawal is advisable. Our bodies are complicated. Many things affect us during withdrawal: not only the chemicals we've used, but how much we've used, how long we've used, our liver function, our health history, the medications we're taking, our emotional stability, our hormonal activity, other aspects of our physical condition, and much more. Getting medical consultation and advice during withdrawal is important.

Most of us don't think we need medical help because we've withdrawn before on our own. That may be true. However, this disease is progressive, and our bodies get in increasingly worse shape over time. Just because we didn't convulse or die in withdrawal in the past doesn't mean it won't happen this time. We *don't* know how it will go this time. We really don't.

I went through the DTs in early recovery. I remember when I was in the situation with these other people who were also getting sober, we'd be holding hands, and my hands would be shaking and my palms would sweat. I remember at night it was so hard to sleep in the beginning, because I would have the night sweats. I'd be in my apartment, and I'd feel bugs crawling on me—and they weren't there. But I could have sworn they were. Or I would see things that weren't there. It was so scary. I was still a young person. It was just horrible. Bottom line, it just took a long time for me to get past the initial physical pain of not drinking. I don't know how I was able to do it, other than I had a group of people who were supporting me through it. It was so hard.

:: FANNIE MAE

Many of us need the safety of a detoxification ("detox") unit when we are getting off chemicals. A detox is a place with medical staff who monitor the physical process of the chemicals leaving the body. A detox is usually in a hospital or treatment center, although some cities and counties have stand-alone detoxes. Most detox units only take people who need medical monitoring during the detox process.

If our medical advisor says we don't need ongoing medical monitoring, like the kind that is done in a medical detox setting, we still may want to go away while we're detoxing. It's good to get away from the triggers for using in our own environment. Also, detoxing from some drugs generally means needing lots of sleep. Some women stay in the home of a friend, family member, or another woman in recovery. Still others go with a friend to a hotel for a few days. Of course, staying at home is also a choice. The point is to be safe and to break the cycle. We need to seek medical advice first, and then go to the place where we can safely withdraw and begin the process of recovery.

Besides being the safe and, in many cases, lifesaving way to go, seeking medical advice can be the start of "asking for help." One of the key principles in recovery is that we can't do this alone. We need other people. The first word of the Twelve Steps is *we*. In Step One, we admit that *we* are powerless over our chemicals and have unmanageable lives. We're in this together. Remember "can't use/ can't quit"? On our own, we can't quit and we can't stay quit. We need to learn to ask for help in recovery. We need to tell a medical advisor what we've used and how much, so that she can assist us in having a safe detox. This simple act of truth-telling about our chemical use may be the start of getting honest. If we hide certain chemicals that we're using and "forget" to tell or "don't think they matter," we may risk our physical safety, since the medical person won't have the whole picture. It's also important to tell our medical advisors if we can't remember everything we've been using. For many of us, that's the real truth. We can't remember how much and when.

While some of us don't need medical detox, others have a particularly tough physical withdrawal. If we get through a tough withdrawal and are feeling better, we might be tempted to think we're "done." For this reason, feeling good after detox can be a double whammy—we think we're done, and we think we can recover on our own. The truth is that getting the chemicals out of our bodies is the beginning in recovery, but that's all it is. We have a lot of changes to make to stay in recovery. We can't make those changes alone. We need the help of others.

Living Situation

Another major threat to a woman's safety can be her living situation. Many of us need to move to different housing immediately after we decide to get into recovery. In addiction, we don't take

good care of ourselves, and we may make unwise choices in partners or living arrangements. In recovery, we may have to move out
of a crack house. Or we may have to run for our life to escape the
sex trade or other illegal or dangerous circumstances.

If we're living in abusive relationships, we may have to move
to a "safe house." Safe houses are places where people who are in
fear of domestic violence can live safely, with little danger of being
found by the potential abuser. They're usually run by nonprofit
groups and generally are free of charge. They're meant as a temporary living space or refuge for safety. These places are not always
"as nice" as our homes, but they are set up so we can live there
without fear of being killed or beaten up.

Just because someone gets sober doesn't mean the abuse or the
domestic violence will stop. This is true whether we're the abuser or
the person being abused. If we're the person being abused, we may
have heard that we "deserved it" because we were high or drunk.
This isn't true, although thinking this way may cause us to hope
the abuse will stop once we're sober. Other women in recovery will
quickly warn us: don't count on it. We may also be hoping the
abuse will stop if our partner becomes sober. Again: don't count on
it. If we're the abuser, we may think we'll quit abusing when we get
sober because we're only abusive when we're using. Again, women
who've been there will say: don't count on it.

Domestic violence and addiction are two separate issues and
need to be dealt with separately. What's most important is our
safety, and if we have children, their safety. We won't be able to
work on our recovery while living in an unsafe setting. If we're living in an unsafe environment, our focus will be on trying to keep
out of harm's way, on trying to stay alive, on trying to intervene so
the kids aren't abused. It will not be on our recovery. We need to
be able to put all of our attention and energy on recovery, not be
focused on trying to stay alive.

If you're being abused, strongly consider spending some time apart from the abuser. Ideally, while you're apart, the other person will work on stopping the abusive behavior. But the priority is to get you into a safe setting, so you can devote yourself fully to your recovery. If you're the abuser, consider spending some time away also. Again, ask for help. Programs are available to help women seeking safe living situations. They are staffed by people who are experts at helping women dealing with domestic violence. You may get some helpful suggestions from women in recovery, but part of asking for help is also listening to people who specialize in certain areas. Their advice may just save your life.

Leaving an abusive situation completely is not always possible or necessary. If you're incarcerated, you don't have the option of "getting out" at present, but you do have some other options. These may include talking to another addict in recovery who is incarcerated with you and asking her what she does to try to be safe. It may mean watching your tongue and your reactions to others, keeping a low profile. Incarceration is not an ideal living situation, but it's a reality for many addicts who nonetheless stay in recovery. In future chapters, you'll learn some strategies that won't change an unsafe situation such as being exposed to abuse while incarcerated, but they can help to make it more bearable.

This advice is also true for those of us who believe we don't need to leave our current situation or are unwilling to leave, yet need assurances of safety. We have to set up a safety plan, with specific actions we can take to keep ourselves safe. We need to have escape plans ready in case the possibility of abuse escalates, and we or our children become unsafe. Some women keep a packed bag at the neighbor's or an extra set of car keys there "just in case." Others memorize the number for the local domestic violence shelter. Others have someone available whom they can call at any time for help. Bottom line, we do what we can to protect ourselves and our children. We need all the energy and focus we have to get in and stay in recovery.

When All That Changes Is Everything

Immediately, once we're in recovery, everything starts to change. Our bodies are letting go of the chemicals and adapting to life without them. In our bodies and brains, changes are happening that are stressful physically and emotionally. Physically, withdrawal is a dramatic change for our bodies. Also, after withdrawal we may need to heal from the abuse our bodies have suffered from chemical use. Some of us come into recovery with damage to our bodies that is *directly* related to our chemical use. We may have liver damage, gastrointestinal disease, cardiovascular disease, malnutrition, diabetes, hypoglycemia, sores, abscesses, elevated cholesterol, hepatitis, HIV/AIDS, holes in our nasal septum, injuries, and other problems. These and other physical concerns mean our bodies are in need of some dramatic healing.

Our brain chemistry is also changing and adapting, and things are going nuts inside. Beyond the initial withdrawal, our brain may take a year and a half to two years to heal, depending on our drug of choice. During this time, our emotions are going up and down, pretty wildly at first. Moods can change every twenty minutes or so. Some women joke that it's every twenty seconds. We may also experience trouble concentrating, difficulties with sleep (either too much or too little), emotional extremes (either feeling "flat" or overreacting), and even trouble with coordination.

While our bodies may be changing as they heal in early recovery, so is everything else. Our lives change dramatically in early recovery, inwardly and outwardly. Every area of our lives is affected in some way. In addition to all the changes happening because of our physical and emotional upheaval, we're also faced with many changes we need to make in our lifestyles, our attitudes, and other aspects of our lives.

In recovery, we're told that "everything needs to change." At the same time, we're told that we should not make any major changes in the first year. Doesn't seem to make sense, does it? That's another paradox of recovery.

Looking at this paradox a little more closely, though, we can make sense of it. We are to change everything that needs to be changed *to support our recovery,* yet we're not to make rash decisions about changing things right away that are somewhat stable or safe in our lives and *that don't hamper our recovery.* We leave those decisions for later, when we're thinking more clearly. For instance, if we're in a relationship that's physically safe but not very satisfying, we stick with it if we can during the first year in recovery. Because our behavior will change in recovery and our minds will become clearer without the chemicals, it's smart to keep whatever stability we can for the time being. In general, it's best in early recovery to avoid leaving romantic relationships, jobs, friendships, or living situations that are safe, even if they're not the greatest. Our thinking becomes a lot clearer after a year or two in recovery, and we see things very differently. Many of us come to appreciate those people, jobs, and situations that we once disliked. Because change can be very stressful, we need lots of help from others in recovery—when all that changes is everything.

Recovery Is Our Number One Priority

To manage all the changes and to make headway in recovery, recovery must be our number one priority. Unless we stay sober, all else falls apart. Many of us gasped when we first heard this because we thought our children needed to be our first priority. But we had to consider this: Were our children our top priority when we were using? Wasn't our drug number one? Most likely, it demanded our constant attention, and we were more devoted to our drug than to our kids. The truth is, most of us who are parents neglected our children in favor of our drug. Part of recovery is facing that fact, as painful as it is. Clearly, we must take care of our children (or make sure someone does) and be responsible for their safety, but that's not going to happen if we're using.

Those of us who consider ourselves religious may also react in horror to the statement that recovery needs to be our top priority. Shouldn't our beliefs/religion/spiritual practice be our number one priority? Well, again, it's time to get honest. How well did we really practice our faith? How did addiction get in the way of our true practice of our faith? Recovery needs to be our priority so that we're able to be true to ourselves and practice our faith or religion without the distraction of addiction. The chemicals always win for our attention, no matter how much we thought otherwise.

It's as if our life is a bottle that fills up with rocks and sand. The rocks are large and have to go in first. The rocks are like our meetings, our relationships, our spirituality, and our self-care. Without these "rocks" of recovery, we won't be able to stay sober. Even if we're sober, we won't be of much use to others. Our bottle of life also holds "sand," those things that may seem crucial but aren't, such as taking on an extra project at work, making sure our house is spotless, being at every charity event, or being at every soccer game. The sand is important and adds to our lives, but it's not crucial. Many of us try to put the sand into our bottle of life first and then can't fit the rocks in. It's only when we put the rocks into our bottle of life first that everything fits nicely. When we put our recovery first, the rocks are there, solid and firm, and the sand easily flows around them. The bottle of life is full and everything falls into place.

Recovery is our foundation for living. It's literally about keeping us physically alive and so much more. We need to put the same energy into our recovery that we put into our using. As we focus on our recovery, other things generally fall into place. In time, we create lives that we could never have imagined having while we were using. It may seem like a lot of work, yet it's broken down into one step at a time. It's one small step. Then one more small step. Then another small step. Just one small step at a time.

 At one time, my plate was full—meeting child pro-tection standards, meeting probation standards, plus meeting treatment standards, doing this, doing that. But I made it through that, and it's all paying off.

:: GLORIA

More Issues in Early Recovery

Women experience many common challenges in early sobriety. Most of us encounter some of them, if not all of them. They're not pleasant, but they're normal. If we think we're the only one who's dealing with them, we may feel shame or guilt. Many of us, when a problem comes up, are used to thinking that there's something inherently wrong with us. We feel shame, believing we're *a bad woman*. We think, *This wouldn't be happening to me if I weren't so different*, or *This wouldn't be happening to me if I weren't bad*. Sometimes, we feel so shameful that we keep what's happening and what we're doing in our lives a secret. We don't want *anyone* to know. This hiding of our experience leads to further stress and isolation. Knowing that many women have experienced certain types of difficulties in early recovery can help us in our journey. We are not alone. *You* are not alone. Other women have gone before us, and their experience shows that, when faced with these unpleasant and scary circumstances, we can learn to handle them, and they will pass.

Cravings

Cravings for our drug of choice are common in early recovery. A craving is a strong desire or urge to use. Our body is missing the drug. The brain is saying, "Feed me." Sometimes, it feels as if every cell in our body is crying out for the drug. Our nerves are on edge, and all we can think about is using. We may experience shortness of breath, elevated blood pressure, increased heart rate, rapid pulse, or sweating. The craving may be physiological (physical) or it may be mental. Either way, it's all-consuming. All we think about while craving is just that—the craving. We know that if we use, the craving will stop—for a few minutes. But then the dam has broken and the floodgates are open. Once we give in to the craving and use, we induce further and more intense cravings, and we don't know when or where we'll stop.

Cravings are very powerful. They take us over for a short period and can become our only focus, much like an orgasm or a spasm. The compelling urge to use our chemicals is all we can think about at the time, yet the cravings will pass in a relatively short period of time. Generally, the average craving lasts between five to fifteen minutes. Other women in recovery can offer some clues about how to avoid cravings and how to manage them when they do show up.

Slippery People, Places, and Things

Cravings don't usually just happen. Something triggers them. We may never know exactly what sets off a craving, but if we work on keeping possible triggers out of our lives, we're less likely to be triggered. Common advice in Twelve Step meetings is to avoid "slippery people, places, and things." This advice can help minimize our exposure to various triggers.

Certain situations can be triggers. For instance, coming home after work means it's time to use. Having a day off means having a day to use and even getting a head start the night before. Plenty of other situations can trigger our cravings. Certain music, concerts, ballgames, outdoor activities, girls' weekends, romantic dinners, sex, dancing, smoking, and pain are possible triggers.

Other triggers can be situations in which intense feelings come up, such as falling in love, births, weddings, and funerals.

As we become aware of what our personal triggers are, we need to be willing to make changes in order to avoid them. For some women, just having money in their pockets triggers a craving. This is particularly true with cocaine. If money is one of our triggers, it's helpful in early recovery to limit our access to cash. We can put a daily limit on how much cash we can withdraw using our bank card. We're less likely to go on a crack run with twenty dollars on us than with a hundred bucks in our pockets. Granted, the addict inside us will say, "Yeah, but I'll just save up the twenty dollars for five days." Sure, that's a possibility, but it's unlikely. Limiting cash each day buys us time. Time helps us to think more rationally, pass through the cravings, and put things in perspective. Since most cravings only last five to fifteen minutes, buying time can be helpful, as the cravings will pass. Some people who struggle with cash let someone they trust handle their finances for a while. That's "asking for help" in a very practical way.

> *I've been very close to the program this whole time, so there have been very few times when I've wanted a drink. I think there are the triggers, like if I fly on an airplane, I'll have the thought that I used to like to drink on an airplane. But I don't actually want the drink.*
>
> :: BONNIE

Drug paraphernalia, such as needles, pipes, and glass cleaning preparations are common triggers. Baking soda, flour, sugar, cornstarch, and other white, powdery substances can be triggers for some women. For most women, seeing or smelling the actual drug is a trigger. We need to ask ourselves, what are our triggers? What items get our cravings started? Keeping away from them can reduce sharply our chances of having cravings. We must go to great lengths, if necessary, to avoid them. If seeing white powder is a trigger, we get it out of our living space for a while. Getting rid of white powders may seem like a radical measure to some people, but for those of us in recovery, it could be lifesaving. In addiction, we took radical actions. In recovery, we need to be willing to do things that may seem radical to others. Recovery is our priority. In the great scheme of things, living without certain things in our home for a period is really no big deal.

Sometimes when we're having urges to use, our greatest asset is our feet! If we're triggered by a situation, we may need to turn on our heels and leave. We learn from other women in recovery: don't think about it, just move. If we're on the bus and someone offers us crack, we waste no time getting off the bus. If we realize we're driving by our dealer's house (which we should avoid in the first place), we make sure to get past it in a hurry. Next time, we drive down another road. If we're at a party where we're triggered by alcohol, we get out of there. We always, always, always have a plan for where we can go that's safe. We think ahead of time about where we can go or whom we can talk to if we're triggered. We plan to get someplace safe—perhaps the home of a trusted family member or friend where there is no alcohol or other drugs.

What's safe and what's a trigger will vary for each of us. Some women feel safe in a shopping mall, while others say that a mall is a trigger. Some women feel safe in a church, and yet women who were abused in a church setting may find this a trigger. In early recovery, we learn to avoid anyplace that may trigger more cravings. For most women, the safest place to be is with another woman in recovery. We can lessen a craving by talking about it. That gets the secret out and takes away some of its power. We need to choose someone to talk to who will understand and help us keep from using. People who aren't addicts may not understand. Active addicts may understand, but two addicts early in recovery talking about cravings can soon be off using again. We need to pick someone who has a commitment to recovery. If we think the person we're talking with is on shaky ground in her recovery, the safest move is to involve a third person with more solid sobriety.

It's important to avoid slippery people, places, and things. Anytime we go to the places where we have used before, anytime we're with people we often used with, we're in a slippery place. A common saying in Twelve Step meetings is "If you don't want to slip, don't go to slippery places." Other common sayings are "If you sleep close to the railroad track, you'll eventually get hit by a train" and "Don't go to the beauty shop if you don't want a haircut."

While we can find ways to avoid certain slippery people and places, such as our favorite bar, our heroin dealer, or the doctor who supplied us with lots of pills, some places may not be as easy to avoid. Going to our home can be a problem if that's where we did much of our using. If we used at home, we can ask someone to go into our home and remove every single drug (including all alcohol). If that's not possible, we can ask someone to go through our home with us. As addicts, we use when we're alone, so it's not smart to clean out our stash alone. It's likely to be a triggering event. We have to ask for help. If our home is a trigger, we may consider living somewhere else for a period of time if possible.

> *Most of my friends now come from AA. The people that drank in my life, I stay away from them, my own family members even. Although I love them, I'd rather keep that distance between us, because they are still in the throes of their addictions, and I can't deal with them. They'll drive me crazy!*
>
> :: DENISE

As a backup plan, we need to prepare a "fire drill" for what we'll do if we come across drugs in our possession in the future. Many women tell stories of finding their drugs after they think they've cleaned out their stash. They find pills in the pockets of a jacket they haven't worn for a while, bottles stuck away with seasonal decorations, drugs in shoes, bottles in the back of a closet, a joint in the car, or some powder in a little baggie somewhere. However thorough we may think we've been in cleaning our drugs out of our area, we aren't likely to remember all the places we left things.

Before we come upon a forgotten supply of drugs unexpectedly, we need to have a plan. For many of us, our plan is to dispose of what we find immediately, and that doesn't mean in the garbage, where we can go back and get it. If we find something, we hand it immediately to someone who won't be triggered. If we're alone, we get rid of it immediately (and permanently), and then tell someone about it right after we get rid of it. It's important not to keep it a secret. We talk about it, but first we take action. It's like fire. If the house is on fire, we do what we can to get out of there, and then we talk about it. If we come upon some chemical or trigger, we do what we can immediately to get rid of it.

Some women live with spouses, partners, or family members who want to keep certain chemicals in their household, particularly alcohol and certain mood-altering prescription drugs. If that's true in your case, ask the people you live with to keep the chemicals they use elsewhere. If they're not willing, then set up some way to keep the chemicals where you can't get to them. For example, you can ask them to put locks on their liquor cabinets or to keep their chemicals in their cars or someplace off site. In the case of alcohol, you can ask them to bring it into the house only for a party and then get it right out. The more difficult it is for any of us to get access to chemicals, the more time it buys us to figure out how to keep from using. When enough time passes, the cravings will stop. If we find ourselves conniving about how to get the key to the liquor cabinet or get to the drug some other way, we tell someone. We do our best to close the back door to using.

We don't know when a craving will hit, and when it does, time can be one of our greatest allies. If the drug is not readily available, we're less likely to use. We do everything we can to make it hard to use when a craving shows up. We do what we can ahead of time and don't wait for a craving to hit.

Euphoric Recall

A major part of our disease of addiction is denial. It's present when we're using, but it also follows us into recovery. In recovery, however, it shows up in different forms. One of the most common forms is "euphoric recall." We remember the good times of using and forget the bad times. There were good times, or we wouldn't have gotten addicted. There were also bad times. In fact, there were terrible times.

Sometimes when we're sober, our disease will try to get us to focus on the good times. This focus on the good times is called euphoric recall. We remember the euphoria. We think back fondly to the soothing feeling, the intense high, the connection we felt to the people we used with, the relief from anxiety, the energy, the relaxation—whatever was pleasant. These memories can be dangerous. They may make us long for our chemicals and start us down the slippery slope to using again. Even reading about the good times can induce this euphoric recall. We need to be careful about putting our attention on these "good times." There were indeed good times, but there were terrible times, and it's easy to forget how bad things got if we reminisce about how good we felt.

One thing that many of us find helpful in dealing with the memories of good times is to "keep it green." Keeping it green means to keep the memory of the pain and consequences of using fresh in our minds. We keep it green and fresh. We remember the pain, the loneliness, the shame, and the things we did that were against our values. We bring to mind the humiliation, the degradation, the sneaking, and the hiding. We recall feeling petrified, feeling paranoid, living a lie. We remember what our life was really like. If we're having trouble remembering on our own, we talk to others in recovery. Going to meetings and hearing the stories of others in recovery is a way to remember what it was really like. They'll help us remember as they share their stories and their pain. They'll help us keep it green.

> *I keep reminding myself what it was like before I came in and how bad it was, and that anything is better than that. There's never really been a situation where I thought,* A drink is going to make this better. *I've thought,* Oh, I'd like one. *But not,* I'll bet drinking will totally make this situation work itself out perfectly.
>
> :: BONNIE

Another way we help ourselves is to "play the movie through" or "finish watching the movie." When thinking about "having just one" or using "just tonight" or "just with this person" or "just . . . ," we play out in our minds what will take place once we start. If we have just one, then what? And then what would happen? And then what? "Watching the full movie" helps get the whole story in front of us. It's not having just one. It's loneliness, degradation, sneaking and hiding, being petrified, living a lie, and all the other horrors of addiction. The first part of the mental movie may look great, but the ending is anything but a happy one.

Monkey Chatter

Those tempting thoughts of "just one" or "just tonight" are examples of the many voices that keep coming up in our minds, urging us to use again. They're the disease of addiction talking to us. The disease tells us, *Try this instead,* or *That sure would feel good,* or *I can't stand this craving,* and a whole host of other messages that can lead to relapse. Some people call this constant mind talk "monkey chatter." It's as if we have a monkey on our shoulders talking into our ears about using or recovering from using or how we can't stand what's going on so we *have* to use, and the list goes on.

When the monkey chatter starts, we need to talk with someone. We need to let someone else see and hear what's going on in our head. Talking about our tempting thoughts takes away some of their power. When we hear ourselves speak them out loud, we realize how crazy they are. Other people who are listening can help us put other thoughts in our head to counteract the monkey chatter. For instance, when the monkey chatter starts saying, *I can't stand this craving; I have to use,* others can say to us, "It's only a craving," "It will pass," "You don't have to use," or "Let's go for a walk and talk." Others can help us use tools such as "keeping it green" or "playing the movie through." We don't have to talk back to the monkey chatter on our own. In fact, on our own, we may believe the thoughts and use. We need others. We need the other "we's" in recovery.

> The most important things in order to stay sober
> in your first year are accountability and connection.
>
> :: JULIA

Special Concerns in the First Month

On top of the concerns already discussed in this chapter, a number of other issues can arise in very early recovery, especially in the first month or so. This section addresses these concerns, which may be especially strong early on but usually subside as we move further along in recovery. They affect some women and not others. If they affect you, know that you're not alone.

Sleep Disturbances

Many women find that they have sleep disturbances in early recovery. They sleep too much or have difficulty sleeping. People detoxing from cocaine and meth sleep more initially. In fact, they sleep so much, they are said to be "crashing." With other drugs, such as heroin, benzodiazepines, and alcohol, people may have trouble falling asleep or staying asleep. Sometimes people feel as if they have to use to be able to sleep. Generally, the body adapts, but this takes time. Sleep disturbances in early recovery can last several weeks or longer.

What can help is to get on a regular schedule and to avoid sleeping during the day. Eventually, most women find that their bodies adjust, and soon they're sleeping like babies. Some women need to seek medical or mental health assistance for dealing with their struggles with sleeping. It's okay to ask for help from professionals to deal with sleep disturbances. However, taking *any* mood-altering chemicals (including some sleeping pills) is not advisable in recovery. The brain doesn't know if the mood-altering chemical came from the liquor store, the pharmacy, or the streets. It just knows that it triggers cravings for *more!*

If questions or concerns come up, we can seek out the advice of a professional. Of course we can't assume that all health care professionals have extensive knowledge about addiction, so we seek out those who do, if possible. In some cases, we may have to help educate our family doctor or other professionals about our disease, perhaps asking them to consult with addiction specialists before offering us any type of prescription.

Some women have nightmares or very vivid dreams when they quit using. They may also have dreams about using chemicals. They wake up feeling as if they have used and aren't quite sure at first whether they did. The brain is healing, and the vivid dreams or nightmares are a rebound effect from using. These using dreams happen less and less often over time, although some people with long-term recovery speak of occasionally having them. The dreams can seem so real that they're scary. More than one woman has spoken about waking up paralyzed with fear, thinking she had used. Sometimes it takes several minutes to process what's happening and to realize it was just a dream.

No one is sure why some of us have these dreams, but when we do, it helps to talk to someone else in recovery about them. We can also use them as a reminder to "keep it green" or to return again to the First Step: "We admitted we were powerless over alcohol— that our lives had become unmanageable." Addiction is powerful, whether we're using or not, and even when we're sleeping.

The Pink Cloud/The Gray Cloud

Some people find themselves on a "pink cloud" during their first month or so in recovery. While they may feel lousy for the initial week or two, after a period of eating and sleeping regularly, connecting with others, learning about their disease, and realizing they're not alone, they feel very hopeful—on top of the world. For women whose lives have been in shambles, this experience can be a gift. For some women, the pink cloud is the start of a wonderfully changed life. If it happens to you, enjoy it. Be grateful and make the most of it. Also, be aware that pink clouds may not last forever, and they don't guarantee ongoing recovery. What's most important is to faithfully go to meetings, to talk with others, and to keep learning about and working the Twelve Step program.

While some of us have a pink-cloud experience, others experience a "gray cloud," or low-grade depression, in early recovery. Changes in brain chemistry are one possible cause for this depression. Our brain adapted to being bombarded by the addictive chemicals we used, creating additional receptor sites for them while cutting back on creating our natural feel-good chemicals to compensate. All of a sudden, we're not using our chemicals, leaving the new receptor sites starving for something to pump us up. No wonder we're feeling kind of down. In addition, many of us also have a lot of messes to clean up from our using, causing stress that can leave us feeling anxious and depressed.

Some of us who were "high-functioning" addicts can get tricked by the pink-cloud experience. We start to question whether we really have much of a problem since, after we put down the chemicals, things started going well very quickly. We wonder, *Did I overreact? Maybe I'm not really an addict. Things weren't that bad, and they got better so quick. Maybe now I can control my use.* We minimize or deny the effects of our chemical use on our lives. Sometimes when we haven't lost everything and things are getting turned around quickly, it's easy to slip back into denial.

A common gray-cloud experience for meth users is "hitting the wall." When meth users come off the meth, they typically sleep or "crash" for days or weeks and may continue to have cravings. About fifteen to twenty-five days following their detox, they start feeling better, probably because they're eating again, getting enough sleep, and not using. About day thirty or so, though, many meth addicts hit the wall, feeling a low-grade depression. They're fatigued, lack enthusiasm for anything, and generally feel low. The good feelings they had are gone, and it's easy for them to think they're doing something wrong because they're feeling this way. They may be at particularly high risk for relapse. This is a common occurrence for meth addicts, and the only way past the wall is through it.

> *Addiction for others doesn't necessarily have to be as big and ugly as it was in my life. There are businesspeople out there who are addicts and still function every day, but they're addicts and they have a problem.*
>
> :: KAREN

When we addicts feel lousy, we want chemicals to make us feel better. Women in recovery stay the course during tough periods like this. We take to heart one of the program's slogans: "This too will pass." We know that it takes time, but eventually our brain will heal and our life will get put back together. We talk with others in recovery to learn how they got through it. Knowing we aren't alone keeps us in the solution, moving forward in recovery.

Small Brush Fires

Daily crises are common in recovery. We can be on top of the world one minute and down in the dumps the next and back up in a few minutes. This is normal. What also is normal is that many of us in early recovery have lots of fires to put out. We may have some major messes to clean up. In addition, we may treat everyday events as if they're catastrophic. In truth, our thinking has typically gotten so fuzzy that we don't necessarily know what is a crisis and what isn't. We may overreact and make everything into a big deal. Or we may feel so down that we don't react to anything, even things that are a crisis or are life threatening.

Recovery is about balance. One saying we learn in the Twelve Step program is to "Live life on life's terms." Over time, you too will learn how to respond to life on life's terms, but for the first few months, don't be surprised if you overreact or underreact. Talk over your concerns with others in recovery. Get their perspective on what's a big deal and what isn't.

Making Connections through Meetings and Sponsors

One of the keys to recovery is fellowship, or connection with others who are in the same boat we're in. Many of us may start this process either in a treatment program or in Twelve Step meetings. We may enter treatment in a residential (inpatient) setting, where we live at the treatment facility, or we may go into an outpatient program, where we spend several hours a week but do not stay overnight. Treatment helps us get information on the problem (can't use/can't quit) and on the solution (fellowship and working a Twelve Step program). It helps us recognize how addiction has affected us personally and allows us to talk about our experience with others who understand, as well as to hear stories of others like us. Connections begin through this sharing of stories. Treatment also helps us deal with blocks or concerns that need to be addressed for us to continue in recovery. Treatment is not a magic bullet. It does, however, provide a setting where we can focus on learning more about our addiction and what we need to do to get into recovery. For many of us, it's a place where we feel like we belong and discover that we're not alone anymore. While treatment can be a powerful experience, it doesn't work for everyone the first time. Also, the work of recovery only begins there. We can think of treatment as *discovery,* and then we go out and live life, which is *recovery.* No matter how short or how long the treatment experience is, recovery is lifelong and needs daily work. Part of this work is going to Twelve Step meetings.

What are Twelve Step meetings? They're gatherings of people who are struggling with addiction and want to learn from and help each other stay in the solution. Alcoholics Anonymous (AA) and Narcotics Anonymous (NA) are two of the best-known Twelve Step groups, and they have the largest number of meetings available for people who struggle with alcohol and drugs. There are also specific "anonymous" groups, such as ones for meth, marijuana, and cocaine, as well as groups for addicts who also have mental health concerns. Some meetings are just for women; some are just for men. Most are coed. For those of us easily distracted by the opposite sex, attending only women's meetings can help keep our focus on recovery.

All meetings are based on the Twelve Steps of Alcoholics Anonymous, the original recovery group. The only requirement for membership in a group is a desire to stop using the chemical. You do not have to be chemically free to attend meetings; you just have to have the desire to be free.

Meetings are either open or closed. Closed meetings are just for people who have the desire to stop using. Open meetings are for anyone who wants to attend. Sometimes professionals, concerned persons, family members, or students working on school projects want to learn more about AA or NA, and they attend open meetings to do so. If you want to bring a friend without a chemical problem with you to check out a meeting, go to an open meeting. If you both have used chemicals and want to quit using, then you're welcome at a closed meeting.

Within the two categories of meetings (open and closed) are several specific types of meetings. At *open speaker meetings,* one or more people tell their personal stories of using and recovery. In Twelve Step meetings, when addicts tell their stories, the format they use is to tell "what it was like, what happened, and what it's like now." This is the format that the alcoholics in early AA used to tell their stories to help others achieve sobriety, and this same format, described in these words, has continued over the years. *Step meetings* focus on the Twelve Steps of the program and include the sharing of stories of recovery. At *Big Book meetings,* the people attending read from the Big Book of *Alcoholics Anonymous* and talk about their experience in recovery. A similar format is used for *Twelve and Twelve meetings*, with readings from *Alcoholics Anonymous* and *Twelve Steps and Twelve Traditions.* Those attending *topic meetings* share stories and ideas about a specific topic at each meeting. The heart of all Twelve Step meetings is the sharing of personal stories—stories of how women experience the problem (can't use/can't quit) and how they are working the solution (fellowship and the Twelve Step program). While meetings vary greatly in their structure and focus, what they all have in common is people coming together to share and connect.

> *I think in meetings, for some reason, it's easier for me to be accepting of people because they're alcoholics and because I know we've all been to the same place and we're all trying to get to the same place—just kind of that survivor connection. There are definitely strong personalities involved, and it's not always easy, but for an hour I can practice tolerance. Could I move in with some of these people? Probably not. But can I go an hour? Of course.*

:: BONNIE

Going to our first meeting can be scary. Many people in recovery tell about going to their first meeting and driving around the block several times before pulling into the parking lot, or going to the meeting place but being too scared to go in. Even if we're scared, that doesn't have to keep us from going. We can go to our first meeting with someone else, and that can make us feel more at ease. If no one can go with us, we can remind ourself that the people in this meeting, whether two or two hundred, all started at some point with their first meeting. Also, they like to help newcomers feel at home, so they will most likely do their best to make us feel welcome.

Even once we're in the meeting, we may still feel out of place, lonely, and scared at first. Some of us may be so nervous that we cover up our fear with anger. We may tell ourself that meetings are stupid and we don't need to meet with a bunch of "losers." We may question whether meetings will help anyway. Deep down, we may wonder if we're a hopeless case, and we're scared that this Twelve Step stuff won't work for us. We're terrified.

Fear, anger, doubt, and feeling alone are common reactions

when we attend our first meeting or meetings. What is also common is that very soon we start making connections we never before imagined. We find the honesty and mutual support in the meetings to be amazing. It may take some time, however, for us as newcomers to feel like we belong. We learn to be patient and "keep coming back."

> *Somebody told me to keep going to meetings until I wanted to be there. I thought that that was kind of cool, because it doesn't always mean you want to be there right away, but if you keep going until you want to be there . . .*
>
> :: BONNIE

Meetings vary quite a bit, so it helps to visit several meetings in order to find one or several that feel right for us. Many people in the program also suggest trying out a particular meeting for at least six weeks before deciding whether it's a good fit for us, as meetings can vary somewhat from week to week. It's helpful to put ourselves on autopilot for those six weeks and just show up. We need to go without debating about it in our minds and without judging the meeting. We just show up. We go until we want to go. This may take some time, but eventually we start to connect. The point is to go and to get involved in meetings early in recovery in order to stay in recovery.

Attendance at meetings is helpful, but involvement is the real key. We need to go and participate as often as necessary, even daily, to keep ourselves on the road to recovery. Meetings are where we connect with others and learn how to work the recovery program.

> *I'd say the first two years I went to a meeting every day. I eventually got comfortable enough that no matter what meeting I was at, I would talk. I might not be able to talk about the exact issues that I was really struggling*

with that day, but I was able to talk about "I feel like using" or "I feel like eating" and people understood.

:: TANYA

Once we start going to meetings, we get a sponsor. Generally, it's best for women to get female sponsors. A sponsor is someone who has what we want. It's that simple in the beginning. If someone is sober and we're not, and we want to be sober—well, she has what we want. We ask her to be our sponsor. That's all it takes. Each of us gets to choose who we want as our sponsor. We don't worry if she's not the "perfect" sponsor for us. We can change sponsors at any time, but it's important to get started with someone. Some women ask another woman to be a temporary sponsor as a way to get started.

I now sponsor a young woman out here in the country, and I have a terrific sponsor, which for me was a very difficult thing to attain, because I really was highly suspect of getting close to any woman. This sponsor very gently, very slowly, allowed me to come to her, as opposed to imposing herself on me. And because of that, I have mirrored her sponsoring to my sponsee, and my sponsee is having the same response and reaction that I'm having with my sponsor, which is being very aware that someone is allowing us to come to them—and knowing ultimately that that is unbelievably wise and gracious. My sponsor just sits and listens, makes no judgment, and I do the same. I've really been careful to try as best as possible to do the same with my sponsee. As a result, I have a relationship with a woman, which I have never had before with any other woman. It is one of kindness and of total respect. She respects me. I respect her. When she says to me, "You are just such a blessing in my

life," at first, I was like, "Oh, please, yeah, right. Me a
blessing. Sure!" Today, a couple of years later, I can say,
"Yeah, I am."

:: KRISTEN

Asking someone to be our sponsor can feel scary. We may
think we don't need to be dependent on anyone. We may be afraid
no one will want to be our sponsor. We may be scared that they'll
expect too much of us or that they won't be caring enough. Lots
of fears and doubts, and even anger, can come up about having to
ask someone for help.

While we may be uncomfortable asking, we do it anyway. We
ask the question "Will you be my sponsor?" It's not as if we're asking someone for a lifetime commitment. Even though we may not
even have known this person several weeks, and we're asking her
an important question, it's just a question. We don't personalize
the answer. If the person we ask says no, perhaps it's because she
just can't give us adequate time right now. Maybe she's already
sponsoring all the people she can handle. Or maybe she's not feeling strong enough in her own program to do a good job as our
sponsor. It helps to know that if we get a "no," that probably has
nothing to do with us. True, we feel disappointed, but we do our
best to keep from personalizing her turndown, and we move on to
asking someone else. Having a sponsor is a great start to making
connections in Twelve Step meetings. Someone knows our name.
She notices if we're there or not. She's someone we start to connect
with and who starts to connect with us.

*Use your sponsor. Call your sponsor. If they want
to be a sponsor, if they raise their hand at your meetings to be a sponsor, then there's something that your
calling them is going to help them with. Because they're*

*reaching out the hand that was given to them. With my
depression, having sponsors was very helpful. Even if it
was just calling in and saying, "Hi." It was that contact
with somebody who knew me. They would call me on
my bullshit, excuse my language. They didn't let me slide
when I would say, "Oh, I've got a headache. I don't want
to go to a meeting," or "No, I just don't feel like it." They
would come and pick me up and get me to that meeting,
because that's what I needed.*

:: TANYA

Structure

How do we structure our lives once we're in recovery? Many of
us hate the thought of structure. The Big Book says that we are
an "undisciplined" lot (p. 88). When we were using, we may have
done what we wanted when we wanted, at least when we could
get by with it.

Recovery is about change. We may discover in early recovery
that we have time on our hands because we're not using, thinking about using, or recovering from using. Or we may feel frantic,
trying to clean up the messes we've made while using or trying
to do better as a way to compensate for the time lost while using.
Whichever situation we find ourselves in, having some daily structure will make it easier for us to create a new habit of recovery.
We build in some routines, such as reading a recovery meditation book in the morning, making our bed, and showering daily.
Bigger routines involve setting up a way to spend our days—some
sort of schedule, whether that means going to work or to school
or to a meeting, or possibly taking our kids to the park, or volunteering, or whatever will give order and direction to our life. We

need to have someplace where we "show up" routinely. Much of early recovery is about "showing up"—showing up at meetings, showing up in life.

> *"Progress not perfection," I would say. I used to tell myself that all the time. Or, "I'm doing better today than I was yesterday, or this month than last month." As long as I'm growing somewhat forward and not backward, I'm making progress.*
>
> :: BONNIE

Keep It Simple

> *Be patient with yourself. There's going to be good days. There's going to be bad days. Don't try to do it overnight.*
>
> :: TANYA

Many immediate concerns face you in recovery. You may feel overwhelmed, but just do one thing at a time. So many of the slogans of the Twelve Step program focus on this simple theme: "Just do the next right thing," "One day at a time," "Keep it simple," "Easy does it," "Progress not perfection," "This too shall pass." "Do your best to avoid HALT"—that is, avoid getting too *hungry, angry, lonely,* or *tired.* Any of these states can put you in a tenuous position for relapse. Take care of yourself. Recovery is a lifelong process. You won't get it all down in the first month. Don't get ahead of yourself. Along the way, ask for the help of the women who have traveled this journey before you. Ask their help and hear their stories. You're not alone anymore. Welcome to recovery.

JOANNE'S STORY

It was right around eighth-grade graduation that I started drinking. It was the occasional sip of beer. You're out riding around with friends on the reservation, and they offer you beer, so you take a couple of drinks. I was really afraid to drink. The night of eighth-grade graduation I was so frantic—scared that my friends were going to get in trouble. I was the pep club president and helped put on this big dance and didn't want anything to go wrong. Some of my friends took off from the dance, and I was scared that the police were going to throw them in jail.

Within a month of that, I went to spend the night with a friend, and some of my friend's friends were having a party at their house because their parents were out of town. I remember standing outside of their house, and they had a bottle of whiskey going around, and the object of this whole thing was to pop bubbles. So, you would just swig until you started popping bubbles, and people would cheer you on. That was my first experience of really doing anything other than taking a few sips out of a beer. I blacked out. That was the start of my addiction process. I always went over the edge, ending up in blackouts or getting myself into some really crazy situations. It progressed fairly rapidly into the insanity of the disease. By the time I was eighteen, there was a lot of shame and disappointment and embarrassment and denial. It took me another seven years before I quit.

My parents were both in the middle of their disease as well. I grew up in a home where my father binge drank. My mom divorced him because of his drinking, and I think she had no coping skills to deal with the loss of the relationship, the loss of income, all of that. There were six of us kids, and we ended up with our mother. She started drinking, and her drinking started to progress very rapidly as well. I lived with my mom for a while, and then I moved in with some friends.

Most of my friends drank and smoked pot. It was just the way things were. I wanted to fit in. I think us Natives are pretty predisposed to the alcohol addiction, and I rapidly fell into that mode.

I did graduate from high school. I was in speech, and I did fairly well in school. I was well liked by my teachers, and I think participating in those kinds of things at school was really a saving grace for me, because it took my mind off the trauma of the kind of home life that I had, and the worry that I had about my parents both using.

I noticed all of these things that were wrong on the reservation—the amount of alcohol and drug use, the domestic violence, the child abuse and neglect. I just wanted to get away. I wanted off the reservation. I met a young man and married him after we knew each other for only a few months. He joked around that he saved me from that life. But the drinking was our common bond, the using. We would intellectualize about how bad things were on the reservation, but we were doing the things that caused so many of those problems. And the relationship—it was about the drinking and the weekend partying. We ended up having three children. The children were what caused my initial need to sober up, because I felt so ashamed and guilty for being what I considered myself: a neglectful mother for them.

My oldest child was four and my second son was two when we sobered up. We did the old "fight when you're drunk," and then we'd sober up and try to make things work. I gave my husband an ultimatum, the codependent sort of thing: *It's all your problem. If you would be sober, then our family would be great.* One time, I remember taking the little pamphlet that I had gotten, *Do You Think You're an Alcoholic?* with ten questions like "Have you ever had a blackout?" "Do you drink before noon?" I remember driving out and parking by myself at this lake and looking at these questions. I didn't want to answer "yes," so I answered about eight of them "maybe." We're talking about just a little bit of denial going on here.

I talked to one of the gals that I went to Al-Anon with and said, "I think I need to go to AA." I was going to cry. It was a huge moment. She invited me to her house. We talked and she said, "I'm going to take you to a meeting on Monday night." I was really nervous. We went to this meeting at this place where a man had built an addition onto his house, just specifically for AA meetings. People from the surrounding communities, both Native and Caucasian, would go to the meeting. I remember this was my thinking: *There's going to be a bunch of grizzled old men there, smoking cigarettes without filters, drinking coffee that you probably could stand a teaspoon in, and telling old war stories.* That was my image of what AA was about—maybe because my dad had gone to AA when I was younger. I saw the old guys that would come and pick him up, and I had this image in my head of what it would be.

But I walked in through that door, and there was a guy standing there who was one of my dad's friends, and he just smiled and said, "I was wondering when you were going to walk through these doors." Then I was glancing around and I saw another guy who was a year older than me in school, and he just smiled and came over and said, "Hi," and then it was time to sit down. I sat down and my whole body was just shaking. I was like, *Oh, my God! What am I doing here?* We did a First Step meeting, and this was a powerful, powerful experience for me, because I was important enough to them that they each would tell a part of who they were—for me, specifically for me. I was just amazed. And I'm telling you, I could relate to every single person around that table, from the older guy that could have been my father—one of my father's friends—to the guy that I smoked dope with, to the woman who had double-digit sobriety, which was amazing to me, and a Native woman at that. It sounds so corny, but it was like I knew I'd come home. It was such a relief, because I talked and I cried, and they were so supportive. I felt so blessed.

I started going to meetings and listening. I was like a sponge. Working the Steps was such a relief. I ended up going to treatment, and my husband went to treatment as well. In treatment, the release of working a Fourth Step was such a wonderful thing. It's like, get it all out. Get rid of it. Let it go. Of course there's some fear. *Oh, my God. I'm going to tell them this? What are they going to think?* But then I heard people have humor about some of the things that they had done. That gave me great hope for myself, that anything is possible.

After I became sober, my focus was on maintaining sobriety. I found a group of people on the reservation who didn't use. The first few years of my sobriety, I wouldn't go to the bars. I didn't want to be around any of that kind of environment. After a while, I wasn't fearful of it anymore. I'll go to the bar now to go dancing. I know that in every moment of every day, I have a choice, and I choose not to use.

Recovery has changed every area of my life. Without it, I'd still be fumbling around in the dark. I'd still be afraid of who I am. I'd be afraid to look in a mirror, from an emotional standpoint. I'd still be running from my emotions. I might be going to church, but just so I could go to confession. I still weep—I like to cry. But it's not always tears of grief and sadness. There's a lot more tears of gratitude and joy—gratitude that I see myself as a whole person, that I see myself not as a brokenhearted woman. I'm not a victim. I'm not just a survivor. I choose to live. I choose to breathe deeply. I choose to stop and smell the roses. The corny stuff. I can still get into the grungies as well. But that's a choice. And I know that I have a choice today.

I think the biggest challenge for me was when I had a sibling pass away. I remember wanting to run away from my feelings, run away from the grief. My cousin and a mutual friend and I were driving around the city, and I said, "I don't want to feel this way anymore. Somebody find me some acid. I want to do some acid." So we went to look for some acid. But there wasn't any in the city to be found. Then I remember walking into a convenience store and standing there looking at the alcohol in the cooler. I was thinking, *I haven't had a drink for eight years, and they didn't have wine coolers when I sobered up. I've never had a wine cooler before. Maybe I should give it a try. I just don't want to feel this way anymore.* And I remember the guy saying to me, "You know, you've been sober for too long, and you don't need to do this." That was like just a huge wake-up call, where you kind of shake your head and go, *Am I really thinking this way? Get me out of here now.* It's the whole "but for the grace of God . . ." I feel that God does speak through others, and he was speaking through that young man that day.

When there was so much grief in my life—things that I didn't have any control over—I would just call someone. I had a wonderful group of women friends back home on or near the reservation, and we kept in great connection with each other. And we still do.

I think the big thing for me was about reaching out. Reaching out to others for help. We all need help at one time or another. A lot of us grew up in situations where there wasn't always somebody readily available to us, and I think that AA has shown me that there are ways of finding people who are available to us, that there's always somebody to connect with.

Spirituality

SPIRITUALITY IS VITAL TO RECOVERY. HEARING THIS MAY evoke strong feelings, positive or negative. If we have (or used to have) a well-established, satisfying spiritual life, the word can be a great comfort to us. We're grateful that spirituality is central to recovery and the Twelve Steps, and we look forward to learning more about how it specifically applies to the recovery program. By contrast, some of us have the opposite reaction. We may feel anxious, angry, fearful, or even terrified.

Regardless of our feelings, positive or negative, the gift of desperation that arises from our addiction is often what helps us become willing to take a fresh look at spirituality. We're in a tough spot and our way isn't working. We need to find something that works. In recovery, we learn that there is a solution for addiction and it has two parts: fellowship (connection) and working the program. Both parts of the solution are spiritual in nature.

In trying to understand the concept of spirituality and how it pertains to recovery, several questions may come up for us in the beginning: *What is spirituality? Is it the same as religion? If it's not, how is it different?* We may even find the notion of spirituality so confusing we don't know what questions to ask. If we've had positive experiences with religion, we may think that spirituality means we need to call on our religious faith in order to recover, and our only question may be *How do I get started?* But that's confusing spirituality with religion. If we've had negative experiences with religion, we may be skeptical, critical, suspicious, or resistant about getting involved with anything spiritual. We may even be cynical, thinking to ourselves: *Is this a bunch of stuff made up by men to control women? Is it just a way to get us into a religion?* That's also confusing spirituality with religion. Such concerns about spirituality are so common that a whole chapter (chapter 4) is devoted to them in the Big Book.

Spirituality is not the same as religion, and the difference between these two words is explained later in this chapter. Understanding that difference is important because we need to avoid getting distracted with religious controversy, arguing about whether religion is a good thing or about which religious viewpoint is the right one. Debating theology won't help us recover from addiction. When chemicals have taken over our lives and we're at risk of dying, our ideas and arguments about religion won't save us. We need something that *works*. We need to find a way to *live*. We need a practical program for survival and sanity. The spiritual program of Alcoholics Anonymous is just such a program.

We may think there must be an easier way than to swallow some of this spirituality stuff. Many of us get closed-minded and full of contempt when asked to think about spirituality. This attitude is so common that a phrase describing it in the Big Book is frequently quoted at Twelve Step meetings: "contempt prior to investigation" (quoted from Herbert Spencer in "Spiritual Experience," appendix II, *Alcoholics Anonymous*, p. 568).

An attitude of contempt sets up a roadblock to recovery—and that's exactly what addiction wants. It's the nature of our disease to stay in control. One way the disease can stay in control is to make us think that we're in control. If it can keep us full of contempt and judgment toward a possible solution, then the disease wins—and we keep on using.

We have a disease that is killing us, and we don't have the power to do anything about it on our own. Something pretty drastic needs to happen. Again, open-mindedness and willingness are key to recovery. We may need to reconsider our way of thinking about spiritual matters. If we're rigorously honest, we'll admit that our drugs became our Higher Power. Even if we practiced religion daily, what we actually worshipped were our drugs. We were powerless not to. Our using was the force around which we organized our life. Now we need another force.

One way to approach this topic of spirituality is by saying a "put-aside" statement. Many of us are surprised at how effective this statement is once we give it a try. We simply declare our willingness to be open, to "put aside" any preconceived notions or judgments. We can make this declaration as a prayer or affirmation. If we share it with a sponsor or at a meeting, it will take on even more power. Trying a fresh approach to spirituality by saying the put-aside statement is a great way for us to practice open-mindedness and willingness, which, along with honesty, are the essentials of recovery.

What Is Spirituality?

As important as spirituality is to recovery, defining it isn't easy. If we asked a hundred women in recovery what spirituality means to them, we'd probably get a hundred different answers. Spirituality pertains to spirit as opposed to physical matter. "Spirit" is the essence of our being, the *us* that lives within our bodies. Therefore, spirituality is about our inner life. It's what gives life meaning and direction. While spirituality can seem abstract, it's actually very practical. Spirituality is the quality of our connection or relationship with self, others, a Higher Power, and nature or the world around us. It's the way we live our everyday lives from the inside out.

The practice of spirituality is very personal. If we were to ask a hundred people to define how they practice spirituality, we'd again get a hundred different answers. Even choosing a Higher Power in the recovery program is a personal choice, and it can evolve over time. (You can read more about choosing a Higher Power later in this chapter and in chapter 5.)

It's easy to confuse spirituality with religion. Spirituality and religion are not the same thing. Religions are based on an organized set of rituals, teachings, dogma, and creeds. Some of them have strong spiritual elements, some do not. Many people believe that spirituality is at the heart of religion and that if they are religious, they are spiritual. Other people practice the rituals of a religion and adhere to the dogma and creeds, but don't apply any of this to how they live their daily lives. They may be religious but not spiritual. Other people may be spiritual but not religious. Ultimately, spirituality is about how we live our lives daily in our relationships with ourselves, others, and a Higher Power. It encompasses all we do, think, say, and feel. It's about our spirit.

> When we were growing up, we weren't really involved in our Native spirituality, and it wasn't until I was an adult that I started exploring that part of it. It's become an integral part of my life. I started going to [the sweat lodge] with my friend, and then my mom and my stepdad would have sweats at my mom's house. It was a healing process that was happening with the family.
>
> :: JOANNE

What is our spirit? While *spirit* is not easy to define, we can think of it as the vital essence within us. It's the force that makes us living beings. We feel this spirit or sense of aliveness inside ourselves. Others also experience our spirit as the "energy" we exude to the external world. Spirituality, then, is the way we live and express our essence or inner life. Spirituality is highly personal and subjective.

The "Spiritual Experience" appendix in the Big Book focuses on spirituality. It describes a spiritual awakening as a "personality change sufficient to bring about recovery from alcoholism" (p. 567). A spiritual awakening is about change inside us. It can be a little change or a huge change. We "awaken" and continue to awaken to the spiritual side of ourselves and become open to doing something about it. We experience a simple yet profound shift in awareness about our spiritual nature. In some cases this change is dramatic, but more often our spiritual awakening is of the "educational variety," as the Big Book describes it, borrowing from a term coined by psychologist William James (*Alcoholics Anonymous,* p. 567). We experience a series of small or mini-awakenings. One small awakening makes us ready for the next as long as we remain open-minded and willing.

Embracing spirituality will change us inside so we can recover from addiction. Each of us changes in our own way. It's an inside job, very personal, and it ultimately affects how we behave. Chapter 6 in this book discusses the need to change our thinking in order to change our feelings. As we adopt a spiritual way of life, our thoughts, attitudes, and behavior all change. They change enough that we can recover.

This spiritual way of life is open to all who want to experience it. It's not just for "good" people or people of a certain faith. It's open to everyone. No one is excluded. What a gift.

> *I had tried AA for a year, and, unfortunately, at the time, this woman came up to me and said, "I'm going to be your sponsor." I said, "Okay." It turned out she was very Christian, and she told me that the only way I was going to get sober was to do religion her way. I kept telling her, "Look, that's all fine and well, and I really respect that you're into your religion, but I'm a Buddhist, and I've been a Buddhist since I was eighteen years old.*

*I'm ordained, and I'm a Buddhist." No, no, no, she told
me, I had to give up my faith. So I stopped going to meetings. Very shortly thereafter, I started drinking again.
I figured AA was for religious people, you know. That's
why I never went back again for many, many years. It
wasn't an option for me.*

:: KRISTEN

We don't earn our way into the spiritual realm. It's a gift. It's
grace. Grace is something that is given that hasn't been earned.
The longer we practice recovery spirituality, the more we become
aware of how much grace we are receiving. This growing awareness prompts us to become more and more grateful for the won-
drous things in our lives that we never noticed before. It's as if we
put on a new pair of glasses and see the world differently.

Admittedly, *spirituality* is a pretty abstract term. It can't be
fully described. One thing *is* very clear about spirituality: it's not
addiction. Addiction kills our spirit and our authentic spirituality.
It tricks us by offering a false sense of spirituality. It's an imposter. Addiction is such a close imposter for spirituality that another
word for *alcohol* is *spirits*. We substituted a false spirit for what we
really needed: genuine spirituality.

Why Do We Need Spirituality?

Remember "can't use/can't quit" and the dilemma it puts us in?
We know we get in trouble when we use, and yet we can't quit
or can't stay quit because we're restless and irritable and discontented until we get the relief that comes from using chemicals. Tough stuff. How do we get out of that dilemma? Although
the problem is with our body (can't use) and our mind (can't

quit or can't stay quit), the solution is spiritual. The need for a spiritual solution is another paradox in recovery. It doesn't seem to make sense, but it works.

Through addiction, we come to realize that our real problem is lack of power. That's what Step One is all about. We're powerless over chemicals—can't use/can't quit. We don't have the power to get out of it by ourselves. *Will*power alone won't do it. We need to find some other power to help us. That's where Step Two comes in. Step One tells us that our problem is powerlessness, and Step Two talks about the solution: power, specifically a Power greater than ourselves, also called a Higher Power. The words *Higher Power* are usually capitalized to help us know that they're not referring to the usual power we think of when we try to control our using. That self-driven power obviously isn't effective enough. Something greater or "Higher" is needed.

For many of us, that Power starts out being people: our counselor, our sponsor, or people at meetings or in our treatment center. We see in them the hope of recovery, and that brings hope to us. They represent a Power that is greater than just us. We can feel the power or the energy of hope and joy at meetings. Eventually, many of us choose another Higher Power that we can count on to restore us to sanity. We may name this Higher Power Creator, God, Allah, Jesus, Buddha, Great Spirit, Spirit of the Universe, or other names. In Twelve Step programs, the word *God* is sometimes used as a general overarching name for *Higher Power*. It is meant to be inclusive.

Whatever we choose as our Higher Power, we need to make sure it's something we can rely on. While, in theory, anything can work as a Higher Power, if we don't choose something substantial, we may have a hard time trusting it will be there for us through thick and thin. Relying on a Higher Power outside of ourselves is a central part of the Twelve Step spiritual program of recovery.

I think the spirituality part was pretty easy for me. I remember people saying you could put your faith in a lightbulb, you could put your faith in a doorknob, and you could put your faith in whatever, just as long as you have it.

:: JOANNE

Hearing that we need to base our lives on a spiritual program to keep from dying may not be an easy pill to swallow. Our addiction has brought us to a point of desperation. Despite feeling hopeless, we may find it hard to imagine that basing our lives on a "spiritual" program could possibly be the answer for us. But that's what it comes down to.

Questioning spirituality can be a healthy sign. It may prompt us to start looking deeper, asking others about their experience, and getting out of our comfort zone. We may come to realize that if we had all the answers already, we wouldn't be where we are. It could be that we're ready to try some new ideas, check things out, and become open to change.

Even those of us who think we know all there is to know about spirituality and who have practiced our religion consistently for years have something to learn in recovery. What we know from past experience of religion or spirituality clearly hasn't been enough. If it was enough, we would have been able to put down the chemicals and keep them down. We wouldn't be in this predicament of addiction. We need to be open to more. This doesn't mean we need to drop all our previous practices. Rather, we need to consider being more open. We need to be humble and willing to making some changes. Our way hasn't worked. We need to find a way that works.

But this particular time I was so desperate that I didn't care. I thought, screw them—they can have their Christianity. Me, I'm a Buddhist; I just don't want to

*drink. It's finished. I'm going to end up dead if something
doesn't happen.*

:: **KRISTEN**

We can learn from people who are living on a spiritual basis. Do
they have anything that we want? Typically, people who live a spiritual program of recovery have a fair amount of order in their lives.
They seem peaceful. They're usually patient, kind, and loving toward
themselves and others. They "keep it simple" and lead useful, meaningful lives. These people are happy and enjoy a sense of freedom.
They're true to themselves and able to call their souls their own.

When we're first coming into recovery, if we're honest, we have
to admit that we have few, if any, of these qualities. We would more
likely describe ourselves as feeling defeated, restless, irritable, discontented, steeped in misery, despairing, lonely, drowning, living
in self-pity, terrified, hopeless, living in self-delusion, frustrated, resentful, trapped, and fearful. The words in the previous paragraph
reflect qualities mentioned in the Big Book. They describe what happens when we live the program of recovery. The words from this
paragraph reflect the Big Book's descriptions of the addict, whether
using or not. Addiction is addiction, and unless we work a program of
recovery, we'll likely stay stuck in our negative feelings—even when
we're not using. If all we take away from *alcoholism* is the "alcohol,"
we still have the "ism." The "ism" is what is sometimes referred to
as the dry drunk syndrome—being "restless, irritable and discontented." We may not be using, but we clearly are not a joy to be around.

Living Spirituality

Spirituality is about how we live. It's not something we just read or
talk about. It's something we practice daily by living it. It's at the
center of everything we do.

It's a Process

Spirituality isn't a commodity. We can't go out and buy it. Learning to live a spiritual life is a process, and the process is different for each person. It may seem like a slow process and not easy to define or measure, yet others will see evidence of our growth before we do. They'll notice us being calmer, more honest, and less self-centered, and they'll observe many other changes in us as time goes on. Sure, there will be twists and turns and hills and valleys, but the process of spiritual growth is ongoing as long as we're open to it. The program tells us to focus on "progress, not perfection."

One tool that many of us start using early in the process, and continue to use frequently, is the Serenity Prayer. This prayer is regularly recited in many Twelve Step meetings. It's a short statement that opens us up to receive the guidance we need. It focuses us on either acceptance or action. Really, that's about all we can do about any situation. Accept it or do something about it. The wisdom of this statement has been used by many.

> God, grant me the serenity
> To accept the things I cannot change,
> The courage to change the things I can,
> And the wisdom to know the difference.

Of course, although the prayer was created using the word *God* and is recited in its original form in meetings, we can substitute in our mind whatever wording helps us connect with the Higher Power we choose for ourselves.

Varieties of Spiritual Experiences

The two founders of Alcoholics Anonymous had very different experiences in their life changes. Bill W. had a "white light" experience that created a sudden and total change inside him—right then and there, instantaneously. It was a spiritual awakening that was like someone coming out of a deep sleep and being instantly awake and able to run a marathon. It was a whopper of a spiritual experience. While this type of experience is very rare, many of us seek this. Of course we do. We're addicts. *We want it now!* We'd like to be able to place an order for the solution and have it delivered immediately. That's not likely to happen, however. Even though Bill W. had a sudden, life-changing experience, he still had to work to maintain the changes. He reached out to others, worked the Steps, and did what we call the "daily disciplines" to stay sober. Daily. One day at a time.

Dr. Bob, the other cofounder of Alcoholics Anonymous, had an experience that many of us find more typical. He changed as he worked the Steps. His spiritual experience was a gradual process that happened over time. It was more a series of mini spiritual awakenings. It was like a person slowly waking up and doing the first thing and then the next thing and then the next: getting out of bed, brushing her teeth, taking a shower, getting dressed, and then she is ready for the day. It's one step after another.

While our spiritual development may feel slow to us, our progress is quickly evident to others in our Twelve Step group. They've been down that path, and they get excited when our eyes start to light up, when the fog starts to clear from our heads, when we first share in a meeting, when we start to listen, and each time we show signs of spiritual growth. Before long, we too feel good as we notice small progress for ourselves. As we do one thing and then the next thing and then the next thing, our confidence increases a little. We feel tiny bits of joy inside, and we wonder what it is. We may not be used to being happy with what we're doing since we spent so much of our time in addiction sneaking and hiding, then being fearful and ashamed. The joy comes from doing the next right thing and then the next thing and then the next small step. One step at a time.

For most of us, recovery is a process that happens quickly but feels like it happens slowly. We may wonder if we're living "spiritually," but then we start to see the quality of our relationships with ourselves and with others change. What happens in just a few months of recovery is amazing. Once we put down the chemicals and make a decision to work the Twelve Steps, our lives are different. The Big Book uses the phrase "sometimes quickly, sometimes slowly" when it talks about how we realize the promises that come about as we work the Steps (p. 84). Although it does sometimes feel slow and other times fast, if we practice living spiritually, we're always moving in the direction we want to go: toward recovery.

Practical yet Radical

> *I read daily meditations from different books. And when I'm struggling, I find somebody, I don't care who it is, and chat. I go to church on a regular basis. I rely on contact with my Higher Power to help me.*
>
> :: TANYA

Recovery spirituality is practical. We follow certain principles to lead us along a spiritual path. We *do* certain things. We *do* spirituality. In recovery, the Twelve Steps guide our way. The Twelve Steps contain principles of spirituality that we practice as we work them. We may add some other practices and principles depending on our belief system, religion, or culture, but the principles of the Twelve Steps are at the center of our program of recovery. They're a proven, practical way to get sober and to start to change. The Twelve Steps tell us how to do it, and they work, provided we follow the directions.

Follow directions? That's a tall order, since many of us don't like to do things someone else's way. We may not want to admit it, but most of us are pretty defiant. We want to do things our own way. We've done that for years—and look where that got us. We don't want to listen to others. But the reality of our addiction gives us the gift of desperation, and we finally get to a place where we humble ourselves and start to listen to others. We become open-minded and willing to follow the suggestions that have worked for millions of addicts. We see people who live on a spiritual basis and learn from them.

Spirituality is not only practical. In many ways it's also radical. When we follow the directions, it changes us drastically. We go from a life of addiction to a life of recovery—from taking to giving, from isolation to connection, from misery to joy, from restlessness to serenity. We may still look like the same woman, but we become different inside when we consistently work the Twelve Steps. Spirituality encompasses wonderful qualities that make life worth living, such as tolerance, patience, kindness, and love. In fact, love is so much a part of recovery spirituality that we're told in the Big Book "Love and tolerance of others is our code" (p. 84). These are the kind of changes we can expect to happen when we live our lives on a spiritual basis.

At first, we may wonder if this kind of radical change is possible for us. The answer is yes! It is possible. We see it in others, and if we do what they did, we get what they got. We work the simple program of recovery prescribed in the Twelve Steps of Alcoholics Anonymous. They're a guide for living, a program of action that changes our thoughts, hearts, attitudes, and behaviors. The Twelve Steps and their principles are so powerful and so fundamental to our recovery that the next chapter is devoted fully to them.

Ongoing Process

Spirituality is a lifelong process. We need to be patient with ourselves. Others in recovery will most likely see changes in us before we will. We'll gradually become aware of the changes we've made, and eventually we'll look back and be amazed at how many changes we've made. Changes that make us feel right with ourselves and the world. Changes that make us feel like we belong. Changes that allow us to look the world in the eye. Changes that aren't done to please others but confirm for *us* that we're on the right path. This process of change will happen again and again as we live by the Twelve Steps and live by the principles of willingness, honesty, and open-mindedness. These principles are key to our recovery and our spirituality. We live them one day at a time, one step at a time, doing the next right thing.

 KRISTEN'S STORY

I grew up around theater people in a family with a lot of money. My father and his family are from the upper echelons of New York intelligentsia, very upper crust. When I was a baby, we ended up in the south of France in a very, very idyllic setting. We had a beautiful farm—fourteen goats, olive groves as far as the eye could see, almond groves, fig trees everywhere, pine trees—and we looked out over the Mediterranean. We lived that way for the first six years of my life. I often look back on those memories with great fondness and wish it had continued!

I had my first drink when I was about two. We had this gardener who would let me sit on his lap while he ate his lunch. He'd give me sips of his wine, and I would drink. I would sleep under a fig tree for the whole afternoon because I'd been given wine. Alcohol affected my life early.

Then we moved to England because my father had a job change. I did not speak a word of English, and I was sort of catapulted into a whole transition without a whole lot of support, because my parents were starting to have serious problems. My father decided to have an affair with his secretary and get her pregnant, and he left my mother and me. The last memory I have was my mother completely clumped on the floor by the door, crying, screaming. I was on the landing and my father was walking out the door, and I remember screaming, "Daddy, where are you going?"

My mom and I moved to America, and I was put in a private school. With my British accent, doing my numbers differently, spelling differently, I was put back a grade and tortured by the teasing, because that's what American kids do. My mother worked, and in those days, women did not work. My parents were divorced, and in those days, that was just absolutely scandalous, particularly in the upper echelon of New York society. And my mom liked to get a snoot full and call other mothers and chat. Eventually, word got around that my mother drank. The next thing I knew was that—and I was told this to my face—I was not allowed to go to other little girls' homes because my mother was a drunk.

So many things were different when we moved to America—even my drinking. I was horrified when I went out to dinner and turned to the waiter and said, "Yes, I'll have a glass of wine, please." I was all of eleven. They looked at me like, "Excuse me?" I looked at my mom and said, "What?" She was a little embarrassed and didn't handle it well at all. In France, that's what we did—we had wine at restaurants. That was normal there, but it wasn't normal in America.

My mother and I left for California, where I introduced myself to pretty wild times because those were the days of the Vietnam War demonstrations and the budding of the drug culture. I skipped school and participated fully in that world of dope and got drunk. I remember my first blackout. I was maybe about fifteen.

My mother told me that she was going to send me to reform school. So, I pulled it together and I went back to my number one love, and that was dancing. I threw myself into it, dropped out of high school, and ended up going to London to study dancing. I stayed with a half-brother, a drug dealer, who turned me on to opiated hashish, which I really liked. By day, I was this very disciplined and focused dancer, and by night, I was an addict. I ended up coming back to America, predominantly because my visa ran out. I was accepted into a prestigious music school, and my New York days were filled with Studio 54, Club Regine's, really going with the fast crowd. It was nothing for me to be sitting next to big-name people in the music or political world. I mean, it was just this really fast life. And cocaine was also very prevalent in that life, because I could do several lines and pull it back together to get back in the studio.

The next thing I knew, I was going on twenty-one and had a boyfriend and so got on the Pill. It was making me gain weight, and dancers have to be very thin. So the doctor recommended that a birth control device be inserted into my uterus. One day I was hailing a cab because I was late for class, and the next thing I knew, I was in an emergency room and in intensive care. The new birth control device had pierced my uterus.

The doctors said, "Good news is that you're alive. Bad news: you are not going to be able to dance again the way you used to, and we're terribly sorry, but you'll never have children." As far as I was concerned, I was dead. My career took a nosedive. I did try for at least a year and a half, or two years, and all I ended up doing was drinking myself to sleep every night. And ordering booze from the local liquor store and having it delivered.

And then I did the first of many, many geographicals. I ended up going to Colorado. Went to school there and I was really doing pretty good. I was still drinking, but controlled. And then I met someone who did a lot of cocaine, and I got back into it. My life tail-spinned out of control. So I did another geographical. I dropped out of school and went to California and hung out there for a while. I drank every night and sometimes during lunchtime. The next thing I know, the FBI is chasing my ass because I had been hanging out with a major coke dealer who apparently was wanted on charges of murder. In order to escape from the FBI, I moved down to Florida, which was where my mother was living with her new husband. The next thing I know, I'm in Palm Beach, on the island, and I'm working at very good money, on boats.

This young man was very nice to me and we started dating. Well, this relationship ended up in a marriage, which was two alcoholics and the days of wine and roses. And that was one low point. My story is a series of bottoms that just got increasingly worse. I lost everything with the boat company. Another geographical to Spain, where I opened up a restaurant. Lost everything there. Bottomed out. Another geographical back to America, where I invested in another industry. And again another bottom, because I was just drinking progressively worse and worse and worse. Then I met someone at a bar, drunk. Married him in three weeks, drunk. Ten days later, he left me and had taken my credit cards, my bank cards, and wiped me out and left me with zero money, except the money in my pocketbook. So it had gotten worse and worse.

The next thing I knew I was in government-subsidized housing because that's all I could afford. I got some help from my mom and went back to school to finish my bachelor's in social work. While I was doing the social work, I went to a well-known treatment center to take a short course in addictions counseling. I thought I'd be a great addictions counselor because of all the trauma that I had had with drugs. During that weekend, many, many seeds were planted. I found myself coming home and drinking a liter of wine and coming the next day to class hungover. I knew intellectually that it was wrong, that there was a problem here. But at that point, my addiction said, "Please. They're the ones who are addicts and alcoholics. You're feeling a little bit of discomfort, that's all." Yet, that seed was planted.

After I graduated with my bachelor's, I had a big fight with my father, and there was a six-month span where I went on a bender. I met a guy who was in the program. He didn't know that I drank. I hid my drinking from him. I would drink before he came over, I would siphon bottles off, and I would put all of my bottles in my neighbor's garbage. In my mind, it was because I was protecting him.

One night he came over unexpectedly and I had a glass on the coffee table. I can only describe the look in his eyes as one of extreme pity, sorrow, and disappointment. As I looked at him, as if in a mirror,

I saw my mother. In that moment—I'll never forget that look in his eyes—I had this brain flash: *Oh, my God, if I keep this up, I'm going to end up like all of them.* I remember going outside to the football field. I was sitting on the grass, and I literally gripped on to the grass because I thought I was going to fall off the planet with the realization of—looking up to the heavens—*Oh, my God, I'm an alcoholic!* The next words out of my mouth were, "Please, dear God, please help me." It was the first time I had actually stated to the heavens, "Please help me." At which point, my whole ego structure collapsed. I cried until I cried myself to sleep. That night I picked up the phone to find out where meetings were in town.

In November 1994, I walked into the rooms of AA. I sat in the back at the first meeting. After the meeting, when everything was done and they were closing up, I went up to the person who was leading the meeting and said, "Excuse me, can I have a white chip?" because I was damned if I was going to walk down to the front of that room *during* the meeting when they asked if anyone wanted a white chip. I started going to meetings, and I threw myself into the program. I have not had a drink in twelve years.

I completed a doctorate program and landed my first job in Washington, D.C., with a nonprofit and met the man that I was going to end up marrying. The next thing I knew, I was called and offered a job in the White House. I've been with the government ever since.

A few years later, I had uterine cancer. They did a full hysterectomy and a cervectomy, and I still had to go through chemotherapy. *This was the turning point in my sobriety.* Up until then, while I'm a very personable, sort of chatty-Kathy social butterfly, I always kept people very much at a distance. Just so close and no further. Although my career was great and I had a wonderful marriage, my sense of self-worth had always been challenged at best, even in sobriety. What I discovered, through the cancer, was that people in the meeting rooms really did like me. When I couldn't get to the meetings, they brought the meetings to my house. This experience of cancer enabled me to let go of the person I used to be and to become the person I always wanted to be, which was an authentic self, a mindful self, a caring, giving, and compassionate self. My marriage deepened. My appreciation for all persons who came into my life deepened. I now know that if a person comes into my life, even if it's just to ask, "Can you tell me where I go for XYZ?" or "Is this the office of so-and-so?" that person has been brought to me because of Buddha or God or however you want to phrase it. And each life that I can touch, I can touch with kindness and grace and compassion.

The cancer wasn't easy, but at no time did I want to pick up a drink. But I sure as hell recognized the feeling "get me out of this." If I was still using, I would have been drinking throughout the whole thing. Of course, in the end, I would have been dead. The reason I didn't use was because my husband is also in the program, and we took a vow before we got married: sobriety, God, fidelity to each other. I knew if I picked up, that would be the end of this marriage, and even if he didn't divorce me, I would lose his trust and his confidence and his respect. And I potentially could lose everything I've earned. I've gotten rather accustomed to this lifestyle, frankly. I like my home, I like my garden, I like my sixteen acres of land.

Because of sobriety and because of my cancer in sobriety, I have learned to overcome my fears—my fear of people, my fear of responses, my fear of confrontation. I have taught myself recently that I'm very capable of having a calm confrontation with another person and not have it end up in a screaming match—or not ending up in a ball somewhere crying and being freaked out.

I had a situation where I wanted to strangle someone because she had just done something so incomprehensibly stupid as to potentially embarrass the president. Even two years ago, I would have just let loose: "Are you out of your God-damned mind, you stupid bitch?" Instead, I sat down and I said, "Now, so-and-so, I need to talk to you about some protocol here in government." For me to talk in that tone of voice, that's unheard of. That's new. I never knew how to express frustration or anger, or how to confront people, or how to resolve differences. I would run a mile before confronting. Or if I did have to confront, I'd start shaking. I'd start getting sick to my stomach. I would throw up. It was horrible. I'd have panic attacks. And there I was in front of this woman, fifteen minutes of basically chewing her out, but doing it very respectfully, very calmly, very quietly. I'll admit I was patronizing to her, but while I was patronizing to her, I thought to myself: better that the voice is patronizing than screaming, yelling, or totally inappropriate. So, years nine, ten, eleven, and twelve in sobriety are the ones where I've been learning about interpersonal relationships—how to deal with complex situations, how to resolve, how to nip things in the bud, how to express to someone: "You know, that made me kind of uncomfortable, what you said. Can we talk about it?" instead of not saying anything and seething and ending up hating the person and having resentments. I can now do that, and I have not had knees shake or vomited or had panic attacks for about three years now.

CHAPTER 5

The Twelve Steps: A Way of Life

THE TWELVE STEPS ARE A PLAN OF ACTION FOR RECOVER-
ing from addiction. They guide us step by step out of addiction and
into a new way of life. The Twelve Steps are the basis for working
the program. At first, we work them around our chemical use, but
over time many of us work them into other areas of our lives. They
are truly a guide for living.

This chapter provides just a taste of the information available
on the Twelve Steps—an introduction to the Steps and a few ideas
for working them. It cannot begin to address adequately all aspects
of working the Steps. It's a humble undertaking even to summa-
rize them here, since the wisdom of Twelve Step work has been
shaped by so many people in recovery over the years. Specific directions on how to work the Steps are in the Big Book and other
Twelve Step literature.

"Working" the Twelve Steps

Learning about the Twelve Steps is not enough. The Steps are meant
to be *worked*. While we usually think of *walking* or *climbing* steps,
the program refers to "working" the Twelve Steps or "doing" them,
since each one requires significant effort on our part. Typically,

we work the Steps in order. There is no set timetable for getting through them. We work each Step. We don't skip any of them. We always work them with the guidance of our sponsor.

Many of us work the Steps right away when we put down the chemicals in order to help us "stay quit." We may work through all the Steps any number of times. Sometimes we go back and work one particular Step again, such as making amends in Step Nine, when we become freshly aware of how we hurt someone in the past. Or we go back to work a particular Step more deeply, such as understanding more fully in Step Two that we need help and can't do it alone. The longer we're sober, the more deeply we understand the Steps and want to work them. We never concern ourselves about whether we do them perfectly; we just get busy and *do* them. They not only help us to stay quit, they bring us freedom beyond our wildest dreams.

As mentioned in chapter 4 on spirituality, in Twelve Step groups and in recovery literature, the word *God* is sometimes used as a name for a Higher Power. We may have a variety of responses when we see the word *God* in the Steps. Some of us may be surprised, others comforted, and others offended.

It's important to remember that the Twelve Steps were written in the 1930s, and at that time *God* was used as an all-encompassing term for a Higher Power. The masculine pronoun was also used throughout the early AA literature to include male and female. In meetings, some people may refer to a particular definition of *God* when talking about their Higher Power, but in the program literature, the term *God* is purposefully vague and left to our own individual interpretation. It is meant to be inclusive and not to dictate the specifics of our Higher Power. While Step Three refers to God, it goes on to say *"as we understood Him,"* leaving the way open for our own individual definition.

The Twelve Steps are listed in chapter 2 on pages 38–39. They also can be found in *Alcoholics Anonymous* (pp. 59–60) and throughout recovery literature. Of course, while the First Step of the Twelve Steps of Alcoholics Anonymous refers specifically to alcohol, in other chemical recovery groups, the First Step refers to other drugs. What we do for recovery, however, is similar for all mood-altering drugs. We work the Steps.

Steps One, Two, and Three

Much of the earlier part of this book was about Step One. Can't use/can't quit. What a dilemma. Talk about powerlessness. We need power. We think we have power, but it isn't working, no matter how hard we try.

How are we to find power? How is this to happen? That's what Step Two is about. Finding a Power greater than ourselves. Trusting that there is a Power greater than our addiction. Many of us once thought *we* were the power, until the great equalizer—addiction—knocked us down for the count. One way to think of a Higher Power is as something or someone outside of ourselves that has more experience and knowledge about something (recovery, in this case) than we do. In finding a Power greater than ourselves, quite a few of us start out with another woman in recovery, our sponsor, a counselor, or our group—anything but ourselves. *All we have to know is that there is a Higher Power and that we're not it!* The first three Steps are sometimes summarized as "I can't. Something else can. I'll let it."

We may find comfort in the idea of a Higher Power, or we may struggle with the concept of a Higher Power at first, just as we struggle with the idea of spirituality. That struggle can take many forms. We may not be able to accept the existence of a Higher Power because of all the bad things we've seen happen in the world. We may resist because of early religious experiences that were negative. Or we may struggle because we think that we know all there is to know about a Higher Power, and we're unwilling to consider any change in our thinking. We may not even be sure why it's so hard for us to accept a Higher Power.

At first, all we're asked to do is to become *willing* to believe in a Power greater than ourselves. That's the place to start. We just need to grasp that there's a Power greater than ourselves and that we're not it. Our understanding of our Higher Power and of spirituality changes as we grow in recovery. That's one reason that Step Three makes so much sense when it refers to our Higher Power *as we understand* it. This understanding doesn't come to us overnight. We start out with *willingness*. The question we each come to terms with is "Am I willing to believe that there is something out there greater than me that will relieve me of my addiction?" We may start out in recovery with such a low opinion of ourselves that we don't feel worthy of being relieved of our addiction or don't think that a Higher Power would be interested in helping us. Or we think we don't really need the help. No matter our thought process, we eventually need to be willing to believe that there is something out there that can get us out of this mess of addiction.

> *Over and over again, I was shown that God's presence is in my world.*
>
> :: KRISTEN

We're told in the Big Book that deep down inside all of us is a fundamental belief in a Higher Power (*Alcoholics Anonymous*, p. 55). Throughout history, people have always looked to something greater than themselves, though that something has been called by many different names. In meetings and in Twelve Step literature, people use various terms to refer to or to describe this Higher Power. Some people use descriptions such as *love* or *power* or *force* instead of a name to describe their Higher Power. Some use the acronym GOD to stand for "good orderly direction," which is what they get from working the Twelve Steps. Some people use specific names for their Higher Power that are part of their belief system. *God* is a common name and is meant to be an inclusive term in the Twelve Steps. Just as our understanding of our Higher Power is likely to change over time, so too the terms or names we each give our Higher Power may change. Part of recovery is learning what words work for us individually.

> ᴄᴈᴖ *I now know that a person has been brought to me because of God or Buddha or however you want to phrase it. I use Christian terms because it's easier. And each life that I can touch, I can touch with kindness and grace and compassion.*
>
>   :: KRISTEN

Our experiences are all different. Some of us have grown up with a concept of a Higher Power that we're very comfortable with. Some of us have no concept at all of a Higher Power. Others are uncomfortable with or even dislike the image we were given as children. The program tells us our understanding or concept will change over time, and we can select a different one at any time. If our image is of a punishing and judging Higher Power, for example, we might choose to identify for ourselves a loving, guiding Higher Power who wants the best for us. That's quite a leap, and it's a process. It doesn't happen overnight, and we need to be patient with it.

If we're not yet sure about how to define a Higher Power for ourselves, we can talk with other women and ask them how they found their Higher Power and how they describe it. We may learn a lot by asking how their experience of their Higher Power has changed over time in their recovery. Another approach some of us use is to write a want ad for a Higher Power. We describe what we need in a Higher Power. We may include terms such as *loving* and *kind*. Some of us ask for a female Higher Power, others for a gender-neutral one. In particular, those of us who've had negative experiences with men may find it helpful to create a feminine image of a Higher Power or bring more traditional feminine traits into our want ad. This process of understanding a concept of a Higher Power begins early in recovery. As we grow in recovery, our concept continues to change. That's why Step Three refers to a Higher Power *as we understand* it. Our understanding changes over time.

> *I had been raised with a very judgmental God, and over the last twenty-three years, that's shifted 180 degrees for me.*
>
> :: JOANNE

While Step Two is about believing that there is something that can get us out of addiction—"restore us to sanity"—Step Three is agreeing to listen and follow the advice or instructions we're given. We remember "I can't. Something else can. I'll let it." Step Three is "I'll let it." Many of us get quite worked up about Step Three at first. We immediately put up our defenses when we discover that we're being asked to "turn our will and our lives over" to a Higher Power. As women, we may think that this Step is another way to keep us powerless and under the thumb of male society. While the language in Step Three may be upsetting to us, it's also upsetting to men. No alcoholic likes to give up power or control. In Step One we found out that our way wasn't working; in Step Two we saw that there was a way that worked; and in Step Three we agree to make use of the way that works.

Step Three is simply a decision. We decide to embrace the solution and work the program of action, which is to do Steps Four through Nine.

We may wonder what it would look like to turn our will and our lives over to the care of a Higher Power. *How will we know what our Higher Power wants us to do? Is this a onetime decision and we're done? Will turning over our lives turn us into robots with no choice or free will? Will we change instantly?*

Our Higher Power often speaks to us through other people, especially in early recovery. Typically, when we're newcomers to recovery, we don't have much of a direct line to our Higher Power. We may think we hear guidance directly, but usually it's our disease of addiction talking to us. Connecting with others in recovery is our way to do a reality check. They keep us on the path to recovery. Some of us describe other people who help us as "God with skin on." They keep us on the path to recovery. As we talk with our sponsor and others working a spiritual program of recovery through the Twelve Steps, we get help discerning what may be most helpful for us. They help us base our decisions on the principles of recovery, not on our own ideas about it. Alone, we use. Alone, we also come up with some pretty goofy ideas that may lead us back to using. Together, we recover.

After a time in recovery, guidance from our Higher Power can become very clear to us inwardly. In fact, one promise in the Big Book is that "we will intuitively know how to handle situations which used to baffle us" (*Alcoholics Anonymous,* p. 84). We will eventually trust our Higher Power to speak to us through our intuition or inner guidance. This guidance often comes in small promptings, from what's sometimes described as a "small inner voice." It can come as the insight to keep quiet when nasty words of gossip are on the tip of our tongue, the prompting to tell the truth about something we've done, or the desire to do something nice for someone and not get found out. Without the chemicals coming between us and our Higher Power, we start to hear these promptings and respond to them. However, we'll always need others for connection and support.

The Big Book offers us a way to make our Third Step decision clearly through a Third Step prayer on page 63. We can say this prayer or make up our own as a statement or affirmation of our decision to take the Third Step. Saying this statement or affirmation aloud with someone else can reinforce it for us. So can writing it down. These concrete actions help to make it real.

Step Three is making a decision to do our life differently, a way that has been proven by other women to work. We continue to refer to this Step throughout our recovery. We make decisions daily about being willing to live the recovery way. That's a principle behind Step Three: turning over our will, becoming willing to do things differently. (Doing it our way has only gotten us deeper into the problem of "can't use/can't quit.")

The Third Step says that we're turning our will and our life over to the care of our Higher Power. We surrender. We wave the white flag. Our way hasn't worked. We're willing to try something that has been proven effective. All we're doing is making a decision to do what works. Once we've made the decision, we move into action.

While Step Three is originally a onetime decision, once we make that decision, we face many daily opportunities to choose again. We have free will and decide moment by moment what we want to do. We don't become robots who are controlled by our Higher Power. We turn our lives over to what works: recovery through the Twelve Steps. We make ongoing choices about what actions to take to carry out this decision. Most of us don't change instantly when we take this Step, although many women feel a great relief when they do. The proof of the change is in what we *do* after taking Step Three.

There is a story of three frogs sitting on a log. One decides to jump into the water. How many frogs are left on the log? While the answer may seem simple—two—the correct answer is three. Three frogs are still sitting on the log. One decided to do something, but that's all it was: a decision. Action needs to follow a decision for something to happen.

Steps Four through Nine: The Action Steps

Steps Four through Nine are often talked about as the concrete action steps. Of course, some of us already take an important con- crete action before we get to Step Four. We put down the chemicals. Some of us use the first three Steps to help us stop using. Admitting our powerlessness (Step One), asking for help (Step Two), and making a decision to do it a different way than our own (Step Three) make it possible for us to put down the chemicals. Some of us don't get sober until we've done a Fifth Step, and some not until after a Ninth Step. Whatever it takes, we need to be willing to *do* it.

Beyond this most fundamental action of becoming chemical-free, Steps Four through Nine map out for us a series of other actions that take us deeper into recovery. The first three Steps were inward work: recognizing our defeated state, accepting that there is hope, and making a decision. Now we get busy making changes in our outer life.

Step Four starts this outward action. One thing that trips up many of us is trying to do a perfect Fourth Step or being overly concerned about whether we're doing it right. Worrying about doing it perfectly is a way to stay stuck. It's important to just do it. It may not be perfect; in fact, it's not supposed to be. It's supposed to be "searching and fearless."

We follow the directions given to us and make a written inventory. Many of us follow the directions right out of the Big Book and make a list of our resentments and fears and the wrongs we've done to others. We can also use *It Works: How and Why: The Twelve Steps and Twelve Traditions of Narcotics Anonymous* or other books or pamphlets published by various sources. We may attend a Fourth Step workshop for guidance. We also work with our sponsor to receive guidance in doing our Fourth Step.

In all cases, our task is to identify our harmful thoughts and actions. We look to see what *our part* was in the difficult relations we've had with others. What did *we do* that contributed to the problem? It's not anyone else's Fourth Step; it's ours. We are to do an honest review of our own thinking and behavior. We are to start taking responsibility for what we do. Though having this disease of addiction is not our fault, it *is* our job to clean up the mess we've made. The Step Four inventory is the way to identify the mess and to make a list of all the damage we've done.

Some of the mess happened before we even took our first drink or drug. The Fourth Step takes in our whole life, not just our drinking and drugging days. It helps us identify what the program calls our character defects, such as perfectionism, grandiosity, low self-esteem, self-pity, resentments, fear, control, self-centeredness, rage, self-pity, and dishonesty. We all have those certain ways of thinking and behaving that have dogged us all through our lives. Recovery is about changing our insides, and we need to know what's in there. That's why we do an inventory that is thorough, to find out what is really inside us.

Doing our Fourth Step list may be one of the most liberating things we've done in a long time. We feel a sense of relief. Writing what we did on paper gives our past some definition, puts some limit on it. We admit we've done some unhealthy and even bad things, but now we're very clear what they are. We no longer have to hide from them, and we know that future steps will help us to deal with them. We may feel some initial shame (thinking we're a bad person), but then we move from shame to guilt, and there are things we can do about guilt. (Steps Eight and Nine help us with that.) Shame will just eat us up. Dealing with guilt will lead us to freedom. Our Fourth Step can be a real taste of freedom.

While we work on our Fourth Step, we stay in close touch with other people. As we look closely at what we've done in our past, harsh feelings may come up—not only shame but fear, anger, and others. As we reach out to others, share our struggles with this process, and get support, we know we are not alone anymore.

In the Fifth Step, we share our written Fourth Step with another person and with our Higher Power, admitting our wrongs to others. That may seem like a tough assignment. We may say along with the Big Book, "What an order! I can't go through with it" (p. 60).

We wonder, *Do we really have to share our deepest, darkest secrets with someone else?* Absolutely. We learn from others in recovery that if we don't, we may not get or stay sober. We need to get the "junk" *out.* As long as this junk from our past is known only to us, it swims around inside us. Talking about it with another person takes some of the power out of it.

In Step Six, we embrace willingness again. At this point, we become willing to let go of our character defects. These are the destructive patterns of behavior that we've identified in our Fourth Step and acknowledged in our Fifth Step. Step Six asks us to be willing to let them go. It's a simple Step, yet a hard one in some ways because we may *like* some of our character defects. They may have served us well at times, but we need to become willing to let them go. When we're not willing, we ask our Higher Power for willingness. That's all we need to do in this Step: become willing.

We can't change until we're ready, and Step Six is about getting ready. There's a saying: "Can't push ready." Maybe we can't push it, but we can become willing for it to happen. We can adopt an attitude of willingness and openness. We can talk to others about this attitude, ask for help, pray, hope or wish, write about our desire to be ready, or share our unwillingness. We may find it helpful to use prayers, affirmations, or statements such as "I'm not willing, but I want to be willing," or even "I want to be willing to be willing to be willing to be willing . . ."

Removing our character defects is hard to do on our own. In fact, it's impossible. In Step Seven, we ask our Higher Power to remove our defects. We may wonder, *How do I ask? Whom do I ask? How long will it take to have my character defects removed?*

By the time we reach Step Seven, our relationship with our Higher Power has changed. It has become deeper. More and more, we trust this Power, listen to it, and follow its guidance closely. We know that when we ask for help, we'll get it if we're honest, open, and willing.

In Step Seven, we ask our Higher Power to remove our character defects. We may use the Seventh Step prayer in the Big Book (p. 76) or a simple statement or affirmation of our own choosing. We ask, and then we do the footwork. We do what we can to change our behaviors. For most of us, it's a gradual change process. The change comes gradually through our behavior and attitude change. We "act as if." Our part is willingness and openness. If we could have let these defects go on our own, we most likely would have. It's almost like working Step One again. Except in working it, we're not admitting we need help with chemicals, as we did in Step One, but with our character defects. Just as we're powerless over our chemicals, we're also powerless over *total* removal of our character defects. While doing what we can to change our behavior helps in the transformation process, a full removal of a character defect is up to our Higher Power.

Of course, we'd like our character defects to disappear instantly once we're sober. That's typical for addicts. We want things done quickly—our way. However, these defects are habits we've developed over a lifetime, and they're usually deeply ingrained. Getting rid of them generally won't happen overnight. Occasionally, our Higher Power does a quick intervention, which we can call a "miracle." But generally, it's a gradual process. We need to keep reminding ourselves that our recovery is about progress and not perfection. Either way, it is a "miracle of recovery" as we change.

Willingness is key to our progress. We're willing to use the tools we have and not just sit around waiting for our character defects to be removed. Tools are things we can use. They work when we use them.

We learn various tools that we can use in recovery through a variety of sources. They can be learned through recovery literature, in treatment, at meetings, through other women in recovery, and through professionals. The list of tools we use in recovery is limitless and is talked about in many places in this book. Some can include talking with others, learning from others, using affirmations, praying, reading, writing, getting information on the Steps through recovery literature, reaching out, using slogans, changing our thinking, breathing, pausing, writing about it, and using other tools we've learned through treatment or through our recovery.

In using the tools, we take action. If we're blaming others, we use the tool of praying or asking for good things for them, or we use the tool of keeping our mouth shut. Inside we may still be blaming, but as we pray or ask for good things for others, our heart starts to change toward them. We can ask our Higher Power to teach us tolerance and patience. We can practice changing some of the messages we tell ourselves about others, such as thinking they should do something our way. We can also talk with another person in recovery about our blaming attitude and ask what she does when she starts blaming. We have various tools to use, and we need to use them.

Steps Six and Seven sometimes get glossed over as fillers between the work in Steps Four and Five and the work in Steps Eight and Nine. While there are only two paragraphs in the Big Book about these Steps, the chapters on Step Six and Step Seven in *Twelve Steps and Twelve Traditions* provide some very powerful insight. They remind us that these are Steps we will do and redo throughout our recovery. They may seem simple, and they are, yet they need to be practiced over and over and over again. We need to remain willing, as some of our character defects raise their ugly heads repeatedly.

In Steps Eight and Nine, we write another list. This time, we make a list of the people we have harmed. Referring back to our Fourth Step can help us with this list. In Step Eight, we become willing to make amends to them all, and then, in Step Nine, we go ahead and make the amends. Many of us have found it vital to work closely with our sponsors in this process. We may think we've harmed a lot of people, and our sponsor can help us figure out whether we've really done harm or not. She can help us see where we've done harm and didn't realize it or where we haven't done harm but thought we did.

Many of us early in recovery want to go out and make amends as soon as we get sober. We feel so bad about what we've done while using. We probably said we were sorry quite often while we were using, though we went out and did the same thing again, or something very similar. Our apologies were meaningless. Step Nine is not something to rush into. We need some time to get our own house in order and for people in our lives to see that we're genuine about our change. Words are empty without change. Amends are about change. A good amend has three parts. The first part is to acknowledge and take responsibility for what we did. The second part is to apologize. The third part is to make the change. Acknowledge, apologize, and amend (change).

After the Ninth Step is explained in the Big Book, a set of "promises" is listed (pp. 83–84). They are so powerful and inspiring that they have come to be known among recovering people as "the promises" and are often referred to that way in Twelve Step meetings. These promises provide hope. Although they are listed after Step Nine in the Big Book, many of us find that we experience some of them earlier in our recovery, showing how quickly our work on the Steps leads us toward saner living and peace of mind.

Steps Ten, Eleven, and Twelve: The Maintenance Steps

Steps Four through Nine are the initial action steps. They are things we clearly *do*. Steps Ten through Twelve are things we *continue* to do. They are called the "maintenance Steps" because they help us maintain our sobriety. Perhaps the most important word in the Twelve Steps for ongoing recovery is *continued*. We continue the actions that will help us stay in recovery and help us grow in recovery. In many ways, the final three Steps are a summary of what we've already done; we just repeat these actions daily. These are sometimes called "the dailies." We continue "doing the dailies." These dailies are vital to recovery.

Just as with any chronic disease, we need to take care of the disease daily. People who are diabetic can't just change their diet or take their medicine for one day and expect their diabetes to be under control for the rest of their lives. The same is true for addiction. We don't expect what we did several years ago or even several days ago to keep us in recovery. We're told in the Big Book that we have "a daily reprieve contingent on the maintenance of our spiritual condition" (p. 85). Our reprieve is daily, one day at a time, just for today, if we work the Steps.

In Step Ten, we take a personal inventory on a daily basis. Many of us follow the directions for Step Ten in the Big Book, which ask us to answer specific questions each day. Another way of doing Step Ten is to check ourselves daily for certain actions or defects that we know cause harm to ourselves or others. In either case, we immediately make amends (changes) where we need to and move on. We don't get lost in analyzing or worry; we get on with life.

In Step Eleven, we practice prayer and meditation. Simply defined, prayer is talking, and meditation is listening. We take time daily to stop and talk with, and listen to, our Higher Power. We pray and meditate throughout our day or at a specific time. Many guides have been produced to offer specific suggestions about how to do these spiritual practices. However we do them, Step Eleven tells us that we are to seek knowledge of our Higher Power's will for us and the power to carry it out.

Many of us talk about doing "the next right thing." It can be that simple. We ask for knowledge of the next right thing, and we do it. Usually the next right thing isn't all that profound. It may be making dinner for our children, shoveling snow, taking a nap, calling someone, or talking to a friend. It's just the next right thing.

*Mostly I just start my day out with my Higher Power
and I end it up with Him, and give most of my gratitude
and my thanks to Him, because I know I would not be
alive today if it weren't for Him.*

:: DENISE

Step Twelve is about practicing the principles of all Twelve Steps in every area of our lives. In order to be able to practice these principles, we need to know what they are. Each step of the Twelve Steps is based on a specific principle. Eventually we start to practice these principles in all parts of our lives, not just around our chemical use and recovery.

The Twelve Principles

The twelve principles, one for each step, are listed in chapter 2 on pages 39–40. Each is discussed in many places throughout this book and in other Twelve Step literature. As we work the Steps, we use these principles in more and more of our life situations, and eventually they become so natural that we use them in "all our affairs." As we do, our lives become transformed. After a while, we realize we're not the same person we once were. We find ourselves eager to tell others how much better our lives have become and to offer them hope for changing theirs as well.

*No one of us was created to become a drug addict
or alcoholic. God created you to be an amazing person.
And no matter what the enemy—your addict—meant
for evil, God can turn around and use for good. So it
doesn't matter how far down you've gone in your addiction, that story you have is going to change someone
else's life. Something in your story is going to turn another person around.*

:: JULIA

A Purposeful Life

Helping others—being of service—is a key principle for ongoing happiness in life. Step Twelve tells us to live lives of service. Once we've found a new way of living, a way of recovery, we are to share it with others. We reach out to those who have been isolated and lost in addiction as we were. We don't take care of them, but we offer our hand in love. We give an encouraging smile or a pat on the shoulder to another addict; bring a newcomer a cup of tea in a meeting; talk in a meeting about our experience, strength, and hope; listen to others' concerns; or offer an encouraging word. At times, we may even go out and meet people right where they are, in the filth of their addiction, whether they're living in squalor or riches. We share with them our story of hope. Our service to others can be as practical as giving someone a place to clean up or getting them a meal. Whatever we do, we pass on what was so generously given to us, with our hands stretched out in love.

Service is a paradox in recovery. We do it because we need to "give it away to keep it," and it turns out we usually find joy in doing it. We lived a life focused on our addiction. Once in recovery, many of us get excited when we're able to help someone who's lost in addiction. It's thrilling to watch people change and to know that we've been helpful in that process. It's another way for us to connect with others and feel connected.

Some of us struggle with the idea of being of service. As women, we may feel that we give too much already in our everyday lives, and now we're asked to give more? Service is about giving, but it's very different than giving because we have to. It's about giving out of our abundance, giving because we have something to give. It's about being helpful with clean, clear motives: to stay sober ourselves and to contribute to the well-being of others. We don't do service to be used or to be someone's servant. We still do self-care and keep our boundaries, but we learn to give out of love and genuine kindness. We are careful not to use our giving as a way to manipulate or control others. Rather, we give in order to serve our Higher Power and other people. For many of us, this becomes our true purpose, and the joy of giving is immeasurable.

> *When I'm stuck in a rut or I'm feeling self-pity or I'm acting selfishly, it never fails that, if I go do some service work or go to a meeting and try to carry the message, I feel better. Meeting with sponsees is my saving grace, because that's an hour or so that I cannot be thinking about my own stuff. When I focus on them, it keeps me staying in the moment and not getting into my own problems and issues.*
>
> :: BONNIE

Many of us find we absolutely love sharing the program, and we start doing Twelve Step work early in our recovery. In fact, some of us do Step One (learn we're addicts) and jump immediately to the Step Twelve idea of helping other addicts. This tendency to jump from Step One to helping others recover is so common that there's a name for people who do it: "two-steppers." Two-steppers are people who figure out they are addicts and work at helping others but don't work the other steps and change. Many two-steppers don't stay sober long. While it's okay to help others early on, we need to work all Twelve Steps.

Getting Stuck

Sometimes we have difficulty working the Steps. We may become confused, resistant, stuck, or arrogant. When we have trouble with a particular Step, we can do some reading from Twelve Step literature or other spiritual books or ask others for help. We can also go back to the Step before it. For instance, if we're having trouble with Step Two, finding hope, we can go back to Step One and see if we really need to find hope. Are we sure we "can't use/ can't quit"? Do we really need to have a Power help us? If we're having trouble with "made a decision" in Step Three, we can go back to Step Two to make sure we have hope that the program will work for us. Why would we want to make a decision to work something that would only be another disappointment? If we're struggling with doing a Fourth Step, we can go back to Step Three and determine if we've made a clear decision to work a program of action. If we're struggling with any particular Step, going back to the one prior to it will help make sure we have honestly worked that Step.

We don't go back and revisit prior Steps alone. We ask others for help; we discuss our process with others; we pray about it; we read literature; and we stay honest, open, and willing. We don't do any single Step perfectly, but we do it to the best of our ability at the time.

Working the Twelve Steps is a lifelong process. We continue to be willing, open, and honest, and the Twelve Steps guide us on our journey of life. Our experience with them changes at different times in our lives. As we work them, we experience the many things we are promised. We hear many promises from others in recovery, at meetings, and in the literature. These promises are found throughout the Big Book, and they are found as we follow each Step. Ultimately, we are promised—and we experience— freedom beyond our wildest dreams.

The Twelve Steps are the essentials for spirituality. Working them gives us a solid foundation for life. We live them one day at a time, one Step at a time. These Steps lead us on the path to being happy, joyous, and free.

How free do you want to be?

BONNIE'S STORY

There is no alcoholism or addiction in my family, so I didn't have a whole lot of information about it when I was growing up, other than what was portrayed in the media. It was a bad thing, a guy under a bridge with a paper bag. I was very active in school, and I was active in a lot of Jewish youth groups and clubs, and I didn't take my first drink until I was seventeen years old. At first I didn't drink a lot, but then I started smoking marijuana. It didn't take long before I was smoking almost every day, all day.

For most of my college years, I smoked pot addictively. All my friends smoked. I would start in the morning, and I would smoke until I went to bed at night, but I was going to my classes and getting good grades. Then I started drinking more regularly around my junior year of college, and in my senior year, I was drinking almost every night. It wasn't to the point of blackout yet; it was just beer with good friends.

I stayed in Michigan after all of my friends moved away, because I wanted to stay with my boyfriend at the time. I started drinking every night to get real drunk, usually until I blacked out or passed out. I was doing it alone, in my apartment. My boyfriend lived with a bunch of other guys who drank like I drank, so when I was with him, we all kind of drank together. Still, I held it together really well. I was good at drinking and still looking like I was sober, or not way past.

It was affecting my life, though. I only hung out with people who drank like I drank, so that cut out a whole lot of people that I could have been meeting. I was driving drunk a lot and bumping cars in the parking lot, stuff like that. I sat home alone a lot. It was no life. It was very depressing. I went to see a psychiatrist, who got me on anti-depressants, which of course didn't work since I was drinking. That counteracts them completely. So, I was very depressed. Over that year, it started affecting work. I got up and drank before work. I drank during lunchtime, and I either came back drunk or called in and said I wasn't coming back. I then left that job and was nannying for a while, and that was pretty crazy because you can't really call in. So, there was a lot of unmanageability.

Then I got into a huge fight with the boyfriend, packed up all my stuff, and moved back to where I grew up. I was supposed to start grad school in the fall, and so I thought, *I'll just go back there and get my life together and stop drinking as much as I'm drinking.* I was thinking, *It's Michigan that's making me drink.*

I got an apartment by myself and continued to drink the way I was drinking. I was working at a coffee shop, and there were days when I would just wake up and start drinking and go to work drunk. I was drinking until blackout, going to work, sobering up during work, coming home and starting again, and then passing out at night. That's all I did. I lived alone, and I was driving drunk a lot. I got my first DUI in June. On the breath test, I blew real high. My parents were extremely concerned because, while they had just thought I was depressed, they started to realize that it was drinking that was probably causing this. The policeman told them that if I could blow that high and still be walking, there was something wrong. I had a really high tolerance, not normal.

I went to jail and then was sent home, where I was on a home breathalyzer for a month, which I kept failing. Then I was taken off and posted bail. I'd sworn for the entire month that I would never ever drink and drive again. But in my head, I was still going to drink, I just wasn't going to ever drive again. I didn't realize that once I start drinking, I have no control over what I do anymore. I got my work permit five weeks later so I could drive to work, and the next night I got my second DUI. I blacked out and woke up in jail. That was kind of my First Step experience: *I'm totally powerless over alcohol. I have no control when I put the alcohol in me. I don't know what's going to happen.* I had sworn for a month that I would never drink and drive again, and here I was in jail, and in my mind I thought, *I just had that one glass of wine, and now I'm back in jail.*

When I went home, my parents were extremely worried, but they also saw that I was totally broken and saying, "I really need some help." They were very supportive in getting me help. I went to a treatment center in August of that year, and I knew I didn't know anything about staying sober, so I kind of just listened to whatever anybody who had any sobriety told me. The big thing that helped me was the people who came and spoke at night. They would tell their stories, and they all had a year, or two years. This was unheard of to me, that it was possible to have more than a week of not drinking. They told me to go to meetings, get a sponsor, work the Steps. So, that's what I did when I got out of treatment. I went to a sober house and lived there for six months. I got a sponsor and worked through my first nine Steps before I left the sober house.

I did a Fourth and Fifth Step, where I did the personal inventory and then talked to my sponsor and told her everything that I'd done. I love that part of the Fourth and Fifth Steps that has you look at your part when you have trouble in a relationship, because I think it gives me a lot more power than if I'm just a victim of circumstance. If someone harms me and I'm a victim, I don't have any control over the next step. If I look at what I did and what I can change, then it gives me more power to change, to take action, and to not feel like such a victim.

With my sponsor's help, I made a list of all the people I'd harmed. For Step Nine, I had to go back and make a lot of amends. There are still ones that I haven't done, just because I haven't seen the person, or it hasn't been the right time. But I've done a majority of them. I think the first ones I did were the big ones, like my parents. There were a couple of small ones I did at first, just to get comfortable doing them.

The first one was kind of scary. It was a friend from high school who I ditched because she didn't drink like I drank and she didn't party. Then, there was one girl I called in Michigan because it was a financial issue, and I wanted to get that taken care of. The amends rarely go how I expect them. They usually turn out better. With the girl in Michigan, I said, "I stole this money from you." She was so impressed that I was coming clean. I thought she'd swear at me or something, that she would be a lot more angry. Instead, she was telling me how great it was that I was telling her, because I didn't have to, and that was kind of weird.

It was scary at first, before doing the amends. But they're not as scary now, because I'm used to doing them. I started to feel the effects—just walking away after an amend feeling really good, like I had done some action toward recovery. The fact that I was ready to do these amends to stay sober made me feel really good. It kind of gave me confidence in my recovery. I could walk down the street and see some of these people, and I didn't have to be afraid of seeing them. That's especially true of people I'm making amends to in sobriety, because those are people I will see again. There was an ex-boyfriend that I needed to make an amend to, a guy I dated in sobriety. The whole time before I made it—and it took me almost a year or so after we broke up to make the amend—that whole year was uncomfortable seeing him. We kind of avoided each other. We barely said hi. I made the amend just a couple of months ago, and since then, I just feel more comfortable. I don't avoid him. I don't go into a different room. We say hi to each other, and we have just a little bit more of a comfort level than before, because I think we kind of both knew that I needed to do it and I wasn't doing it.

My life is very different since getting into recovery. Before recovery, my life was me and the couch and the bottle and the television. I rarely went out. I've had a couple of summers sober, and I go outside now and I enjoy being outside. I never used to leave my apartment, unless it was to get more liquor. I didn't have friends calling. I didn't have a sense of purpose. Now I do. I have wonderful friends. I have a best friend who I don't know what I would do without. I met her in treatment, and we ended up somehow—just a miracle—that we both went to the same sober house, worked the Steps, are still sober, still working the program, going to meetings, and we're very, very close. I've never had anything like that. We're honest with each other, and I have the intimacy that

I've never experienced with other people. I have a sense of purpose that I'm actually doing good for the world. I didn't have that. Even before I was drinking, I don't know that I necessarily felt like I was making the world a better place. I wanted to, but I didn't know how. Now I think I have a very simple way of doing that every day. When I go to a meeting or I meet with a sponsee or I talk to someone on the phone or call my sponsor, I'm being of service, and I'm having a purpose.

I'm in school now getting a master's degree, and I'm working part time in an after-school program. The program has helped me in dealing with other people outside of the Twelve Step rooms. I constantly remind myself to practice the principles with my mom and dad—patience and tolerance and not acting immediately when I want to lash out or say something that might be harmful. I think about what I'm going to say. My work ethic is a lot stronger now, because I can't call in sick if I'm not sick. I have a conscience now. I can't lie without feeling the aftermath.

The biggest thing that I know keeps me sober is I pray every night, on my knees. And I do the formal Eleventh Step at night, where I look through my day to see where have I been resentful, selfish, dishonest, self-seeking, and that kind of stuff, and then I do my prayers. Also, throughout the day, I do a lot of checking in and just trying to keep in contact with my Higher Power. Usually it's when I'm uncomfortable. But definitely there are times when I'm seeing something that—well, I don't call it a coincidence anymore, I see it as God doing something for me. I say thank you, so it's kind of a mix of that. When I'm resentful, I have to check in, or I have to pray. If I'm just uncomfortable, I check in and say, "I don't know why I'm uncomfortable, but I am, please remove it." It took work, because it wasn't normal for me to do that. But it's definitely become more second nature.

CHAPTER 6

Feelings

EACH OF US HAS MANY FEELINGS IN THE COURSE OF A DAY. Feelings give us clues about what's happening inside us. They are signs of how we're reacting or responding to some event, thing, or person. We need to learn how to be tuned in to our feelings so we can listen to what they're telling us. They may be signaling us to do something—or to not do it.

Just as addiction messes up our lives, it also messes up our feelings. When using, we weren't in touch with our feelings because we covered them with chemicals. When we had a feeling that was uncomfortable, chemicals would soften it. When we had a good feeling, chemicals would heighten it. When using is no longer an option, we need to learn what to do with these feelings.

For me, it was more the psychological craving, I think, than it was the physical. I don't want to feel this way anymore. So if I have a beer or two, that feeling will go away. *I think the biggest reason why I drank is because I just didn't want to feel what I was feeling.*

:: JOANNE

Feelings in Early Recovery

In early recovery, we may be emotionally shut down and feel very little or be flooded with feelings, which can be scary, particularly when the ups and downs are coming rapidly. Both scenarios are common in early recovery. We may need to learn how to contain our feelings and not react so much, or we may need to learn how to express our feelings more. Recovery helps us get our emotional life in balance.

The feelings that tend to overwhelm us the most in early recovery are anger, resentment, fear, shame, guilt, depression, stress, and even joy. We will discuss these at length later in this chapter.

> *I'd love to tell you that when I stopped drinking, all of a sudden I was thrilled, and life was great, and I just kind of skipped along into never-never land. But it was very, very hard, because I had to let go of something that I had been dependent on for years. I mean, for years, when I didn't feel good, when it was raining, when it was sunny, when somebody hurt my feelings, when I was happy—for years, when I had any kind of emotion, I ran to drugs and alcohol. All of a sudden, I'm being taught that that's not the way to celebrate—or to handle feeling bad. I had to substitute some new ways of handling disappointment and joy.*
>
> :: FANNIE MAE

Rapid Ups and Downs

In early recovery, feelings can be pretty intense. Some are so intense they make us want to come out of our skin. Rapid mood swings are also common. One minute we're feeling up, the next down. Our moods can change that fast. We may show our feelings easily and possibly in an overreactive style, or we may stay shut down inside, and no one knows that we're having intense feelings. We may be so shut down, we don't even realize that there are feelings inside us, and the reality is if we were aware of them, we'd be aware they are changing rapidly.

> *I just want women to know that it gets better. And if there's no pain, there's no gain. That you have to feel, and when the feelings start coming back, there's some things that are going to come up that are going to be pretty painful. But it will pass. And that no matter what situation comes up, no matter how life shows up, know that you don't have to use, no matter what.*
>
> :: GLENDA

There are several reasons for our intense feelings and rapid mood shifts early in recovery. The biggest reason is that our brain is healing. As mentioned in earlier chapters, when we were using, our brain became used to having certain extra chemicals in it. It even created extra receptor sites to absorb them. In the meantime, our brain cut back on producing some of its own feel-good chemicals. Once we quit using, our brain is not only missing the natural feel-good chemicals that are in short supply, but it has all these extra receptors that are craving the extra chemicals they're no longer getting. While our body will work to straighten this out over time, it can feel pretty uncomfortable early on.

Hormone levels also influence moods in some women, and these levels can change daily. Factor into these changes a brain that is healing plus the other challenges of recovery, and it can be quite a ride.

Another contributor to our intense, fluctuating feelings may be a lack of emotional maturity. Many of us quit maturing emotionally when we started using. Because our lives were centered on using, we missed out on normal developmental stages and didn't experience the emotional growth that goes with them. As a result, a fifty-year-old recovering woman who started using at age fifteen may still have the emotional reactions of a fifteen-year-old. Many of us in recovery don't know how to deal with our feelings. We blame others, we're moody, and we're scared to death. In recovery, we learn how to grow up both emotionally and spiritually.

Keeping Feelings in Balance

In general, women are perceived as being more feeling-oriented than men. That may or may not be true of women in recovery. We may have been shut down in the feeling area for so long that we have no idea what we're feeling. On the other hand, we may be sensitive to our feelings and freely express them or act on them. No matter where we fall on the continuum, recovery is about balance. Eventually, we learn balance in dealing with our feelings also, whether we begin to open up more or whether we learn not to react so strongly to our feelings. Either way, it's about balance. To do this, we learn tools to help us identify our feelings and decide what to do with them.

Feelings Are Not Facts

Some of us treat our feelings as if they were facts. We think that our feelings make us act in a certain way. Feelings just *are*. They do not *make* us do anything. We get to decide how we respond to these feelings inside us. When we don't feel like going to a meeting, it means nothing other than that we don't feel like going to a meeting. We can still go to a meeting. Just because we feel angry at people doesn't mean we have to yell and scream at them, nor does it mean we have to stuff the feeling.

Feelings are not facts; they are just clues to what's happening inside us. Feelings do not have to dictate what we do, although in addiction many of us let our feelings take the lead. If we felt like using, we used. If we felt like isolating, we isolated. Giving in to feelings has to change in recovery. Often, especially in early recovery, we have to do the opposite of what we feel like doing. If we feel like using, we don't use. We call someone instead. If we don't feel like going to a meeting, we go to a meeting. If we don't feel like talking about something, we talk about it anyway. Feelings just give us information about what is going on inside us. They do not need to dictate our actions.

Misreading the Information

While feelings are just information, in early recovery we may misread this information. Our addiction is active and we can't trust it, even when we're not using. Our addiction talks to us, trying to get us to do things to get us back to using. We need to talk back to it. We haven't learned yet how to distinguish between our addiction and our own voice that is supportive of our recovery. In order to help clarify which is which, we discuss our feelings with others who are grounded in the principles of recovery. They can be helpful as we sort out our feelings. In the meantime, we base our behavior on what we're told to do by our sponsor and by the program literature, not on what we feel like doing. We eventually learn to trust our feelings and act on them when appropriate, but that's not the case in early recovery.

Choices and Feelings

When feelings come up, we have a number of ways we can respond. We can investigate the information, ignore it, dispute it, or act on it. For instance, if we feel upset with someone, one choice we have is to gather more information about the situation. Another is to tell ourselves that, although we're angry, the other person is right or what he or she is doing is none of our business. Another way we can react is to tell ourselves we're not angry, denying our feeling or stuffing it. Other options include pouting, refusing to talk to the other person, or acting out physically or verbally. It's the same feeling—anger—yet we have a wide range of possible responses. We always have choices with our feelings. The feeling does not dictate the action. We decide.

Know and Own Our Feelings

To work with our feelings in a mature way, we first have to know what our feelings are. We have to be able to recognize and name them. One way to name them is to group them by basic categories such as mad, sad, glad, ashamed, and lonely. An even simpler way is to call them either uncomfortable or comfortable. Or we can describe what's happening in our bodies. We might say, "My stomach feels tight," "The hair on my neck is standing up," "My teeth are clenched," or "My forehead is scrunched." As we describe our physical experiences, we start to recognize the feelings associated with them. For instance, "When the hair on my neck is standing up, that means I feel scared." Or, "For me, that means I'm feeling excited." The exact same physical sensation could mean different feelings to different women.

When I first started going to a counselor, she'd ask me, "How do you feel?" and I would give her all these thoughts, and she would go, "No, Tanya, I want feelings, feelings, feelings." And I finally asked her one day, "What is a feeling?" I didn't know. As a kid I was taught that people in our family don't cry. And that's all I knew. We're not supposed to cry. We don't get scared. That's something that I've come to terms with, that I am human and

> *I do have those emotions. They are powerful and not*
> *something to be ashamed of.*
>
> :: TANYA

Once we've identified our feelings, the next step is to own them. They're our feelings, not someone else's. Statements such as "You make me feel mad" are neither true nor helpful, because no one can make us feel anything. No one else is to blame for what we feel. The anger we feel is *ours*. In recovery, we learn to claim our feelings as our own. When we own our feelings, we take responsibility for them and we gain internal authority. Saying "I'm feeling angry" is more powerful than "You make me mad," because we're taking charge of our feeling. We own it as coming from us. If we think someone else is causing it, we're sunk. We can't do anything about other people's behavior, but we do have power over ourselves.

We don't have to be afraid of our feelings. Rather, we need to learn more about them and how to manage them. Some feelings may be more comfortable than others, but that isn't always a good sign. In fact, at times we may be comfortable with some feelings we've had for a long time that are problematic for us. In active addiction, many of us lived in resentment and fear for years. Resentment is about living in the past, fear is about living in the future, and recovery is about living in the now. Fear or resentment might seem normal or comfortable because we've felt it for years. That changes in recovery.

Feelings are fluid; they change. It's when we get stuck in a feeling that we may need to seek outside professional assistance. Even if the feeling intensifies for a while, it still doesn't dictate our actions. If we find ourselves spinning our wheels and caught up in a lot of drama because of our feelings, we can practice the "7 T's": *Take time to think the thing through.* How we think makes a big difference in how we feel, a topic that is discussed in more detail later in this chapter.

*CNSO I talk things out a lot with my sponsor and my best
friend. Therapy helped me get in touch with how I'm feeling about things, but it also helps just talking it through
with somebody I know who understands. My sponsor has
one perspective on things, and my friend has another.*

:: BONNIE

In recovery, we have choices about how we act, no matter how
intense the feeling. This is one kind of power we gain in recovery:
a conscious awareness of our feelings and our actions. At first,
it's hard to believe that's possible. But women with more experience will remind us that we can indeed choose how to respond
and that, in time, the feeling will calm down. As we practice
the tools that we learn in recovery, the feelings will not seem as
overwhelming.

We also have the choice to ignore our feelings and stuff them.
That choice carries some huge risks. When we stuff our feelings,
we bury them alive. They bubble inside us like acid in a cauldron.
If we bury feeling after feeling, the buildup in the cauldron has
to be settled, and as addicts, we think the only solution is our
chemicals.

*CNSO I had such hatred toward God and a resentment
toward all that had happened to me, that I could not
think of my life without drinking. Sometimes I was able
to quit for several months at a time. When things seemed
to be going good, something would happen, and I would
get mad at my mom or get mad at someone else, and I'd
think,* I'll show them! *I would go get drunk. The only one
I really showed was myself, because I ended up hurting
myself more than anything.*

:: DENISE

Once we know and own what we're feeling, we have a number of choices. One is to accept the feeling and do nothing. It's just information. We can accept the feeling and then move on. We can also take steps to keep the feeling from intensifying. When a feeling is particularly strong, we can take some of the following actions:

- examine our thinking
- watch our expectations of ourselves and others
- talk with others
- write about our feelings
- read Twelve Step, spiritual, or recovery literature
- pray
- meditate
- breathe deeply and slowly
- be of service

Examine Our Thinking

In recovery, one tool that is especially helpful in dealing with feelings is to *examine our thinking*. What does thinking have to do with how we feel? It may seem surprising, but *thinking comes before feeling*. Thoughts come first, then feelings. This fact may seem surprising, because feelings come so fast. They do come fast, but as we slow down the process and look closely at what's happening, we'll see that a thought always precedes the feeling. And, almost magically, when we change the thought, the feeling usually changes too.

Simple As the ABCs

Several forms of psychotherapy are based on the idea that as we change our thoughts, our feelings will follow. Dr. Albert Ellis, a famous psychologist, used this concept when he created Rational Emotive Behavior Therapy, or REBT. REBT teaches us a new kind of ABCs.

A = An activating event or action takes place.

> *Someone tells you your office looks messy.*

B = You tell yourself something in your head about what happened— your belief or interpretation about it.

> *I should have a cleaner office. I must be bad for having a messy office.*

C = You have a resulting feeling based on what you just told yourself— the consequence of what you just told yourself.

> *Scared, mad, embarrassed, or other feelings.*

$$A + B = C$$
Activating Event + Belief = Consequence (Feeling)

In life, rarely can we change "A" (what happens). What we can change is "B" (our belief about what happens), which will change "C" (how we feel about what happens).

If we change the irrational belief ("I must be bad for having a messy office") to the rational belief ("I'm a human being, and sometimes human beings have messy offices"), then our feelings will most likely change. They'll become less intense or more positive.

In this case:

$$A + a \text{ different } B = a \text{ different } C$$

A = An activating event or action takes place.

> *Someone tells you your office looks messy.*

B = Your belief or interpretation about the event. (What you tell yourself in your head about what happened.)

> *I'm a human being, and sometimes human beings have messy offices.*

C = The consequence of your belief or interpretation. (The feeling you have as a result of what you just told yourself.)

> *Content, open, accepting.*

When we change our thinking, our feelings change. Though it's not easy, with time and practice, we can change our thinking. Looking at the words that make up our irrational beliefs is a place to start.

Killer Words

Some words are especially likely to conjure up uncomfortable or strong feelings, words such as *should, all, nothing, must, always, never, terrible, must never,* or *should always*. Anytime those words are part of our belief, we may want to soften that belief by getting those words out of there. If we do, we'll have a different "C" (feeling).

Killer words show up in statements such as *"All* people are mean," or "I *must never* make a mistake," or "I *must always* know the answer," or "They *should* know better." Modifying these words so the statement is not so black and white can change our beliefs, which in turn changes our feelings. Yes, it's true: *"Some* people are mean," and "I will *sometimes* make a mistake," and "I *sometimes* won't know the answer," and "They *may* not know everything." It's amazing how changing one word can change our whole tone and belief.

Expectations

Some of our problems with irrational beliefs come from our expectations—expectations of ourselves and of others. We learn in recovery to *examine our expectations* of both ourselves and others. The Big Book tells us that our serenity is "inversely proportional to [our] expectations" (p. 420). This means that our serenity is like a seesaw. If our expectations of ourselves or others are high, then our serenity is low. If we want our serenity to go up, then we need to lower our expectations. This need to lower expectations is particularly common for women. We tend to judge ourselves. Many of us feel we *need* to be superwomen. We *should* work fifty hours a week, *should* have an immaculate house, *must* have perfect kids, *should* not feel down, and the list of demands on ourselves goes on. Any wonder why we feel frazzled?

> *I have these very high expectations of myself, which I believe I was given through my childhood. If I place them on me and I don't need them, then I'm kind of setting myself up for failure, and I'm not going to feel good about myself. It's going to be bad for my self-esteem. So, I just continue to try to be more accepting when I mess up.*
>
> :: BONNIE

When we have trouble figuring out a way to look at our beliefs differently, we can ask for help from others in recovery. Many times they can spot the error in our thinking before we can. They can also suggest ways that we can change the belief in order to change the feeling. In recovery, we often talk about "stinkin' thinkin'" and stress the importance of getting rid of it. Stinkin' thinkin' refers to very negative thinking in general, but it can also mean having irrational beliefs in our heads and thinking we need to act on them.

Changing our thinking can change our whole attitude, which can change our world. The Twelve Steps are a big help in changing our thinking. As we work them, it's as if we start seeing life with a new pair of glasses. Our harsh judgments soften, and we become more accepting of ourselves and of others. The world looks different.

I'm a perfectionist for myself, so then I also hold other people accountable to be perfect. When they're not, if I can look at where I'm not perfect and just accept that I didn't do something perfectly, I'll be more able to accept that someone else makes a mistake. I realize, Oh, I do that too.

:: BONNIE

Changing our thinking is just one tool that can be helpful in dealing with feelings. In order for this tool to work, though, it must be used. Leaving a tool on the workbench does nothing. We need to pick up this "change your thinking" tool several times a day. With continued practice over months and years, we eventually learn to identify irrational beliefs quickly and to change them on the spot.

Other Tools

Many tools are available to help with our recovery. Here are a few more that can be especially helpful in dealing with feelings.

Talking with Others

Sometimes just hearing ourselves say our feelings aloud can help us sort them out. We may need to talk about our feelings frequently. We may feel embarrassed to talk about them, but feelings are neither good nor bad. They're just information. When we share information with others, we get their support and also their feedback. Other women who have gone down this road before us have a lot of wisdom to offer. Sometimes, just listening to what others have to say can help us shift our thinking or leave us more at peace with our feelings.

In early recovery, many of us struggle with poor concentration and aren't thinking as clearly as we will be down the line. We're not at our best and won't be for a while. That's why checking out our thoughts and beliefs with others make sense.

Writing

Writing about our feelings can help us sort them out and iden-tify the thinking behind them. Writing helps us "get it all out" on paper. It helps us see just how big something is—bigger than we realized, or maybe a lot smaller. It also helps us see the whole jumble of thoughts behind the feelings, and once we get them all on paper, our minds don't feel so cluttered with them any-more. It helps us see what's rational and what's not. We also feel some emotional release. Writing diffuses some of the intensity of the feeling. We can put our strongest feelings on paper, writing things we'd never actually say to the person we're upset with. We don't need to give it to the person we're upset with. In fact, sometimes it's good to have a trash can nearby. We may decide, though, to read what we've written aloud to another person in recovery. Sometimes just having someone else know what we're going through can be a relief.

Reading

Reading Twelve Step literature or anything about recovery or spiri-tuality can give us new perspectives. As we are open to new in-formation or a different way of thinking about something, our feelings can change. Reading our writing aloud can also help us sort out our thinking.

Prayer and Meditation

Prayer is talking to our Higher Power, and meditation is listening to it. They're both discussed more in chapter 4, on spirituality.

Deep, Slow Breathing

Another tool that we may find helpful is breathing deeply and slowly. We can use this tool anytime and anyplace to calm our feel-ings and shift our thinking.

Service

Being of service, or doing something for others, can help us get the focus off ourselves and our uncomfortable feelings for a while and give us some relief.

Counseling

Sometimes we can't manage to get on top of our feelings by ourselves. We can seek out professional counselors if we need more help in dealing with emotions.

Feelings Recovery-Style

While we have many feelings in recovery, some are of special concern. Resentment and fear are so common for addicts that when we're doing Step Four, we are asked to examine these specific feelings in depth. (The Fourth Step process is discussed in detail in chapter 5 of the Big Book and briefly in chapter 5 of this book.) We learn that resentment is about living in the past, fear is about living in the future, and recovery is about living in the now. Following is a deeper look at some of the many feelings we may experience in this journey of recovery.

Anger and Resentment

Anger is energy. It's powerful, and it can be destructive or it can be our guide in setting limits and taking action. As women, we may feel particularly uncomfortable with this emotion. If we deal with it correctly, though, it can free up our energy for positive uses. When we're feeling angry, we can practice assertiveness, which means communicating directly and respectfully. That can be very empowering. Most of us need to learn assertiveness skills, and we can get help with this from a counselor or other women in recovery.

Without learning how to express our anger in safe and helpful ways, we may stuff our anger or act it out. Neither is healthy. However, acknowledging it and expressing it appropriately can help us move on in recovery.

Sometimes our anger turns into rage. *Rage* is massive anger. Some of us in recovery get in touch with buried rage. We may have been angry for a long time and stuffed it and stuffed it and stuffed it. All of a sudden, we feel like an active volcano. Feeling this sudden, erupting rage can be quite scary. As with any feeling or thought, we are responsible for how we act on it. Telling others about it can take some of the pressure off. By letting off steam with another person, we take some of the power out of our rage. We can also practice some of the other recovery tools, such as breathing, praying, meditating, doing a Fourth and Fifth Step about it, and possibly getting professional help.

> *If I get upset, I sit and talk to my Higher Power. And if it's somebody that I'm upset with, when I calm down enough, I can go talk to them and work it out. I ask God to go with me, and I'll work it out with them. But I no longer want to drink or drug because of it, nor do I get that angry that I want to show anybody and go out and hurt myself because of it.*
>
> :: DENISE

Resentment is anger felt over and over again. We all are wronged at times (or think we are), and we may get angry when that happens. But, if we keep thinking over and over about how we were wronged and stirring up the feelings of anger repeatedly, resentment has taken over. Anytime we're continuing to bring up anger about old wrongs, that's resentment. Resentment is repeatedly "re-feeling" the anger over a period of days, months, and even years.

Resentment is something we need to work hard to avoid, or we risk relapse. As we "re-feel" our anger again and again, the resentment builds up in us, and eventually we're using again as a way to "get back" at someone or something or to "show" them. In setting out to hurt someone else, we lose. Not only is resentment a huge cause of relapse, it also destroys us inside by making us bitter and keeping us angry and separate from others. Fortunately, the Twelve Steps help us work through our resentments, starting with Step Four, where we look at their causes and effects.

> *Now, without resentment, I'm peaceful. I'm more energetic. I treat my daughter different. I'm not over-protective with her. I allow her to make some of her own little decisions. I'm not being so controlling and so over-protective, making her life miserable, which wasn't fair.*
>
> :: GLORIA

Fear

Many women say that the longer they are in recovery, the more they realize how *fear* has driven them. As we get sober, we may actually get in touch with more fear, since we're no longer covering the fear we have with chemicals. We're told in the Big Book that we are "driven by a hundred forms of fear" (p. 62). It doesn't tell us what exactly those hundred forms of fear are, because we all experience fear differently. It does tell us that fear is a common driver in most of our lives. It's a very basic emotion at the root of many other emotions.

Used as an acronym, FEAR is commonly said to mean "face everything and recover." Most of us don't want to go through fear; we want to go around it. Or we're not sure what to do when we feel fear. Recovery is about feeling the fear, acknowledging it, asking for help with it, and moving on to do the next right thing.

In recovery, we're given a prayer to say in which we ask our Higher Power to "remove our fear and direct our attention to what

He would have us be" (*Alcoholics Anonymous,* p. 68). When we ask for it to be removed and ask for our focus to be on what we should be, we start to move out of fear. We become willing to go through the fear so we can move past it. We start to "face everything and recover."

Another common interpretation of the acronym FEAR is "false evidence appearing real." Fear is not always based on reality. We may be responding to false evidence. We need to check it out with others. Sometimes we find that we magnify things, making them bigger than they are. We need to share our thoughts about our fears with others to get a realistic perspective. There's a saying in recovery that our heads are dangerous neighborhoods, and we shouldn't go there alone. Talking about our thoughts and feelings helps us to process them and brings someone into this dangerous territory with us.

Fear is so common that when doing a Fourth Step, it's one of the feelings we're asked to review most thoroughly. Even the thought of doing a Fourth Step can conjure up fear. We work through that by talking about it, praying, and continuing to do the next right thing. We don't need to do a Fourth Step perfectly. We just need to do it.

A few of us have especially strong fear in the form of *panic or anxiety attacks.* When we have these attacks, we may have difficulty breathing, suddenly become very hot, and feel as if we might pass out. We may be unable to move, paralyzed with fear. All we can think about and focus on is the fear.

Panic and anxiety attacks are different from the fear the Big Book is talking about, although some of the tools that are helpful with fear in general can be helpful with these attacks. We may have panic or anxiety attacks in response to a recent stressor, a fear, or a history of trauma. There's no one single reason for these attacks, and they can be very frightening. We may feel like we're going to die during a panic attack. The fear of having another attack keeps us from doing things or going places where it might happen. It becomes a circular problem. The fear of the problem becomes part of the problem.

If we experience panic or anxiety attacks, we may benefit from seeking professional help. Some things that are helpful in dealing with panic and anxiety attacks are getting off caffeine, deep breathing, meditation, becoming desensitized through therapy, and looking at our thinking through Cognitive-Behavioral Therapy, an approach similar to Rational Emotive Behavior Therapy. At times, medication may be needed, but even by prescription, mood-altering chemicals must be avoided or used with extreme caution, since they may induce cravings.

Shame and Guilt

Shame is feeling bad about who we are. *Guilt* is feeling bad about what we did or didn't do. Guilt can be healthy in recovery. It shows we have a conscience. Shame is not healthy.

Shame comes from thinking we're bad people, that we have some huge defect, or, worse, that we *are* a huge defect. Guilt comes from thinking we did something that we need to clean up or to change. As we talk with others in recovery about the mistakes we've made and the harm we've done, many times our shame turns into a healthy guilt. We see that we're not defective people. As we talk about our shame, we are given feedback, and we learn some ways to deal with it. We discover that although we did some things that were wrong, we're not bad people. We may even realize that some of the things we did were *not* wrong—that we've been unnecessarily feeling guilty about things we don't need to feel guilty about. The Twelve Steps are a formula to help us deal with guilt. As we get specific about what we've done in our written Fourth Step, talk about it in our Fifth Step, and make amends in our Eighth and Ninth Steps, we clean up our past. The feeling of guilt leaves as we clean up our side of the street. We're able to look the world in the eye again.

Depression

One feeling that many of us struggle with in early recovery is *depression*. For some, our state of feeling blue is relatively mild; it comes and goes. Others experience a more serious form of depression called clinical depression (in Western medicine), and we need attention from health care professionals.

In early recovery, as our brains work to get rid of the extra chemicals and extra receptor sites and to build up the production of the natural feel-good chemicals we need, this healing work can feel quite chaotic and stressful. Sometimes people coming off meth or cocaine may feel better at first but then sink into a low-grade depression after being sober for three or four weeks. We call this "the wall." The chemicals in the brain are changing as they heal. It takes time for the brain to regain its normal chemical balance.

At the same time that our brains go through this healing crisis, many of us become aware of some of the messes we have to clean up in recovery. This is not a happy picture. We may feel discouraged and lonely at times, even near despair. These disheartening feelings are fairly normal in early recovery.

We can help our moods in several ways during this time. Getting adequate rest, exercise, and good nutrition, plus watching our caffeine intake, is just the start. Talking with others also helps. Just as with our chemical use, we need others in order to recover. They can tell us about their experience with being blue at times, or even clinically depressed, and assure us that this feeling will pass or that there is help available. We need to seek their advice and support, and then follow it. We may also seek professional help. Connecting with others, working the Twelve Steps to clean up our lives and change our insides, working on changing our thinking, and meditation and relaxation—all of these tools can be helpful. All the tools that we use to change our thinking also work with depression.

If we experience clinical depression, we may need counseling or medications to assist us in recovery from clinical depression. While the tools of recovery are helpful with clinical depression, we also seek help from a professional. A professional who is knowledgeable about both depression and addiction will help us manage both concerns. When we have a mental health concern and chemical dependency, this combination is called a co-occurring disorder. Both need to be treated, side by side.

> *I was on medications for depression for many years. I tried a million different things before we found the right fit. That in itself was a challenge, trying to be patient, because I, like a lot of other people, wanted to be cured. Now. And it just didn't happen overnight like I thought it should. But I have just recently stopped taking the medications, with the advice of my doctor.*
>
> :: TANYA

There is yet another saying in recovery: "Suit up and show up." It means that we are to follow a structure and do the things we need to do even when we don't feel like it. The willingness to do them will come over time if we continue to show up and do the work. With depression, we may sometimes feel so sluggish and unmotivated that suiting up and showing up can seem almost impossible. Yet, being active and working the program is critical to our recovery. When we can't get moving on our own because of depression, we may need to work with a professional therapist or see a physician and possibly use medications. We listen to health care professionals and follow their direction. We may need medications for a short period of time or long term. In any case, we listen to the direction of professionals concerning our medications while we continue to practice other tools. There is help available. The Twelve Steps provide us with a good foundation while we use medications or other tools in dealing with depression.

Happiness

Happiness or contentment is a foreign feeling for many of us. Feeling contentment or serenity may seem so unfamiliar, we may even label it as "bored." That's because it may have been a while since we've felt joy, peace, happiness, contentment, and serenity. Maybe we can't even remember ever having these feelings. Talking with others in recovery about our happy feelings when they come up will help us establish them as normal. It's okay to feel happy. It's okay to feel content. It's okay to feel joy. The first time we identify joy or contentment as a feeling we're having, we may be surprised. In time, we learn to welcome such feelings. We also learn that, like all feelings, these happy feelings come and go.

One of the signs of feeling happy is laughter. Many of us in early recovery find ourselves laughing more than we've laughed in years. We connect with others through some of our crazy stories, and laughing about them with others can be very freeing. Laughter stirs up certain brain chemicals that make us feel good and may be healing. We hear a lot of laughter in meetings about things that in the past we never thought anyone would talk about in public (and that we probably wouldn't laugh about in front of family and others whom we've hurt). Laughter in the midst of our disease is another paradox of recovery. Many times, we even find humor in the things that originally caused us shame or pain.

Stress

Even in the midst of the joy and laughter, we're up against plenty of *stress*. Stress aggravates everything! We're under a lot of stress in early recovery because things are constantly changing. We may feel joyful, anxious, depressed, elated, content, and confused all in the same hour. Our bodies are healing, our living situations and jobs may be changing, and we're making changes in our thinking. In the midst of all these changes, we're also developing new relationships. While all these developments can be helpful, they can produce a lot of stress at the same time. Healing is stressful!

During the first year to eighteen months of recovery, many of us experience certain common symptoms. We may have difficulty with our memory, sleep, or physical coordination. We may have trouble thinking clearly, be extra sensitive to stress, or be inclined to emotional overreaction or underreaction. These symptoms are discussed further in chapter 10, on relapse. For now, it's important to realize that stress will make these symptoms worse. We need to do what we can to minimize the stress in our lives, particularly in early recovery.

Times of stress are times to be especially kind to ourselves. We are reminded often by others in recovery that this whole journey is about "progress, not perfection." We learn to adjust our expectations to reality. During stressful times, we remember to "keep it simple." That requires changing our thinking and changing our actions in many areas of our lives. Making these big changes takes lots of practice.

Another common slogan we hear in recovery is "Do the next right thing." We just do what's next for us to do. As we do that, the next right thing to do after that is revealed. We take one small step. Then one small step. One step. Just one small step.

GLORIA'S STORY

I was born into an addictive family. Drugs were always done in the house and around us. My mother was an alcoholic and addict. My father was also an addict, so I was raised into it. Where I grew up, my house was a party every day. We tripped over people to go to school. We never had nothing to eat in our refrigerator. As a child, I despised it, but I ended up becoming what I despised.

I started using at age fifteen with drinking and marijuana. At the same time, I ran track and I was on the swim team. I had good grades.

I had mentors working with me to keep me in school and to get my ed-ucation. Well, I started smoking marijuana, and I fell off from all that. I found myself skipping school. I wasn't running track no more. At fifteen and a half, I ended up running away from home because of my mother's addiction. I was living with a friend of hers, who was an active lesbian, so I participated in that lifestyle. Everything went downhill for me. I was shot at the age of seventeen by this person. The one woman that I loved so much and trusted wasn't there for me. It got to a point where I didn't go to school at all. I ended up getting my GED in prison.

Forging checks and various other things led me to prison at age eighteen. From then on, I found myself just caught up in failure. I found myself going to prison over and over and over. When I was out of prison, sometimes I was using, sometimes I wasn't. I've been in rehab five times.

I didn't have the skills to get a job. I never maintained my own place, so I didn't have a rental history. I'm a criminal. All those doors kept closing on me. I totally gave up. It was the end for me. At least that's how I felt. So, when I was hurting and frustrated, when I was sad, when I started getting depressed because nothing was working for me, and I felt like I had no way out, I went right back to what was familiar. I medicated.

At the lowest point, I just wanted to die. I'd just sit on the street corner and cry. People were coming past me—"Are you all right? Ma'am, are you okay, or do you need us to call the police?"—until somebody did call the police. I told the police, "I just want to die." They put me in a psych hospital.

At another point, I was in a relationship with a guy that was a stone-cold criminal. This guy's whole MO was burglary. He also was an addict. This guy was going up into houses and kicking in the doors, and I was going up in there with him.

Then came the bomb: I didn't even want to go that day, but he made me go. He just kept kicking in these doors, and the owner walks in there, so we run. I weighed about seventy pounds, not healthy at all—bad off on drugs. No energy, no nothing. The police pick me up and they charge me with three counts of second-degree burglary.

Now, the judge didn't want to do it, and he said it was against his better judgment, but he sent me to treatment. But let me tell you how cunning and baffling this disease is. I had fifty-nine months hanging over my head—that's five years—and the judge told me if I came back in his courtroom, if I violated my probation in any way, that he was sending me directly to prison, and I would never see my kids again.

When I went back out, I didn't use at home, but I ended up abandoning my children to a babysitter so I could go use. I knew that once I took that hit, it was over. But in my mind, the insanity part is *Okay, I can do this. I'll be okay, and I can go home.* That wasn't the case. I took that hit and it *was* over. Everything flashed before me: my probation officer; I'm going to prison; I'm going to lose my kids; I don't deserve my kids; they don't deserve to have a mother like this. It just all went down. That was the lowest of low. I deteriorated within two weeks. I wasn't checking in with my probation officer, and my kids had been taken to a children's shelter, so she put out a warrant on me.

I went before that exact same judge, and he said, "For the life of me, I don't understand this, Gloria. Why would you risk it? You know I said I was going to send you back to prison." But you know what he did? He said, "I'm going to go against my better judgment again and give you another chance." I was in jail for four months, but I was in a treatment program there. Then I finished my six-month aftercare program, and now I have eighteen months clean.

I'm actively maintaining my recovery, going to meetings, hearing other stories, and sharing mine. I've gotten stronger in prayer. I've got a network that's positive. I've got a sponsor. I go out and speak to newcomers. I reach out to a lot of women. And that's what works for me. My children are a part of it. My daughter and my son have been going to my meetings with me for over a year. I do service work in the meetings. I chair a meeting. I just started getting really involved, because this is a lifelong thing. I always thought that after treatment, if I just don't pick up, that's my recovery. It's not that. I have to work on this for the rest of my life. So, I humbled myself. I went on a job search, did all of that. I got frustrated, but that's life. I didn't pick up. I hung in there, and I started volunteering at my daughter's school. I got involved in a work training program there that also helps me be a better parent. I volunteered there, and that volunteer work paid off. Another child care center wanted me. I ended up applying at that child care center, working in their kitchen, and that's where I currently work right now.

I'm not only working at this job. I sit on the policy council for my daughter's school. I sit on the council that interviews new tenants in our building. I'm on the welcome committee to welcome new women in these buildings. See, today, I'm reaching out. I step outside of my self-centeredness in doing something for somebody else—because it's not all about me.

On the rough days, I get on my phone and talk to my network. I pray. I go to meetings. I share it. I get it off of me. I don't hold it on the inside. I talk about it. I'm getting support. See, my sober network is solid, and that means that everybody that calls my house is in recovery, or they never used. I have a whole new circle of people. An addict in recovery can call me at any given time of the night, and I'm there to listen—because it was addicts that were there for me.

In active addiction, I didn't trust nobody and I didn't trust myself. I didn't have no circle of people. You know how people say, "I got friends, and I go to people's house and all that"—I didn't have that. So, it took me a long time to even connect with other people. The rooms of Narcotics Anonymous allowed me to start connecting with women. I had issues with trust. Both the one woman and the one man I loved and trusted wasn't there.

God is first and foremost in my life. God has done for me what I couldn't do for myself. There's no way that I would be where I am today if it weren't for Him. That judge gave me another chance and allowed me to get my children back. So, I know that there's God and I know that He loves me, and I know that I deserve my children. I deserve this recovery. I deserve everything that I've got. And that's why I give it back—because it was so freely given to me. I didn't have to sell my body. I didn't have to do nothing for it. It was free. And there ain't nobody expecting nothing in return. This was freely given to me.

I'm not filled with shame no more. I turned that shame into gratitude, because I'm grateful for my experience and because my experience can help another woman. See, for some women, their shame and guilt won't even allow them to share in meetings. Some women think there's no way out. I know some women that lost their kids and feel like they ain't never going to get them back. I know some women did some things that they ain't too proud of. But I'm here to let you know: I'm one of them women.

Of course, I had to do some work to get past the shame. I had to get honest with myself. I had to stop pointing the finger, and turn them fingers back at me. I blamed my mom and my dad for so many years for what I went through: *It's your fault. If we wouldn't have lived like that . . .* Who am I to say? I have a sister now who never picked up a drug in her entire life, and she lived in that exact same household. So, I had to stop blaming. I also had to get rid of those resentments, which took a lot of work. It took a lot of writing letters and tearing them up. It took a lot of quiet. It took a lot of soul searching, and to this day, I'm still in therapy. I had to get over those resentments in order to even move. See, I'm comfortable with resentments. I've always had them. You know how they say everybody has one good childhood memory? I can't give you one. Honestly. I can't give you one. So I had to let go, which was hard. It took treatment after treatment after treatment, because I didn't want to let it go—because that means I'm letting go of my excuse to get high. Without that, then what's my excuse? Now who can I blame it on?

CHAPTER 7

Cross-Addiction

ALL OF US LIKE TO FEEL GOOD. THIS DESIRE FOR PLEASURE is a natural human trait, and there's nothing wrong with it. In fact, the desire for pleasure is a gift that encourages us to do things to feel good. Some of these things that give us pleasure, such as eating and having sex, are basic to the survival of the human race. However, when we chase after good feelings and they become the central focus in our life, we run into problems.

As addicts, we know this in spades. At first, we got plenty of good feelings from the chemicals we used, but in the end, we were only chasing those good feelings and creating major messes along the way. Most of us were so uncomfortable that we had to use our chemicals just to try to feel normal. We needed them as a substitute for the natural feel-good chemicals that had become depleted in our brain due to our repeated using. What started out helping us feel good turned on us.

As addicts, many of us have used to try to fill some sort of void in our life. One woman described it as "trying to fill the hole in my heart the size of God." We thought we could fill this emptiness with chemicals because they made us feel good. They worked for a time, but then they turned on us.

Once we get into recovery, we may think, *Now, finally, I'll feel good. From here on, everything should be smooth sailing.* We expect to look and feel great every day. We think that if we just do recovery right, we won't have any uncomfortable feelings—not even any pain. Our mantra becomes "I have to feel good all the time." We think we can escape from unpleasant emotions and challenging situations. If unpleasant feelings come up, we tell ourselves that we need to escape from them quickly. Our mantra expands to "If I don't feel good right now, I must change that right away."

When we buy into the expectation that life will be smooth sailing in recovery, we are deluding ourselves. Our thinking is just not realistic. We're setting ourselves up for disappointment. A more realistic mantra would be "Life is difficult at times, and I have tools and support to deal with it." With this kind of realistic thinking, we set ourselves up for feeling some serenity and hope. The truth is that we do have the tools of the program, which we can use to deal with life as it happens. Many of us with experience in recovery have come to a place of being content and serene despite life being life.

Cross-Addiction: What Is It?

 Cross-addiction is like changing seats on the Titanic.

:: **KAREN**

Cross-addiction is a term used to describe trading one addiction or dependency for another. We're cross-addicted when we substitute one drug for another drug or when we replace our drug use with some other addictive, feel-good substance or behavior. Being in an addictive relationship is an example of cross-addiction. A relationship is addictive when almost all of our attention is focused on the other person or the relationship. We think about this person so much that we can hardly concentrate on anything else. Just as we did with drugs, we look to this relationship to "fill us up," to make us feel good. Just as with chemical addiction, the relationship may have many intense highs and lows, creating emotional havoc for us, and yet we continue to stay with it. We may give up our family and friends, homes, jobs, and pretty much everything to pursue an addictive relationship. In an addictive relationship, the relationship is the problem. In many respects, it's like our chemicals in the way it takes over our lives and brings us down.

Other behavior patterns or substances that become addictive for some of us are gambling, sex, food, spending, nicotine, Internet use, shopping, exercise, work, caffeine, television watching, and self-mutilating behaviors such as cutting. In excess, any of these substances or activities can be cross-addictions and can bring us down emotionally, physically, spiritually, and mentally. They can also lead us back to our chemical use. Cross-addiction is a relapse issue.

The Pleasure Center

We can better understand how cross-addiction happens when we remember how our brains work. As chapter 1, "What Does It Mean to Be an Addict?" explained, our brains produce certain chemicals that make us feel good. The brain is wired to ensure that we repeat life-sustaining activities such as eating and reproducing. In order to ensure that humans do these things, the brain creates these feel-good chemicals whenever we do them. It also produces feel-good chemicals for many other activities we do, such as exercising, dancing, and laughing. These chemicals, or neurotransmitters, carry messages between neurons in our brain. When we experience something that gives us pleasure, the neurotransmitters fire off and move from cell to cell. The good feeling or pleasure comes as they move between cells. One particularly powerful feel-good neurotransmitter is dopamine. It's the chemical that gets activated when we're having sex. It's also released when we eat chocolate. Other powerful feel-good chemicals in our brains include serotonin, norepinephrine, and endorphins. As these chemicals move between cells in our brain, we feel good.

These neurotransmitters, or feel-good chemicals, are active in the "pleasure center," located in the brain's limbic system. Alcohol and other drugs increase the activity of these neurotransmitters, and we get high. Chemical use leads to pleasure, which leads to more chemical use. It's a pleasant circle at first, but it eventually becomes a problem.

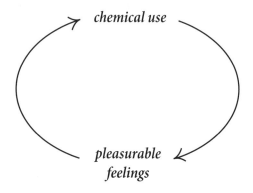

We may know in the analytical part of our brain that something is bad for us, but the limbic part of our brain remembers how good this something has felt in the past. We may say to ourselves, *I get in trouble when I use cocaine,* but our limbic response is *Dopamine jackpot! Bring it on!*

Motivation, Desire, and Decision-Making

What further complicates this whole process is that the area of the brain that holds our pleasure center—the place where dopamine is pumping out the feelings we like—is the same area where we get our motivation and make decisions. Logically, it seems as if we should be able to "decide" to quit using and then quit. However, even if we're highly motivated and make the decision to quit, our chemical use is adding dopamine to the area of the brain where we're motivated and make decisions, making sure we *don't* quit. The dopamine buildup *reinforces* our using by adding more and more pleasurable feelings. Oddly, our brain is working against itself as we try to get sober. This conflict going on within the brain, caused by our using, is why we cannot "will" ourselves to get or stay sober. It takes much more than willpower. This "can't quit" part of the addictive process is particularly true with alcohol and other drugs, but it can happen with other addictive behaviors also.

Cross-Addiction to Other Drugs

When we first come into recovery, we may think that we're addicted to one chemical but not another. Some of us even try to prove it. We may be a cocaine addict and yet think that we can drink in recovery, since we've never had a problem with alcohol. We may claim that smoking marijuana never got us a DUI, so we can smoke pot with no problem. We may think we can take certain addictive, mood-altering pills because we got them from a doctor. Some of us even get fooled when we learn in treatment about other chemicals we didn't know existed or didn't know much about. We think we can try these chemicals.

Addicted to "More"

As addicts, we're addicted to the feeling of intoxication or the mood-altered state of feeling good or "high." We may think we're addicted to cocaine, for example, and that may be true, but the bigger picture is that we're addicted to feeling good. We're addicted to "more." Our brain doesn't know what the chemical is called or whether it came from the drug dealer, the liquor store, the pharmacist, or even over the counter. It just wants more of the good feeling, and it will take it from wherever it can get it.

Judgment and Motivation Affected

A few of us have made the mistake at some point of using various chemicals that we didn't think would be a problem. The result was disastrous. We either went immediately back to our drug of choice, or it took a while longer before things went down the tubes. But down we all went. We didn't want to believe that *any* drug would cloud our judgment and suppress our motivation to steer clear of the drugs that got us into trouble in the first place. Even the judgment of normal users is affected when they use. Having our judgment clouded *and* our motivation to stay sober suppressed is not a great combination.

Some of us decided to drink alcohol, determined we weren't going to use crack cocaine. But the alcohol clouded our judgment, and our resolve to abstain from cocaine weakened. All of a sudden we were back on the rock. Some of us smoked pot, thinking that we'd never go back to alcohol, because things always fell apart when we drank. That didn't work, either, as pot took away our motivation to stay sober. Our brains liked the high from the pot and wanted an even greater high, and soon we found ourselves with drinks in our hands or smoking pot more addictively. Some of us got mood-altering sleeping pills from our physicians, thinking that we could use them and that no one would know since they couldn't smell them. Eventually, we were hooked on them, or they led us back to our drug of choice. Our brains liked the high from the different chemical, and off we went.

Equal Opportunity for Disaster

All mood-altering drugs provide equal opportunity for disaster for the addict. Remember "can't use/can't quit"? That's true with all chemicals and not just our drug of choice.

Cross-Addiction to Other Behaviors or Substances

    Something that I struggle with is replacing alcohol with other things that are harmful, like replacing it with a guy or shopping or food. If I'm uncomfortable, I think I

can go eat and I'll feel better. It doesn't work, and I know
that if I keep acting that way, I'm going to eventually go
back to drinking, because that's what people have told me.

:: BONNIE

Although we abstain from all mood-altering chemicals while in recovery from our addiction, we may struggle with other chemicals
and behaviors, and may even be addicted to them. Many substances
and behaviors can become addictive. Nicotine is one well-known
example. As with other chemical addiction, regular nicotine use
involves increased tolerance over time, attempts to control or quit,
problems with withdrawal, and problematic consequences around
using it, yet we still continue to use. One difference between nicotine and other mood-altering chemicals is that nicotine is not
intoxicating. Granted, we experience a little high each time we
smoke, but we don't become intoxicated. We may exhibit similar
behaviors to our other chemical use, such as protecting our supply,
using to relieve the withdrawal symptoms, hiding and sneaking,
denying, using despite health or emotional consequences, using
alone, organizing our life around it, or trying to control it.

We may do these same things with certain foods. Some of us have
an addiction to sugar or other foods. We hide and sneak, deny, lie
about what we eat, eat differently in front of people than when we're
alone, use to relieve the withdrawal symptoms (yes, sugar does have a
withdrawal associated with it), use despite health or emotional consequences, organize our life around eating, and try multiple ways to
control it through diets, plans, and health farms. While nicotine and
excess food aren't intoxicating like other chemicals, they can take
the same, or even a greater, toll on the body and the spirit. Addiction
to these substances has serious consequences.

Not all compulsive behaviors meet the full technical definition
of addiction, but for simplicity's sake, they're called cross-addiction
in this chapter. All of the issues talked about here as cross-addictions

clearly get worse and worse without intervention, and they lead to some sort of can't use/can't quit dilemma. They often become barriers in our relationships with self, others, and our Higher Power, and our recovery depends on keeping these relationships healthy.

Compulsive behaviors are a way we try to fill the void inside. They are a means to escape the fact that life is difficult. They can be mood-altering in that we get some sort of high from them. Once we've crossed the line to addiction, we may feel as hopeless with any cross-addiction as we did with our chemical addiction. We can become powerless and hopeless with any addictive behavior. The same feel-good chemicals released in chemical addiction are triggered in other compulsive habits or addictions. These chemicals may be triggered differently and in different degrees, but they still make us feel good—feel comforted—for a while. Eventually the behavior or preoccupation with the substance or activity becomes relentless, and we're in the cycle of cross-addiction. The addiction can be just as severe as with chemical use. Some people lose everything or die from cross-addictions.

What is similar for all cross-addictions is that they have seriously messed up the lives of some of us who are in recovery from chemical addiction. They become a centralizing focus in our lives. We give our full attention to our addictive interests, thinking about them, recovering from acting on them, or sneaking and hiding so others don't fully know what we're doing. As our lives become organized around these cross-addictive interests, our behaviors, thoughts, attitudes, and relationships are all affected, and we don't focus on recovery from chemical dependency.

Some of us had cross-addictive habits prior to getting into recovery. Some of us pick up cross-addictions while we're in recovery from chemicals. If we had them before our chemical use started, we may have stopped acting on them while using chemicals, but then found that we returned to these addictive patterns when we put the chemicals down. Resuming old patterns is particularly common with food issues. We may have struggled with eating disorders when we were young and may even have started chemical abuse (meth, speed, cocaine) as a way to lose weight. We switched to chemicals but then were surprised that the eating issues resurfaced once we put down the chemicals. Some of us practice other cross-addictive behaviors throughout our chemical addiction.

However we find ourselves in cross-addiction, most of feel a lot of shame about our addictive behaviors and do not want to tell anyone about them. Shame, which is a huge part of any addiction, can be relieved by talking about it. Yet, that's not always easy for us. We already feel shame about our chemical use and find it hard enough to talk about that. Add to that having to talk about our obsession with something that has also become self-destructive, such as food or sex or nicotine, and the shame can feel overwhelming. In fact, we don't even want to acknowledge it. We hide and sneak and live in shame, thinking that we're "bad" people because, after all, even though we're sober, we're still doing *this*.

Cross-Addiction: A Relapse Concern

Cross-addiction is a huge area of relapse concern for women in recovery. Take, for example, the woman who is getting sober from alcohol but doesn't tell anyone about her gambling addiction. Her family and work colleagues don't know why she disappears for hours at times, her friends wonder why her phone is off, her partner is wondering why they're getting overdrafts, and people start to think she's using chemicals again. She gets fired from work for embezzlement, which people think she did to pay for her drugs or alcohol, and instead of getting honest about the gambling, she ends up going back to drinking.

Another example is the food addict who eats huge quantities of food. She may be purging through vomiting and laxatives, so while her weight is up there, it's not as high as it could be with those quantities of food. In treatment, she is put on a special diet with nutritious food, but no one knows about the ice cream sandwiches and candy she stuffs in her pockets every night as she heads back to her room to binge and sometimes purge. The shame she feels about the secret is huge, and yet she feels as if she'd just die if anyone knew how much she was eating. She goes home and into Twelve Step meetings thinking that she "should" be able to do something about her food addiction since she's now working the Twelve Steps. The shame only worsens.

> *I have overcome an eating disorder, which had been very active before my drug addiction and during my drug addiction. I was a little chunky when I left Iowa. Then I got to California, where the body image thing was big. I was so fearful of gaining weight that I started exercising and running. But a lot of times, I wasn't disciplined enough to continue, and I started purging whenever I would overeat. In early recovery, bulimia was also my way of rebelling against control. Whenever the housemother at the clean and sober house called me on not doing the chores or coming home late or not calling her about my change in plans, I would act on my bulimia. I have to be aware that this is an issue that the enemy—my addict—can use at any time to take me back out. I have to keep my recovery principles in place.*
>
> :: JULIA

Addiction Is Addiction

Ultimately, any addiction needs to be treated as an addiction. We may think that we can treat our cross-addictions as we would character defects. We may think we can go to Alcoholics Anonymous or Narcotics Anonymous meetings, get support there for our other addictions, and work Steps Six and Seven around them, as we do with our character defects. However, addiction is addiction, and attempting to treat it as a character defect just doesn't work. Each separate addiction is a First Step issue.

We need to be with people who speak our language, people we can truly identify with. An alcoholic may be helpful to a food addict, but there's nothing like hearing the story of another woman who used to eat like we do to help us break the denial and isolation and, more important, to provide hope. For the gambling addict, there's nothing like hearing other recovering women talk about how they spent countless hours and money at the casino, neglecting to pick up their children on time at day care, and wondering who else in the family they could get money from to "chase the loss." For the sex addict, there's nothing like hearing about the hours spent cruising or masturbating, or the all-encompassing focus on having to get a partner and the obsession with keeping the relationship. For the spending or shopping addict, there's nothing like hearing another woman tell about how her life was centered on what she bought and how her kids didn't get their needs met, and yet she still kept buying. For the workaholic, whose value is in what she does and who feels totally empty apart from it, there's nothing like hearing another woman talk about being an empty shell with work as the filler. For the Internet addict who misses work, neglects her kids, jeopardizes her job, and lives in front of the computer in a corner in the basement, there's nothing like hearing another woman talk about how that same type of behavior destroyed her family or got her fired.

Many Twelve Step groups exist to help us with a variety of cross-addictions. Examples of these groups are Gamblers Anonymous, Overeaters Anonymous, Anorexics and Bulimics Anonymous, Sex Addicts Anonymous, Nicotine Anonymous, and Debtors Anonymous. Many other specialized groups also exist. In communities where no groups are available, the Internet can be a helpful resource. Some groups have online meetings. Another type of meeting is done on the telephone using conference call technology. It may take a bit of research to find it, but the Twelve Step fellowship is available in various forms for many addictions, not just mood-altering chemical addiction. Again, we are not alone, and we can find help in other people.

For some addictions, we need to maintain total abstinence. That's certainly true for mood-altering chemicals, but it's also true for addictions such as nicotine and gambling. We're faced with "can't use/can't quit," and that means no using at all. None. One is too many; one thousand never feels like enough. With some addictions, however, we need to set limits, because abstinence isn't an option. For example, we need to eat food. Food addicts, however, may need to eliminate eating certain binge foods. Common binge foods are sugar, flour, wheat, nuts, and certain fats. The abstinence needs for each woman are very individual and unique to her particular addictive patterns. One woman may lose control when she eats wheat and nuts, while another may binge on oatmeal. Just as an alcoholic discovers that she may be able to drink beverages such as water, milk, and soda but not alcohol, the food addict also needs to determine what her body reacts to—what gets her craving going—and then no longer eat it. The sex addict may or may not go through a period of abstinence, but will make choices, with the help of others in recovery, to live within healthy sexual limits. For many addictive behaviors, having a strong sponsor and accountability are essential to setting and keeping appropriate limits.

Any addiction, be it gambling, chemicals, food, sex, work, television, busyness, or something else, gets in the way of our relationships. Addiction stands between us and our self, others, and a Higher Power. Cross-addictions keep us from living in freedom. Ultimately, the solution to fill the void is working a spiritual program with the principles of recovery. Spirituality is connection with ourselves, others, and a Higher Power. It fills the hole in our heart that we try to fill with so many other things. It's an ongoing process. We need to be willing to apply this same program to cross-addictions and to take them as seriously as we do our chemical addictions.

There is a solution! The freedom that we find from working our program of recovery is immense. Many of us are just as grateful for the grace that keeps us willing to do the program for our other addictions as we are for the grace that is keeping us sober today. One day at a time. One step at a time.

TANYA'S STORY

I grew up in a very conservative family in Texas. I had a history of sexual abuse from a family member when I was younger and didn't tell anybody at the time. When I was around thirteen, I found that when I would take some pills, I would sleep better. I felt better and didn't have to worry about stuff. I continued with pills and then alcohol. I would take any kind of pills I could get my hands on. I'd do pharmacy and doctor shopping, illegally going from one place to another to get Percocet or oxycodone. When I couldn't get those, I would get myself doped up on over-the-counter stuff, Benadryl, Robitussin, anything I could get to get a buzz, or to just completely check out—to make myself kind of sleepy so I wouldn't have to worry about anything.

I basically didn't have a life. I lived in a trailer house that I rented twenty-five miles out of town. I worked in an adolescent girls program in New Mexico. Our shifts were seventy-two hours, and when I would get off shift, I would go to town, get whatever I needed to get through the weekend or through the next seventy-two hours, and go home and stay there. I would get myself doped up on my drugs. I didn't go anywhere or do anything. For seventy-two hours, I'd be pretty much unconscious. When I went to work, I would have Robitussin or NyQuil because I always had a cough. I just kept myself as comfortable as I could without compromising my job.

I had never been a real go-getter. When I was in high school, I was in sports. When I got out of school, I just kind of faded away. I had never been an outgoing type of person who wanted to go to the parties in school and all that stuff, so I really didn't know what was out there.

The low point happened when my boss came to me and said, "You know, you cannot work with the kids." They took me off direct line with the kids and stuck me in a file room, because they were concerned about my mental health. I didn't have a clue there was anything wrong with me at the time. The kids that we were working with were very emotionally challenged, and they needed all of us to be 100 percent there for them, and I couldn't be. Sometimes in group meetings, when girls would talk about abuse that had happened to them, I'd just walk out. I wasn't there to support my co-workers. I was depressed. Basically, they saw me giving up on life, and finally they sent me to a treatment center for my addiction.

I went simply to keep my job. I didn't think I had a problem. I didn't go get drunk. I didn't go out and get DWIs. I didn't have any legal issues. So I didn't really think I had a problem. But in treatment, I had to follow all the recommendations, which is always a catchall that gets you into getting more help—I know that now. They wanted me to go to a halfway house. So I decided, okay. I was just going to go, to say I went, so that I would get my job back. Things didn't quite work out that way.

I was starting to realize that maybe there is something to this. I was talking about stuff, I was making friends, going to meetings, doing stuff that I had never done before. I was going places with people, hanging out at friends' houses. I was starting to come out of my shell. I thought about going back to school, doing something to help people like I'd been helped.

I was also going to counseling, dealing with the sexual abuse issues and coming to terms with who I am as a lesbian. I'd had a little inkling of being a lesbian when I was working in New Mexico, and, when I went back to school, I attended some GLBT meetings. One day I was talking with my counselor, and I said, "I want a little bit more to life than just being by myself." And she said, "Well, when you find the right guy . . ." I just looked at her and I said, "Does it have to be a guy?" That to me was the major coming out, when I said it out loud to her, somebody who I trusted, it was affirming it to myself, that this is who I am, and I don't have to hide behind it any longer.

At the AA meetings I was going to, there was nobody who could really relate to the stuff that I had been through. I finally found a lesbian meeting, where I felt like I fit in—for once. That was very freeing to me, and then when I would go to GLBT celebrations or gatherings and run into them, they always knew who I was, and it's nice to be known.

One of the high points in my recovery has been meeting my partner, who also is in recovery. For a long time, my partner and I would go to the same meetings, so we didn't tell people that we were together. Once we did start talking about it, the reactions that we got were "Oh, cool."

Another high point for me in recovery is being able to be honest. When I go home to see my family, I can go and hold my head up. I don't have to have my stash and worry about, is one of my brothers or my sister going to go through my stuff? I don't have to worry about driving around—if my sister will let me take my nieces somewhere. I like just being able to be normal.

Recovery has made a huge change in my life. The promises have come true. I'm free. I don't have to hide behind chemicals to open up, to be able to go into a room and have a staff meeting. I like who I am. I've got a good job that pays the bills. I go out with people. My partner and I are starting the process soon of my becoming pregnant. It's something I never thought possible, since I didn't like guys. Now I can do that. I can become a mom. I can fulfill that dream.

Another of the gifts of recovery is that I've learned how to talk about what's going on when it's going on. I realize that if it's happening to me, then it's probably happening to somebody else also. I'm not alone. Somebody can relate, somewhere. I've learned that I have to have other people in my life.

There's been a huge change in my relationship with my family. It used to be that I might call my parents or my sister once a week. When I went to treatment, I took off, and nobody knew where I was. My parents were getting ready to call me in as a missing person, because I just took off and didn't bother to tell anybody. Now I talk to my mom or my sister every day. We live way across the country, but they're an important part of my life. They've been able to see the difference in who I am and in my behaviors and my integrity. When I say I'm going to do something, I do it. It's none of this "Oh, I forgot" or excuses why I can't do it.

Since I've been in recovery, I've also been able to work on my eating issues. I was a binger. I thought it was normal to eat a whole bag of cookies at a time. At the halfway house that I went to, we had eating disorder groups. I wasn't watched, but I was helped to monitor my eating, and I got that pretty much under control. I also had stomach stapling surgery, and I lost 145 pounds and am able to manage my weight through exercise and just watching what I eat now.

When I had the surgery, that brought up all kinds of issues about "What am I going to do when I'm in physical pain after the surgery and need to take pain medications?" I worked very closely with my sponsor and my partner. When I needed medication, she would give it to me, initially, so I wouldn't be tempted to take more than one, or more than what was prescribed. If I felt at any time like I needed more, I would have to wait for a little bit before she would give it to me. And if she wasn't there, I just wouldn't take any more. Because for me, when I'm in pain, I have to really sit back and say, "Is this real pain, or is this me looking for medication?" I do that even with Tylenol today. "Oh, I've got a headache." Do I really have a headache, or am I just looking for a fix?

I've had several surgeries in my recovery. I talked to my sponsor several times a day whenever I was recovering from surgery, because I just didn't want to take a risk. We set up a plan ahead of time as to what would happen: if I took more than I'm supposed to, or if I found myself searching it out of its hiding place, what were we going to do? We had a plan.

I've pretty much plateaued now at about 199 pounds. But I'm very happy there. I do things that I could never have done before. I ride bikes. I rode in the Ironman last year, and I don't think I could have even gotten on a bike before.

Because of my depression, there were times that I wanted to kill myself in early recovery, when I just didn't think that it was worth it. I didn't think I would make it through. And now I can look back and say, "I got through that, so I can get through anything if I have help and support, and if I'm not trying to do it alone." Back then, I felt like a burden when I was talking to people about what was going on at times, in early recovery. I thought they'd be better off without me. And now, it's like, well, I might have helped somebody else going through the same thing. So I don't look at myself that way anymore. But it took some time to get to that point.

CHAPTER 8

Self-Care

WHETHER WE'RE NEWLY SOBER OR HAVE YEARS OF SO-briety, we need to take good care of ourselves physically, socially, emotionally, and spiritually. Each of us is in charge of our own well-being. That includes care of our "self," or self-care. Taking care of ourselves may be a new concept for us, as we may not have taken responsibility for anything while we were in our addiction, let alone ourselves. Or we may have concentrated on taking care of other people but neglected ourselves. Failure to care for ourselves keeps us from living life to its fullest and puts us at risk for using chemicals again. Self-care helps us keep our life in balance. This chapter offers guidelines for physical self-care and also touches on the emotional, social, and spiritual aspects of self-care. These other aspects will be addressed more fully in later chapters.

> *I have mentors in my life professionally, spiritually, and recovery-wise who I invite to tell me if they see me going off the path. They catch me when I slip back into unhealthy patterns. I have to always make sure that I eat right because I have a history of eating disorders. I have to make sure I sleep right, stay spiritually strong, and stay connected to people—that I don't isolate, that I reach out, that I don't stuff my feelings. I make sure that my Higher Power is the most important*

thing in my life. I have to keep spiritually fit that way, just like I physically keep fit.

:: JULIA

What Is Self-Care?

Our addiction made us pretty selfish. While actively using, we may have driven drunk with kids in the car, not thinking of their welfare. We've called in to work sick because we were hungover, not thinking about the burden it would put on our co-workers. We've missed events that were important to others. We've used people to meet our needs. We've put ourselves and our chemical use first at the expense of others. These are all examples of selfishness, which program literature tells us is at the heart of our addiction. Why, then, the push to take care of ourselves? Haven't we been too self-absorbed already?

Self-care is not the same as selfishness. Self-care is treating our body, mind, and soul with respect and kindness so that we can show up for life and be genuinely present for others. It's doing those things consistently that help us feel better in the long run, and maybe even help us live longer. We're *not* being selfish when we take care of ourselves in healthy, positive ways.

> *We're often taught as women that if we're thinking about ourselves, we're selfish, and God forbid a woman should want to be considered selfish. We'll act out all over the place just so somebody doesn't think we're selfish. And I say, get rid of that. I had to learn to be selfish. Not in a negative way, but I had to* learn *how to put me first, how to take care of myself.*
>
> :: FANNIE MAE

HALT

Self-care is so much a part of Twelve Step programs that in recovery we often warn each other to be careful when we get too *hungry, angry, lonely,* or *tired* (HALT). Some people add an S and make it HALTS. The S can stand for *sick* or *stressed.* Being hungry, angry, lonely, tired, sick, or stressed makes us more vulnerable to using chemicals again. Any of these conditions makes us vulnerable to other potential dangers too, such as falling asleep at the wheel, failing to think clearly enough to handle our responsibilities, and developing major health problems. Self-care is about doing what we can to prevent becoming too close to HALTS. No matter how long we've been sober, we're still vulnerable when we experience any part of HALTS.

Sometimes the best thing we can do for our recovery is to take a nap when we're tired or get something to eat when we're hungry. Pretty practical stuff. That's what self-care is. Very practical. It's such common sense that we might think it's too simple to work. When we're tired, we may get into thinking about why we're tired, what we should and shouldn't have done, how we shouldn't be tired, and on and on. The most practical thing to do is to quit thinking and get some rest. As addicts, we tend to complicate things. Complicating things is so common that one of the sayings in the program is "Keep it simple, stupid" (KISS) or, as some people say, "Keep it simple, sweetheart."

Physical Self-Care

We're physical beings. That may seem obvious, but many of us tend to believe that the rules of nature don't apply to us. We think we're unique. For some reason, we think we should be superwomen and don't need to bother with self-care. We assume an almost arrogant attitude. We don't need to eat healthy because we haven't ever done it, and we're doing just fine. We don't need rest because we know how to stay awake, no matter what. We don't need to consult a health care professional because we're not sick, and besides that, we know more about ourselves than anyone else does. We may be so busy taking care of other people that we think we can't take time for ourselves. These ways of thinking cause us to neglect our bodies, yet our bodies *need* care.

> *I would always look for that easier, softer way. Those rules—they don't apply to me. I thought,* I don't have to do that because I'm different, I'm unique.
>
> :: JULIA

What if we kept our car running in high gear through rutty areas and never took it in for a tune-up or repair? What if we put bad gas in it and didn't change the oil? Our car might work fine for a while, but it will have serious problems before long. Many of us treat our bodies like that. They were created wonderfully and beautifully to house our beings, but we put in poison, don't give them nourishment, fail to exercise them, neglect to give them needed rest, and then wonder why we're feeling sluggish, tired, and empty. Not surprisingly, when we start to take care of our bodies, we feel better overall.

Getting Information on Our Health

Previous chapters emphasized the importance of seeking medical assistance during withdrawal. The need for getting good health care doesn't stop there. We may use Western medicine, complementary health care, or some other mode of health care. We may even use some combination of these. We need to do our best to make sure that the types of health care services we receive are safe. Not all forms of treatment have a proven track record, and they may have unpleasant or dangerous side effects or other harmful consequences. In order to make health care decisions that are best for us, we need to ask lots of questions. Whatever modes of health care we choose, we need to make use of them. We need information about our bodies and about treatments that may be helpful.

Many of us have neglected our recommended yearly health checkups or other important procedures. In recovery, getting information about our health is another way to ask for help. It's also a way to listen to others. Not only do we need to schedule a regular medical physical, we need a dental checkup, a mammogram, an eye exam. While using, we neglected what was recommended. Now it's time to take charge.

Most of us need be tested for sexually transmitted diseases, including hepatitis C and HIV. We may resist getting these tests, saying we haven't had multiple sexual partners and don't use or share needles. That may be true. However, if we've ever had a blackout and can't remember a period of time when we were with someone, or don't even remember who we were with, we're at risk. Substance abusers are at high risk for sexually transmitted diseases.

How do we find a health care professional? There are several ways. We can ask people we trust whom they would recommend. Twelve Step meetings are full of people who practice self-care, and many of them go to health care professionals who understand addiction. (Some health care professionals do not have a lot of familiarity with addiction.) We can choose from the list provided by our health care payment program (if we have one), whether that's insurance, a government-paid program, or some other program. We can look in telephone directories or on the Internet under *health clinics*. Other women in recovery may know of health care providers who are sensitive or knowledgeable about addiction. In the United States, a physician specializing in addiction is certified by the American Society of Addiction Medicine. Other countries may have a different process for identifying such specialists.

It's a good idea to ask some preliminary questions of any professionals we're interested in seeing for our health needs. This will help us decide if we want to work with these individuals. In particular, we can ask about their experience in working with women in recovery from chemical dependency, as well as other questions about the specialty we're seeing them for.

If we meet with medical professionals who can prescribe drugs, we need to tell them that we're chemically dependent. We ask them not to prescribe anything for us that is mood altering or addictive. When going to the dentist, we insist on an alternative for any anesthetic or tranquilizer the dentist may use that could produce a high. We don't use nitrous oxide (laughing gas) because it produces a little high. Anything that is mood altering and produces even a little high is not for us. Our brain doesn't know if that little high is from the doctor, the liquor store, or the crack dealer. What our brain knows is that it feels good and it wants *more!* We're very careful about what chemicals we put into our bodies. On our own, we "can't use/can't quit," and even a little buzz from a chemical can induce the craving for more. Sometimes we may need to use mood-altering chemicals such as pain pills—when we have surgery, for example. Chapter 10, on relapse, talks about ways to use them with enough accountability and structure to get us through those periods in our lives.

Because we're so sensitive to even a little bit of mood-altering chemicals in our bodies, we don't take this matter lightly. This means that every time we're given a medical prescription, we remind our medical professional that we're chemically dependent, and we ask if the substance is mood altering or addictive. Every single time. Since some medical professionals may not have much knowledge about addiction, we may also seek out an addiction professional to get more information about what we're taking. While addiction counseling professionals should not give us medical advice, they can tell us what chemicals are mood altering and bring up any concerns they may have about an addict taking that chemical. At that point, we can go back to our medical professional with this information. We talk about our concerns and ask for something that is not mood altering. Ultimately, what we put into our body is our individual responsibility. Sometimes we need to do some footwork and gather information. That's part of taking care of ourself. That's part of knowing we're worth the time and the effort.

As women, we also need to take care of our gynecological health. Depending on our stage in life, we may be dealing with pregnancy planning and birth control, pregnancy itself, childbirth, hormonal concerns, mammograms, premenstrual syndrome, perimenopause, menopause, or other matters. We ask for help. Our sponsors and the people in Twelve Step rooms know a lot about recovery, but they aren't experts on our health conditions. In recovery, we learn to go to the right source for what we need and not expect one person or group to have all the answers. For information about our bodies, we go to people who specialize in health. We may, however, ask others in recovery for recommendations about which health care providers to see.

Keeping on top of our health takes time and planning. It takes time to find out which health care professionals to see and then to set up and keep the appointments. It also takes time to follow through on the recommendations we're given by health care professionals and to make and keep further appointments. We may think it's easier to just ignore all this. In the short term, that may be true. However, neglecting to consult with professionals about our special physical needs as women could have life-threatening consequences in the long run. Basic self-care includes attention to our gynecological health.

Hygiene

Many of us didn't take good care of ourselves outwardly when using. We clearly weren't at our best, and at times we may have neglected showering, brushing our teeth, or even combing our hair. Chemicals like meth may have rotted our teeth and caused sores on our bodies. In recovery, we take care of our basic hygiene. If our bodies smell, others don't want to be around us, leaving us feeling isolated and ashamed. Poor hygiene is clearly a distraction that can interfere with recovery.

We can take simple steps to keep ourselves clean and presentable. We need to do the basics of bathing, brushing teeth, and cleaning and combing hair regularly. Doing these simple things faithfully makes us feel much better about ourselves. Other people also feel more comfortable around us. If we're not sure whether we smell, we ask people we trust. If they seem uncomfortable with this question, we tell them we need their help with this for our recovery. If we have never learned good hygiene practices, we ask other women what they do to take care of themselves. It's okay to ask for help and suggestions. It's also humbling. Being willing and open-minded is essential to our recovery. We don't know what we don't know. It's okay to learn it.

Rest

As mentioned in the chapter on getting started, many of us struggle with sleep issues in early recovery. This is normal. We need to do what we can to get the proper amount of rest. When we're rested, the world looks brighter. Things don't take on the darkness they do when we're exhausted. Rest is so important that it's listed as one of the HALTS. *T* is for *tired*. We're much more vulnerable when we're tired—vulnerable to using, to making poor choices, and to other dangers. Sometimes the best thing we can do for our recovery is to go to bed.

In early recovery, many of us regret all the time we wasted

while using. In recovery, we may want to make up for lost time and live life to the fullest. However, in early recovery, our brains and our bodies are healing. Throughout our recovery, we'll continue to grow emotionally and spiritually. Just as a growing child needs rest, we also need rest during these times of growth.

Some of us need more sleep in recovery than when we were using. When we were lying on the couch all day, we didn't need a lot of sleep. Now that we've become active throughout the day—being present, giving to others—we need rest. In recovery, we expend a lot of energy just in being present. We may forget how much our lives have changed. Our bodies aren't used to being so active. They need rest. It's okay to take a break, catch a nap, or go to bed early. We don't need to be superwomen and do things twenty-four hours a day, seven days a week. We're physical beings. It's normal to need rest. Getting on some kind of normal schedule will help ensure that we get needed rest consistently.

Our bodies do better when we get the sleep we need in a consistent, routine manner. Consistency, structure, and routine are key components in many areas of recovery, and particularly with sleep.

Nutrition

Eating or not eating can be a huge concern for some women. Many of us have made unhealthy food choices for years. On top of that, we may have gained or lost weight, depending on our chemical of choice. Some of us have a history of eating disorders—restricting our eating, purging, overeating, binging, using laxatives, over-exercising, or engaging in other self-destructive behaviors related to eating and body size. As women, many of us have body image problems. Preoccupation with body size may be a symptom of an eating disorder. We may have started using chemicals like meth just to lose weight and were soon in over our heads.

Once we're sober, food can grab too much of our attention again. We may have had food issues earlier in life, switched to chemicals, and now, in recovery from chemicals, we switch back to obsessing about food. Some of us have either pigged out or passed out most of our life.

For some of us, food is a major issue. It may require more than ongoing self-care. We may be dealing with a cross-addiction. Chapter 7, on cross-addiction, talks about the importance of treating any addiction as addiction, including addiction to food. While some of us may have an addiction to food, others have diagnosable eating disorders. It's beyond the scope of this chapter to discuss the difference between food addiction and eating disorders, but with either condition, we may not be able to make good nutritional choices on our own. It would be like asking drug addicts to make good choices about which drug they can use. Many of us need outside help, such as counseling or Twelve Step groups that focus on eating issues, to get into recovery in this area. We may participate in treatment or recovery programs for eating disorders. Dealing with food addiction or eating disorders takes more than good self-care. We need outside help and accountability. It's okay to ask for help.

We may need to call on that help at various times in our recovery. It can be an issue early on while we're getting sober, or it could be something we deal with in ongoing recovery, after years of sobriety from chemicals. Just as our chemical addiction may need periodic intervention from professionals, so may our food concerns.

Regardless of whether we're dealing with the extra challenge of food addiction or eating disorders, part of our ongoing self-care in recovery from chemicals is to treat our bodies with respect. We give them the right kind and amount of food so they can function at their best. We can start by following a few basic nutritional guidelines.

One of the basics of good nutrition is giving our bodies enough water. Our bodies are made up mostly of water, and this supply of water needs to be replenished often for us to function well.

Common advice is to drink at least sixty-four ounces, or eight eight-ounce glasses, of water a day. Our needs for water may vary based on our size and body condition, so getting personal guidance from a health care professional can help us determine what's right for us.

Some of us have found that eliminating sugar decreases our cravings for chemicals. We may even feel better when we eliminate sugar substitutes, since for us sugar substitutes are like having sugar and can increase cravings. Not using sugar or sugar substitutes may be harder than it sounds. We may crave sugar itself in early recovery, particularly if we used a lot of alcohol. It makes sense, as there is a lot of sugar in alcohol, and our bodies are used to it and continue to crave it. A few of us are so sensitive to sugar that we need to read labels to make sure our foods don't have *any* sugar in them, as even a tiny amount of sugar can cause cravings for us.

Eating in a healthy way keeps our blood sugar at steady levels. Women who have fewer episodes of low blood sugar are found to have fewer alcohol cravings. To keep our blood sugar at stable levels, we may need to eat several times a day.

Many nutrition experts say a healthy diet includes a balanced mix of protein, fat, starches, dairy, fruits, and vegetables. While some people may avoid dairy or another category of food because of personal or cultural standards or health problems, they still need to get an adequate mixture of certain vitamins and minerals. Variety in our diet ensures that our bodies get this mix. Some women also take a multivitamin supplement or other supplements according to their health needs. However, a supplement is just that. We need to get our primary nutrition through foods directly.

Beyond these basics, we can seek out the abundance of information now available to the public on nutrition. If we have trouble finding it, we ask for help. Many of us have never sought support or advice concerning what we eat. We made up our own rules, and we think we know what our bodies need. In recovery, we can benefit by seeking outside help. We can consult with a nutritionist, dietician, doctor, or other professional. By getting advice from professionals and following it, we can get smart about our eating and overcome the bad food-related habits we've acquired. As we heal, we become more tuned in to our body and its needs, but at first we rely on others for information and support.

Movement

Our bodies are meant to move. Good self-care involves physical activity that includes a regular exercise program. In addiction, most of us weren't very active physically. In early recovery, we may jump into a crash exercise program to make up for lost time, and the result isn't good. We overdo it and then injure ourselves, or quickly wear ourselves out and quit. When our bodies first start to heal, most of us are in poor shape.

We need to ask for help to learn what's safe and best for our personal health needs. Health care professionals who specialize in exercise and movement can tell us how to start out, what our body can stand, and how we should proceed. Most of us need to start out slowly. We're not in a race. We get moving, a little at first, and then more as time goes on. It's about feeling good and being strong and healthy. Many of us have had no experience or skills in exercising our body or in healthy recreation. Developing a healthy body takes time. The key is consistency. A little at a time in the beginning, but consistently. Recovery slogans that are very helpful as we become more physically active are "Easy does it," "Progress not perfection," "One step at a time," and "Just for today."

Variety in an exercise program makes us feel the best and keeps us from getting bored. Doing a mix of aerobic exercise (which gets the heart and breathing going), muscle-strengthening activity, and flexibility exercises meets the various needs of our bodies. An exercise partner keeps us accountable so we stay with it, or we can join a team or league or take part in some group exercise. Others prefer to exercise alone or to walk or run with their dog.

We start out slowly and build up our exercise program over time. We get advice and support from others. We're not in this alone. We ask for help.

Nicotine

Nicotine is highly addictive. Nicotine releases some of the same feel-good chemicals in the brain that other chemicals do, and it's highly addictive and damaging to our health. While nicotine may not be as totally intoxicating as alcohol and meth, it's highly addictive. If you're a smoker or chewer, some of the tools used in recovery from alcohol and other drugs can help you quit. You can learn more in chapter 7, on cross-addiction.

Some women first start using nicotine while sober and in recovery from other chemicals. If you're considering taking up smoking, don't. Talk with women who smoke and get their input. Smoking may help us to feel a sense of belonging, because smoking is commonplace in some treatment programs and some recovery meetings (though many are smoke-free). Many of us have started smoking to lose weight we put on while using or while newly sober. It's especially tragic when we start smoking in treatment or early recovery. Not only are we picking up another addiction, we're picking up a deadly one. A research study by one leading health care institution found that, out of one thousand patients who completed chemical dependency treatment, more died from nicotine use than from returning to chemical use. The bottom line is that nicotine is addictive, numbs our feelings, interferes in our relationships, and kills us, just like our drug of choice would. It's a very hard drug to stop using. Just as with our chemicals of choice, many of us find we "can't use/can't quit." For those of us who haven't starting using nicotine, we can practice self-care and choose not to start. For those of us addicted to nicotine, we can seek help and support. We have an addiction. Alone we use. Together we recover.

Caffeine

Many Twelve Step groups serve coffee as part of their meetings. Caffeine has long been a mainstay in Twelve Step groups. At the home of one of the founders of Alcoholics Anonymous, the coffee-pot that was used by the two founders when they first met is on display. Many an alcoholic has found fellowship over a cup of coffee with another alcoholic. While it's a tradition to have coffee available at meetings and gatherings, coffee is not helpful for everyone. For some of us, caffeine becomes another addiction. We focus on when we're going to have our next cup and stay buzzed most of the day. If we struggle with anxiety or panic, caffeine can make matters worse. Caffeine is in many soft drinks also. Some soft drinks contain more caffeine than coffee.

If we quit drinking caffeine, we may go through some withdrawal. That usually takes the form of headaches, irritability, or tiredness. If we're planning on getting off caffeine, it's helpful to plan a time to do it when we know we can get some extra rest. As with breaking any addictive habit, we'll have an easier time of it if we talk with others and get their advice and support.

Getting Sick

Most of us have found that we're more vulnerable to many things when we're sick. We're more likely to be irritable or demanding, to say things we wish we hadn't said, to isolate, or to make unwise decisions. We're also more likely to go back to using, because our defense systems are weakened and our minds are less clear than usual. Many of us tend to push ourselves to keep up with our daily activities when we're sick. It's common for us as women and caregivers to think that we need to be superwomen and keep going no matter what, because people are depending on us. We may think our sickness is a punishment for something bad we've done, so we feel shame about being sick and keep pushing on. Or, we think that because we're sick, the world should stop and everyone should pay attention to us. None of these ways of thinking are helpful.

We accept that we're sick, and we take care of ourselves. Of course, we need to do what we can to prevent it in the first place, but when sickness strikes, our first priority is to take care of ourselves. We need to slow down and get any necessary help from health care professionals. If we have responsibilities such as a job or taking care of children, we let others know that we can't manage all the usual tasks while we're sick, and we ask for help. We slow down and ease up on our usual expectations of ourselves. It's okay if not every single thing that we usually do gets done. "First things first" is a slogan in the program, and when we're sick, we need to focus first on getting well.

Good self-care will strengthen our immune system and prevent some illnesses. Eating wisely, exercising, and getting adequate rest are extremely important. They make a remarkable difference in our well-being. We may also prevent some illnesses by working our program of recovery. Because of the link between mind, body, and spirit, our thoughts and beliefs can affect our health, and our recovery program strengthens us mentally and spiritually. Clearing up our resentments and fears and reducing stress take a huge burden off our immune systems.

No matter how well we take care of ourselves, though, sometimes we'll still get sick. During these times we ask for help from those around us. We seek outside guidance from health care professionals, if necessary, and follow their support and advice. Again, the principles of recovery come into play. We ask for help and listen.

Mental Health Self-Care

Some of us have emotional concerns we need to deal with in recovery. Many of these concerns are helped by getting and staying sober and working the program of recovery. However, we may need professional help in dealing with our mental health troubles. The most common mental health concerns for women in recovery are depression, anxiety, trauma, and eating disorders.

Just as we had to learn about our chemical dependency and what we need to do to recover, some of us have to learn how to handle mental health difficulties. We may feel shame about our problems, thinking that once we're sober, we should be feeling good and shouldn't have to struggle with any other issues. Not true.

Our drinking and drugging may originally have been an attempt to self-medicate and cover up common concerns such as depression or anxiety, or to hide schizophrenia, bipolar disorder, or other less-common concerns. We may be surprised to discover some sort of mental health disturbance now that we're sober. Our using may have kept us oblivious to it.

The fact is, some women in recovery have mental health concerns. Part of self-care is to address these concerns. We begin by letting others know the difficulties we're having. As we do, we no longer feel so alone in the world with our symptoms. We may see a therapist or counselor. It's okay to ask for help. In fact, it's necessary.

Twelve Step groups help us deal with recovery concerns, but the members are not professionals. We may need more help than they can offer. The Big Book recommends being open to outside help. The Big Book even includes comments from professionals in various fields. It's possible our mental health problems are caused by a chemical imbalance in the brain, in which case medical experts may be able to help by prescribing medications for us. There's no shame in taking medication for a chemical imbalance. If we need medications, we need them. We swallow our pride, become open-minded and willing, ask for help, and follow directions. We tell our medical advisors that we're chemically dependent and work with them to make sure the medications we take aren't mood altering. If we start feeling better after taking medications, we might think we can cut back on them or stop taking them, but we always check with a medical professional. When discontinued, many medications (including antidepressants) cause considerable discomfort, and medical monitoring is necessary. We don't make these decisions alone. We ask for help and we listen to the advice we get.

Managing Our Time

Many of us in early recovery have extra time on our hands, time we used to spend pursuing and using our chemicals. Part of self-care is to manage our time well. Many of us either overbook or underbook ourselves. We're very busy or we're bored. Recovery is about balance. Many of us need support and guidance from others in figuring out how to balance our time. Otherwise, we get so overcommitted that we exhaust ourselves, or we become couch potatoes, spending our days sprawled in front of the TV or computer with no interest in our own lives.

 I'm going to school for my food management certificate. Then later on, I'll get into culinary arts. I'm taking the baby steps because I don't want to overwhelm myself or raise my expectations too high to meet, and that's working for me.

:: GLORIA

Structure helps us keep our activity level in balance. We set up routines, creating a planned schedule every day. In early recovery, we may get what we call "recovery jobs" even when we don't need to work. A job provides the needed schedule and structure. Other ways to build structure into our lives are always to attend specific meetings, have a set time to do our meditation, get up and go to bed at regular times each day, and even do simple things like making our bed every day. Consistency and structure help us stay in balance as we move along the road to recovery.

> *So I look forward to the next thing. See, there was a time when I didn't want to wake up, when I didn't want to get out of bed. It feels good to go to sleep and wake up fresh now. It feels good to have a clock to punch in, to be productive. That's the way to be every day. It feels good to hear my four-year-old daughter say, "My mom got a job," and to be a part of her school activities. It feels good that all her teachers know me, because I've been so active over there for months. It feels good just to hear the positive things other people have to say about me.*

> :: GLORIA

Just for Today

We do recovery "just for today." We also do self-care "just for today." When we think too far ahead of ourselves, we may quickly get discouraged. If we're thinking about exercising today, for instance, and then we jump ahead to think we'll have to exercise five days a week for the rest of our lives, we may not even get ourselves to exercise today. We exercise "just for today." We eat healthy "just for today." We take care of ourselves "just for today." When we stay in the day, our lives are manageable. We're present—one day, one experience, one mistake, and one victory at a time.

JANET'S STORY

I'm seventy-four years old, Jewish, and a mother of four. I was addicted to codeine and Valium for over twenty years. I had chronic pain, so I took tranquilizers and pain pills. What I did was go from doctor to doctor to get my drugs, and then I went to several drugstores at a time to fill the prescriptions. I didn't realize I was an addict. It was ridiculous. I had knee pain. I had two knee replacements. I had back pain. I had migraine headaches all the time. I thought it was okay to take pills because the doctor gave me pills. But in my drugged head, I'd even get the drugstores mixed up. I'd call the wrong drugstore with the wrong prescription.

I slept half the day. I had four children at home, and I was sleeping while my kids were managing by themselves. It was horrible. My whole life was just on drugs. My voice slurred. I just walked around like a zombie. I was a nonperson in my house. I was so vegged out on pills.

Finally, twenty-six years ago, I went to a pain clinic where they taught me relaxation, and I had to exercise every day to change the stress in my life. I had to learn that I don't always have to feel good all the time, every day of my life. That was hard for me to accept. I also learned that I was an addict. I was told that I had to go to Alcoholics Anonymous at least once a week for the rest of my life. I was shocked. I thought Alcoholics Anonymous was just for people who used alcohol. I didn't use alcohol because I was afraid it would kill me since I took so many drugs from so many doctors.

At the time, my husband was president of a synagogue of 1,400 families, and I thought I would die if anybody found out about me. There was a terrible stigma about being chemically dependent. I was so full of shame. *I was sure I was the only Jewish chemically dependent person in the entire world.* It was awful.

When I went to AA meetings, I wanted to put a bag over my head. I thought somebody would recognize me. Here I was, a Jew, going to a church basement. They were talking about the Twelve Steps, and I was sure they were trying to convert me to a different religion. On top of that, I was told I had to do this for the rest of my life. However, I found out that AA is not Christian. They taught me there to live one day at a time, and to put my faith and trust in a Power greater than myself. Of course, for me, that is God. I belong to this AA group—a women's group, a wonderful group of women. They're the kindest, nicest people I ever met. I'm very thankful for all of them.

At the time, I was the only Jew in my AA group, and after a year, another woman walked in. She and I talked, and we decided to start a Jewish recovery network. We thought that if we went to many AA and Al-Anon meetings, we could find some other Jews. So we found, I think, half a dozen, and we met in my house. After a year or two of doing that, I broke my anonymity at the synagogue, which was horrendous, because the executive director of the synagogue said, "Not you!" which intensified my pain and guilt. But they gave us a room at the synagogue, and we're still meeting there at that synagogue.

We have meetings once a month. We have professionals speak on all kinds of subjects that pertain to us as Jews, like depression, guilt, shame, grief, forgiveness, many things. The first hour we have an open meeting, which is a Twelve Step meeting that's open to everybody. We have a freedom Seder every year, which is the celebration we have at Passover, celebrating our exodus from slavery and our freedom from addiction. We get close to a hundred people there.

We have a picnic every year, besides having our meetings once a month. We're putting on workshops for the community, which is just wonderful. I get phone calls regularly from persons in our community looking for help with their alcoholism and chemical dependency. I'm not a counselor; I just give them ideas of where to go, what to do. I belong to a group of chaplains that meet every other month, a spiritual group, and we talk about what's going on in the community, which is wonderful.

I go to a treatment center a couple times a month and meet with Jewish patients. They all ask me the same questions: "Am I the only one?" and "What do I do about the Lord's Prayer?" That seems to be a tough thing for Jewish people. The Lord's Prayer is a Christian prayer that's said at some AA meetings. We tell people, it's no reason not to go to AA. Just say your own prayer—say something to yourself if you're uncomfortable saying the Lord's Prayer.

Getting into recovery is probably the most wonderful thing that ever happened to me. I learned a different way of living, one day at a time. Now, my Jewish support network is my life. Trying to help other people is my life. Calling on people in treatment. Doing the Seder. The picnic. I do a mailing once a month to the five hundred people on the network mailing list. I talk on addiction and recovery whenever I can. I guess it's my whole life.

When I first gave up all the pain pills, I was in terrible withdrawal for a whole year. I wasn't functioning well at all. I was a mess. I really thought I wasn't going to live, going off the drugs. I was terrorized. My skin jumped, and I had terrible insomnia. It was a nightmare. My mind was gone. I couldn't think. But I kept it up. I was finally able to talk to somebody else who had gone off of drugs, and that gave me hope to stay there. I made it through, but it wasn't easy.

I had been living with pain for more than twenty years and taking all these drugs. Actually, a lot of my pain, I found out, was caused from the stresses in my life and by poor self-esteem. I had gone through some really tough things in my life. My first husband died at age thirty from cancer, and I had three children under the age of four and a half, one of them a newborn. My mother and father died of very long, drawn-out diseases, and I took care of them. All the while, I had physical pain, and it was intensified by the way I was reacting to what was going on in my life. When I learned that everything that happened to me wasn't a crisis, and I learned how to handle my life, the pain was so much better. I'm not saying I don't have pain today. I still have chronic pain. But I've learned to live with it.

As part of my recovery, I went to each pharmacy and told them not to fill any drug prescriptions for me. I tell the doctors to put their hands behind their back, so they don't write prescriptions for me. Of course, many of them have offered me drugs, and when I've had surgery, then I've had to have drugs. It's inhumane to go through surgery and not have drugs. I had my husband hand me the pills that I had to take, and every day I had to check in with my sponsor about everything. This is what I have to do, because I'm a druggie for life. I don't like being treated like a drug addict. I hate it. But there's nothing I can do about it. It's back to the Serenity Prayer. I have to accept that I have a disease, like diabetes or anything else.

When I'm in pain now, I talk about it. I'll announce to my husband, "Today is a pain day." And once I talk about it, I can live with it. There are many times that I'll say, "Pain, pain, pain, pain," because I know I'm having it and I have to live with it. I call my sponsor. I try to exercise. I walk in a warm pool at a health club, and I have to rest a little bit each day. There are certain things that I learned at the pain clinic that I have to do, and that's what I do to live with it.

My husband picked up the slack for me all those years I was taking drugs. It was pretty tough when we had to rearrange power afterward, because I changed a whole lot after treatment. He was used to making all the rules of the house, and all of a sudden, I became a human person, and we had a lot of adjusting to do that first year. I learned to take back some of the power of my life. I learned how to take care of my children, how to handle money, how to do everything. My husband has joined me in this Jewish recovery network and all that I do with the community. Believe me, without his support, I couldn't do it all.

I just feel I'm so lucky. I feel very blessed. At first I couldn't believe it when people said they were a grateful recovering person. I thought,

That is ridiculous. How could anybody feel that way? Now, believe me, I'm grateful that I'm in recovery and that I have this program.

One thing I'm especially grateful for is that, when I was so concerned about being converted, I started interviewing rabbis and finding out more about my own religion. That really helped me a lot. I found out there is nothing that is in AA that is against my religion. The Jewish people believe that we are in partnership with God. But I didn't know that at the time. I learned that. Now I can talk to my Higher Power all day long if I want to. I have a personal God that I can talk to anytime, anyplace, anywhere. That never entered my brain before. My brain was so full of *I have pain, where am I going to get my next drug? How can I find enough drugs to get me through the next day?*

Now, I love life and I'm doing so wonderfully. I'm really blessed, and the more people I can help, the better it is. Anything I can do for other people makes me feel good.

CHAPTER 9

Relationships

THE QUALITY OF OUR LIVES HAS A LOT TO DO WITH THE quality of our relationships. All of us have relationships with many different people in our lives: friends, family, spouses or partners, co-workers, roommates, and other people who are part of our community. Many of us in recovery have difficulties in our relationships with others. In fact, most everyone has concerns at times about particular relationships or the lack of them. Figuring out how to get along with other people is part of being human.

This chapter talks about how addiction affects our relationships and how the principles of recovery can be helpful in making our relationships healthier and more satisfying. It identifies some of the blocks or ways of acting in relationships that can leave us feeling lonely, frustrated, and ashamed. It also offers some insights about getting along with people—insights that many of us in recovery have found useful. Although this chapter is long, what it offers is just the tip of the iceberg when it comes to understanding our behaviors regarding relationships. Twelve Step literature such as *Alcoholics Anonymous* (the Big Book), *Narcotics Anonymous*, and *Twelve Steps and Twelve Traditions* provide further insight into using the principles of recovery in relationships.

Addiction and Relationships

During our active addiction, our primary relationship was with our chemical. We may deny that, arguing that our primary relationships were with other people, but when push came to shove, what won over our time, focus, and attention was the addiction. Because of this preoccupation with our chemical, most of us did things that hurt others who mattered to us. We may have pulled away from people entirely, leaving us with only our chemical for companionship. As our addiction progressed, many of us crawled into the bottle of isolation and didn't even know we were doing it.

We sometimes spoke of our drugs in terms of relationships: "Crack was my true love." "I never went to bed without Jack Daniels." "I lost my lover." "That was my brand." "I fell in love with my pills." When some of us came into recovery, the only relationship we had left was with our drug. Even if we had some relationships with co-workers, family, partners, friends, or others, they had been greatly affected by our addiction.

Addiction puts great stress on our relationships. It interferes with our connection with self, others, and a Higher Power. As women dealing with addiction, we have a special challenge. Women are usually seen as caregivers and as central to the stability of the family. Many of us are also seen as having a central role in our jobs, volunteer organizations, or other situations in our lives. When we're using, we disrupt the stability of our family or other situations; some of our relationships and roles don't survive the addiction.

Let's face it. Most of us haven't been too successful with relationships. Even if we've had loving relationships at various times in our lives, our addiction interfered with them when we were using. Relationships require work and engagement, and our primary focus was on our chemical, not the relationship. The Big Book compares an active addict to "a tornado roaring his way through the lives of others" (p. 82). Once sober, the addict is usually oblivious to the havoc that's been wreaked on others. Like the addict described in the Big Book, when we put down the chemical, we may think that our problems are over. Getting sober is a great start, but there's a lot of work ahead to fix our damaged relationships.

A basic problem for many of us is connection. Even in a room full of people, many of us have felt alone. We may have no idea how to be an equal partner or a regular, contributing member of a group. We have hardly ever felt connected to any group or relationship. We may have blamed others for leaving us out, but in truth our self-centeredness has been the biggest barrier between us and others. We may have felt we were better or worse than others and acted accordingly. We rarely acted like a partner in a true partnership. We weren't seeking to treat others equally or to contribute what we could to the individuals and communities around us. We really didn't know how to be any different.

Recovery and Relationships

Recovery is about connection, and we experience this connection through relationships of various kinds. We practice our spirituality through our relationships. We practice living our program through our relationships. We cut off relationships with people who are not safe or who were our using buddies. We change "people, places, and things." We form a support system of other people by taking part in the fellowship. We clean up the mess we made in our relationships when we were using (Steps Eight and Nine). For many of us, this is the beginning of feeling truly connected with others. We form new relationships.

Developing healthy relationships is an ongoing journey. Just as we're never finished with recovery, we're never finished with learning how to live in relationships. It's an exciting adventure, learning to develop healthy relationships. It's also difficult at times. In recovery we learn to base our relationships on the principles of recovery.

Patterns of Relating

Some of us get stuck in relationship patterns that are self-destructive or hurtful to others. We may tend to lead with anger, sullenness, isolating behavior, or superficiality. Perhaps we default to aloofness or passivity or aggressiveness. We generally have some sort of pattern in the way we relate to people. For most of us, these patterns fall into one of two categories. Either we try to be in charge and pretend we are the Higher Power, or we let others be in charge and act helpless, depending too much on them. The patterns discussed in the rest of this chapter fall on one end of this spectrum or the other: control or dependence. They include codependency, control, people pleasing, dependency, fear of commitment, and "one up, one down" relationships. These are just some of the ways we can get stuck. In order to get unstuck, we first need to know a little about these patterns so we can identify them in ourselves.

Codependency

Codependency is a term that was originally applied to the partners and spouses of addicts. It referred to the way they were affected by the addict's disease and the way they tried to control the addict's drinking or using. Although the word is still used in that manner, over the years its meaning has broadened and can apply to anyone.

Codependency is the habit of trying to control others or situations in an unhealthy way. This attempt at control takes a number of forms, such as being nice in order to manipulate, putting the feelings and needs of others first so they won't get mad at us, ignoring our own needs and then getting angry or resentful (at least inside), and being focused on others and their behavior. Codependency often includes obsessive thinking about certain people or situations. Thoughts about them overtake our mind just as alcohol and drugs did when we were using. Our focus is not on ourself, nor on helping others in a healthy way, nor on our Higher Power. It's on how we're going to control a situation or change someone or something. We may even go so far as to think our worth comes through another person. We get into living a secondhand life. It's not our life we're thinking about or focusing on, it's someone else's.

If codependency is an issue for us, just working our recovery program may help us focus more on our own lives and less on others and what they're doing. We learn that what others are doing, thinking, or even feeling really is none of our business. What is our business is what *we* are doing, thinking, and feeling. Focusing on ourselves in a healthy way takes us out of codependency. It gives us back our lives.

> ⟐ *The biggest challenge for me is not letting other people and their problems affect the path I'm on. It's easy to get caught up in a lot of the drama going on with other people, so I'm learning to set boundaries for myself. Also, I sponsor women, and at first if I sponsored somebody and they went back to doing what they were doing, I took it really, really hard. I would wonder,* Should I have done something better? Did I not do something? Is it my fault? *I've had to learn that each of us is responsible for her own actions.*
>
> :: KAREN

Having a practicing addict, or even a dry drunk, in our lives can be frustrating for us and can cause us to slip into codependency. But, just as with our own addiction, we didn't cause this person's condition, we can't control it, and we can't cure it. We can, however, get help with our codependency from Al-Anon, Families Anonymous, Nar-Anon, Parents Anonymous, and similar groups. While the focus of each of these Twelve Step groups is a bit different, in general they have the same purpose: to help people affected by someone else's alcohol and drug use. Co-Dependents Anonymous (CoDA) is another group that can be helpful. CoDA is for anyone who desires to develop healthy relationships, regardless of any involvement with addicts. Many of us have seen how helpful these groups have been for our families as they recover from living with our addiction. These same groups can help us if we're codependent.

Just as it can be difficult to acknowledge in Step One the powerlessness we have over our own addiction, we may find it challenging to acknowledge that we are powerless over someone else's addiction. In dealing with someone we love who is addicted, we may have to learn some new slogans—in particular "Detach with love." This slogan reminds us to avoid becoming overly involved in or overly focused on the other person's addiction. It doesn't necessarily mean abandoning that person. We can still love the addict, but we just don't get caught up in the chaos. We learn to *care for* the addict instead of *taking care of* the addict. This detachment takes lots of support and guidance from others. We can also benefit from other program slogans, such as "Live and let live," "Easy does it," and "Let go and let God."

It's really hard to live with addiction—our own or someone else's. Some of us have found it more painful to live with someone else's addiction than to live through our own. Twelve Step groups can offer support and help in this area.

Control

Some of us default into being controlling in relationships. We think we can arrange and control everything so it'll turn out all right. This is particularly true for those of us who live with someone else who is in active addiction. We try to arrange things so that everything will work out the way we think it should. We're convinced that if others would just do things *our* way, all would be well. We're under the delusion that *we know best.*

Our controlling behavior can take many different forms. Some of us become workaholics, trying to control our world through being big shots at work or being martyrs. Others become enmeshed in our families, putting all our energy and focus on their behaviors and issues. We may try to control family members through anger, bossiness, or manipulation. Some of us try to control through being nice and considerate. While we may look good to others by being kind, even virtuous, if our motive is to control people or situations, we won't have healthy relationships. We won't have serenity. Our recovery is not about how we look in the eyes of others. It's about what we see when we look inside ourselves.

People Pleasing

Those of us with low self-esteem may think we're worthwhile only if others are pleased with us. We become "people pleasers." We work hard to do good for others, yet secretly we may resent doing so much for them. Still, we feel driven to do it in hopes of getting their approval. As long as people are happy with us, we think we're okay. The reality is, we're okay even when people aren't happy or pleased. In fact, many times when people are upset, it has nothing to do with us. Some of us personalize everything. We see a stranger on the street with a stern look and think we did something wrong. In recovery, we start to change our thinking and realize *it's not all about us.* We're not the center of the world. We don't have the power to make people feel anything. Others have a right to their thoughts, feelings, and behaviors, just as we do. It's respectful to let them be who they are and where they are emotionally, physically, and spiritually. It's disrespectful to try to manipulate their feelings so we feel good.

Our job is to live the principles of recovery and "to thine own self be true." That doesn't mean we live selfishly. Quite the opposite. "Love and tolerance of others is our code" (*Alcoholics Anonymous*, p. 84). People pleasing is not our code. We're responsible for the effort (love and tolerance) and not the outcome (people feeling pleased). In truth, sometimes when we practice healthy behaviors that are true to our own recovery, people won't be pleased. For instance, if we tell someone that we're not going with her to a particular event because we're concerned about alcohol or drugs being there, and she gets upset with us because of that, that doesn't mean we shouldn't have said it. It's okay when people get upset with us when we put our recovery first. We may find their response hard to take, but we can talk about it with others who will understand, such as others in recovery, and then we let it go. We learn to "live and let live."

> *I was raised codependently, so I had to learn what boundaries meant, what taking care of myself meant, that it was okay to say no. I remember my sponsor saying, "No is a complete sentence." I can still be a giving person, but I can also say, "No, I have plans tonight," when my plans are just to stay home and do nothing. I have learned that boundaries are important.*
>
> :: JULIA

Dependency

A common problem for some of us in relationships is that we come to depend on certain people too much. They become our all and everything, and we feel like we would tip over if they weren't there.

In some cultures, women are taught to be overly dependent. Some of us are highly dependent on our spouses or partners. Our whole world revolves around them, and we can't make a decision for ourselves. Some of us come into recovery thinking we should be able to depend completely on our sponsors for everything and that they should have all the answers. However, our sponsors are not our moms, therapists, or even necessarily friends. They are people who are sober and working a program of recovery. They have what we want. We ask them how they got it and follow their suggestions. We don't depend on them for everything.

Instead of putting all our eggs in one basket (our sponsor's), we turn to a number of people for support—our friends, home groups, families, other women in recovery, therapists (if we have them), faith communities (if we have them), and other members of our community. We don't depend totally on one person. We avoid exclusive relationships: we need more than one friend in recovery. What if something happens to that person? What if she relapses? What if she moves? We develop a community of support and eventually become "citizens of the world" (*As Bill Sees It*, p. 21).

Eventually, we learn to trust ourselves to make more of our own decisions. This takes a long time, though. In early recovery, we need to depend pretty heavily on guidance from others who are further along in the journey. Gradually, we learn how to draw on their help without becoming overly dependent on them. Even when we become more confident in our own decisions, we maintain a broad community of support to help us stay honest and grow in our recovery.

Fear of Commitment

Some of us hesitate to commit fully to any relationship. We keep to ourselves, or we appear very friendly and may even be a leader. But we keep ourselves at arm's length from others emotionally. Regardless of how sociable or introverted we are, we avoid committing to any relationship, whether with a partner or spouse, friend, support group, home group, family, co-worker, roommate—anyone.

We may keep so busy that we're not available for relationships. We may be so scared of getting close to people, of having them discover who we really are inside, that we isolate, dreading and avoiding interactions with others unless absolutely necessary. Another tactic is to get involved with people who really aren't available for us emotionally. Or, we get romantically involved with someone who's married, knowing that we won't have to commit ourselves fully, or with workaholics or other addicts, knowing subconsciously that we won't have to get to know them deeply. Some of us use humor to avert serious discussions with people. We don't allow ourselves to become vulnerable. We tap dance around relationships to shy away from letting people get to know us. We keep on the move, switching work places, changing meetings, staying busy—whatever it takes to keep people at a "safe" distance. As long as we're moving, we don't have to commit or let people get to know us. These ways of thinking and acting pose problems in a recovery program that's about relationships.

Healthy, close relationships are based on intimacy. Intimacy involves opening up our lives to others. We become vulnerable, letting other people close to us know who we are, inside and out. We share with them our feelings, thoughts, and beliefs. We let them in on our hurts, joys, disappointments, mistakes, and dreams. We talk with them about our everyday life and activities. Much as we do when we shared our Fifth Step with another person, we let people who are close to us know who we really are.

One Up, One Down Relationships

Some of us get into relationships in which we think we're better or worse than the other person. In Twelve Step rooms, the ground is level. It's also level in the world, though we don't always recognize that. The book *Twelve Steps and Twelve Traditions* says that we always "tried to struggle to the top of the heap, or to hide underneath it" (p. 53). Many of us struggle with being just one of the family, one of the group. Recovery is about being one among many. We're not the best (there is no best!), and we're not the worst (there is no worst!). We have a lot to add to any situation, just as others do. We have our individual gifts, preferences, knowledge, skills, quirks, and abilities. That makes us valuable, but no more or less valuable than another person.

Recovery Changes Relationships

As we work the Twelve Steps in recovery, we change. We change inside and we change in our relationships. We take stock of our mistakes in how we've handled relationships; we make amends; we learn how to manage our feelings and resentments; and we practice behaviors that help us to be safe and to keep our focus on recovery and taking care of ourselves.

As our behavior changes in recovery, our self-esteem increases. Improved self-esteem affects our relationships and how we handle them. As we feel better about ourselves and our behaviors, we hold our heads up a little higher, look people in the eye more, ask for what we need in direct way, and avoid playing games. In the past, we may have said we didn't care about something and then got resentful or silent when someone didn't do what we wanted, even though they had no idea what we wanted. We may have expected people to read our minds and never said what we needed. As our self-esteem increases, we feel our worth as an equal partner in relationships. We don't grovel and we don't control. We get more honest with ourselves and thus more honest with others. We become direct with ourselves and with others. We become more present—more invested and available. We're not swallowed up with feelings of guilt over what we just said or did. We're able to deal with what's happening in the moment.

Our relationships can be compared to a mobile, with its parts dangling and moving in the wind. Each of us is one piece of the mobile. The mobile tries to stay in balance, keeping an evenness or "homeostasis" in the system. When some part of the mobile is moved, the other parts are moved in some way along with it. The mobile is trying to get back to balance. It may swing wildly for a bit to make balance happen, or it may move smoothly with little notice. Either way, it is attempting to get back in balance.

As we change in recovery, our relationship system is thrown out of balance, just as when someone pulls down on one part of a mobile. As we change, and then as people around us change in response, we need to learn how to respond differently to create a new, healthy balance in this system. We practice the principles of open-mindedness, willingness, and honesty. We realize we don't know a lot about being in balanced, healthy relationships with others, and we become willing to learn. As we go on in recovery, we become open to even more change. We learn to develop partnerships, to become one among many, a sister among sisters, a friend among friends. We learn to be givers rather than takers. When people fail to meet our expectations, we learn to give them the same understanding we would want them to give us. That's a lot of learning to take on. We need both willingness and openness to take in these life-changing lessons.

Healthy Relationships

What does a healthy relationship look like? Healthy relationships are safe and respectful. They are flexible and change over time as circumstances change. People in healthy relationships communicate about things that matter to both people, including feelings. Each person gives and takes, compromises when needed, and sometimes agrees to disagree. Both people are committed to the relationship itself. They admit to mistakes and forgive mistakes.

Unhealthy relationships are the opposite. They are neither safe nor respectful. They have rigid roles and rules that aren't flexible as life happens. The two people may rarely communicate, particularly about feelings. If they do communicate about feelings, it may be done in anger. There isn't mutual give and take. One may almost always give, and the other may almost always take. Forgiveness may be one-sided.

Relationships are on a continuum. They usually aren't all good or all bad. Most of them could use some work to move toward being healthier. That's the "dailyness" of being in a relationship, whether a friendship, sponsor relationship, family relationship, or romantic relationship. They all take work. Part of the work is setting up healthy boundaries and communication.

Boundaries

Boundaries help define us. They are limits we set that separate us from others and things around us. They help define us as individuals and help to separate us from others. We can set physical boundaries, such as the physical distance we want to keep between ourselves and another person. More often, we set emotional boundaries, such as determining when we want to spend time alone or not letting people talk to us a certain way. We can even set spiritual boundaries, choosing to avoid being around someone who is constantly angry or who gossips a lot, if that puts a damper on our spirit. Boundaries are very individual and personal. We set them.

Granted, certain cultural norms and rules exist to guide our boundaries. Some may be based on religious beliefs, ethnic traditions, or regional or national customs or laws. Others may be shaped by families, workplace guidelines, or educational settings.

For example, in most countries, it is against the law to force someone to have sex (rape) or to take someone's life (murder). These are very clear examples of boundary violations. Other laws, such as those against stealing, robbing, and trespassing, are based on boundaries. Driving through a stoplight is a boundary violation because it could result in harm to the person driving and to others. While some boundaries are defined by society, others are individual and personal. They are defined by us and not by law or norm. While it's usually pretty clear when someone crosses a boundary established by law, it can be harder to know when someone crosses a personal boundary.

Boundary Violations

Many of us have experienced personal boundary violations and have also violated the boundaries of others. One example of a boundary violation is when someone tells us we're not feeling a certain way when we *are*. For instance, we may be feeling scared, and someone tells us, "You're not really scared of that, are you? That's silly." Or we may be feeling concerned about something, and someone tells us, "Don't worry about that. That's nothing to worry about." Sometimes people may tell us we *should* feel a certain way: "You *should* be happy to have so much" or "You *should* feel really guilty about that." Sometimes they may use a combination— telling us both what we should and shouldn't feel. For instance, "You *mustn't* feel jealous, you *should* be happy for her." However others try to convince us that feelings are right or wrong for us, they don't know what we're feeling inside. They've crossed a boundary—the boundary that defines who we are and what we're feeling.

More blatant boundary violations are physical or sexual abuse. These are clearly physical, emotional, and spiritual boundary violations. Sometimes people get too close to us physically. That's a boundary violation. Sometimes people tell us they love us deeply after they just met us. That's another kind of boundary violation. They're getting too close too soon. Boundaries are about balance. They keep us safe and separate from others, and they help define who we are.

Setting, Adjusting, and Respecting Boundaries

Boundaries change depending on the relationship. They're flexible. For instance, most of us are much more comfortable being physically close with our family members than we are with strangers. We may be more comfortable sharing our emotional life with friends and people in recovery than with people at work. That's appropriate. Boundaries vary depending on the relationship.

As women, many of us play various roles in our lives. We may be employers, caretakers of children, partners, employees or employers, daughters, aunts, sisters, parents, students, sponsees, or sponsors, to name a few. Sometimes we get our roles confused, blurring the lines between them and losing our own boundaries in the process. We may let our sponsees treat us the same way we let our kids treat us, thinking that we're totally responsible for their well-being. This is a boundary concern. We may have to change our boundaries as circumstances change. For instance, we have different boundaries with our parents as they age than we did when they were younger, especially if we move into a caregiver role. Boundaries are meant to be flexible, and we're responsible for adjusting and holding boundaries depending on the situation.

Just as we're responsible for creating and communicating what our own boundaries are, we're also responsible for respecting other people's boundaries. For example, if we like to hug at Twelve Step meetings, and we know someone doesn't like it, we respect that and don't offer a hug to that person. We listen to what people tell us about their boundaries, and we respect them. Most of the time, people don't talk about their boundaries out loud. Physically, they may back up if we get too close. Emotionally, they may get quiet if we're too prying. If we're in doubt, we can ask if we've offended them. They may not always give us a straight answer, but we can ask anyway. We don't have to be mind readers, but we do the best we can by asking. In general, we try to be respectful of someone's boundaries if we know about them, and when we aren't aware of them, we're willing to learn about them so we can honor them. Love and tolerance is our code.

The Twelve Steps help us learn how to set and accept boundaries. They get us to stay focused on our own recovery and not on what other people may be doing or saying. Even starting with the First Step, we're asked to take responsibility for our addiction and not blame others for causing it. All through the Steps, we're asked to work on our own recovery and then told when to share what we're discovering with appropriate people. In Step Nine, we're asked to make amends to people we've harmed—but not to those we haven't harmed. That wouldn't be appropriate. Earlier, in Step Five, we share our inventory with another person and our Higher Power. We're not asked to do our inventory in a Twelve Step meeting, though. That would be too much openness and a violation of our boundaries as well as the boundaries of the meeting. Not everyone wants to hear our inventory.

Some of us cross others' boundaries by telling too much about ourselves. We need to look at the appropriateness of what we're saying and to whom we're saying it. We may have had secrets for so much of our lives that we go to the far extreme when we start to tell our secrets. We feel such a sense of relief and freedom that we get caught up in telling everyone. That's a boundary violation.

Some of us have so little understanding of what appropriate boundaries are that we need to talk over our concerns with other women in the program. We may have been violated so often and in so many ways that we don't even know when or how we're being violated. We may be crossing others' boundaries and not even know it. Some of us get so involved with others that we "take hostages," expecting too much of people who just want to be general friends or acquaintances. We need other women in recovery to mentor us as we practice having healthy boundaries in relationships.

Improving our communication skills can help us to improve our boundaries. Many books, seminars, workshops, and other means are available to help us learn how to communicate better. One basic technique is to use "I" statements rather than (blaming) "you" statements. We can say, "I feel _____ when you _____ because _____ . I think/want/need/would like/prefer _____ ." If we're angry at someone because she continues to call us late at night after we've told her not to, we can use the above tool to help us flesh out what we want to say. "I feel angry when you call me late at night because I've told you before that I need to get my sleep. I would like you to call before ten o'clock unless it's an emergency." When we use this kind of approach, we're being assertive.

Assertiveness is a part of good communication and boundary setting. It is asking for what we need. "I feel hurt when you tell me what so-and-so said about me behind my back. In the future, I don't want to know what she says about me," or "I want you to let me know the next time you take money out of our savings, so I can keep a handle on our money." When we make requests, we ask for what we need or desire respectfully. We don't insist that the other person give us what we ask for. Boundaries are not about controlling others. They are about setting healthy limits for ourselves. Another way to set a boundary is to say no when that's our choice. "I appreciate the invitation to the party, but I won't be able to attend," or "No, I won't be available to do that." We don't need to explain.

Many of us think we owe everyone an explanation for everything we decide. We don't. In fact, sometimes explanations negate what we are saying and make it harder for us to keep our no firm. As some women in recovery say, explanations are undignified.

We don't have to explain everything to everyone. We may decide, though, to give a brief explanation to people close to us out of respect for the relationship. If our partner, for instance, asks us to go along to a work party, and we're concerned about being around alcohol, we might want to share our reason for not going with our partner. This is much more respectful than a simple no. Also, it will let our partner know more about what we're experiencing and that we're putting our recovery first.

Setting healthy boundaries is about being true to ourselves. It's also about being respectful of others and at the same time being direct and honest with them. Sometimes the most loving thing to say to someone is the truth. Just as we need to be told the "truth in love," so may others. It may be up to us to be the messenger, particularly if we're someone's sponsor or close friend. If we're close to these people and care about them, we do it in a kind and loving way. Before we say things to people that may be hard for them to hear, we can ask ourselves several questions about what we're going to say:

1. Is it kind?
2. Is it loving?
3. Is it necessary?
4. Does it need to be said?
5. Does it need to be said by me?

Using this process before speaking keeps our focus on being helpful and may save us from having to make unnecessary amends.

The Principles of Recovery and Relationships

We learn many principles in recovery that can help us in our relationships. Reviewing the principles associated with each of the

Twelve Steps (they're also listed in chapter 2, "A Way Out") is a good place to start:

Step One: Honesty
Step Two: Hope
Step Three: Faith
Step Four: Courage
Step Five: Integrity
Step Six: Willingness
Step Seven: Humility
Step Eight: Compassion
Step Nine: Justice
Step Ten: Perseverance
Step Eleven: Spiritual Awareness
Step Twelve: Service

Additional principles that support healthy and satisfying relationships are reflected in some of the Steps. For instance, the principle of forgiveness is embedded in Steps Four, Five, Eight, and Nine. The principle of love is embedded in Steps Two, Three, Five, Six, Seven, Eight, Nine, Ten, Eleven, and Twelve. The principle of humility underlies all of the Twelve Steps.

> *This is the first healthy, normal marriage that I've been in. I didn't know what that was. It certainly wasn't modeled for me. I had two disastrous marriages before this one. My mother had six. My father had four or five. So I'm learning how to get along with a man who's also my husband. Men's egos are not something you want to tackle with. Because then you're going to get in fights, and they're not going to back down. Just as I have learned to humble myself in terms of my work, or in terms of the program, I am now learning also to really*

humble myself a little bit with the guy. He's a very
powerful man, and he's got a very powerful ego. And
even though he's in the program, if I humble myself, he'll
back down instantly, and then we can talk from a pro-
gram level with each other and say, "Let's sort this one
out." Someone's got to back down. So I'm learning that,
and that's been many years in the program.

:: **KRISTEN**

The recovery program developed by Alcoholics Anonymous teaches us many other principles that can ease difficulties in rela-tionships. In chapter 2, "A Way Out," we discussed the importance of willingness, honesty, and open-mindedness. While these are key in recovery, they also really stand out as principles that help us with relationships. Some others are patience, tolerance, respon-sibility, taking our own inventory (not someone else's), living on a give-and-take basis, generosity, kindness, and understanding.

The Twelve Traditions, which are used to guide the operations of Twelve Step groups, contain additional principles we can make use of in our relationships. Among these principles are maintain-ing unity, putting the welfare of the group ahead of any particular individual in it, including others, preserving liberty for each group unless it hurts other groups or AA as a whole, creating structure, having focus, being self-supporting (not living off others), avoid-ing arguments, attracting not promoting (avoiding coercion), pay-ing attention to principles and not personalities, and practicing anonymity.

Whole books have been written on the principles found in the Twelve Traditions. *Twelve Steps and Twelve Traditions* was written to provide more information on these principles. While it's beyond the scope of this chapter to explain the Twelve Traditions, a few ex-amples may be helpful in showing how these principles can apply to relationships.

For instance, the tradition saying that the common welfare of the group comes first is also relevant in relationships. Sometimes we need to compromise or give up our own desires for the good of a relationship. For instance, sometimes we spend time with the person we're in the relationship with, even when we would have rather done something else. We do this for the good of the relationship. In healthy relationships, there is a lot of give and take. While we avoid codependent behaviors—such as people pleasing—and other unhealthy behaviors, we do give—and also take—for the good of the relationship.

Focus is another principle talked about in the traditions. Having focus can help us to have an orderly, balanced life. The focus of Twelve Step groups is to help the still-suffering addict. In our personal lives, we may need to set our compass with a clear focus in mind. When we're in school, for instance, we may need to reduce our TV-watching time or set aside some other interests so we can focus on our studies. At various times in a relationship, we need to focus more on that relationship than at other times. For instance, if a family member is gravely ill, we may choose to set aside some other activities in order to focus on that relationship. If we become a new parent, our focus generally goes more toward our relationship with the new child than it will when that child is older. Some companies or businesses refer to their focus as their vision or mission statement. We can create such a statement for our own lives and use it to guide our choices.

Another important principle from the traditions that we learn in recovery is to put the principles of the program before any individual personality. In groups, that means that we keep our attention on the principles of our AA, NA, or other Twelve Step program and don't let ourselves get distracted by the quirks of individual members. We can use this principle in any situation. The nitpicking, bickering, and judgments that can be part of relationships tend to disappear when we focus on the principles that bind us, such as the goals of a project or work situation, a common vision, strengthening the relationship, getting our children through some event, or getting ourselves through some event. We keep our eyes on what we're doing and why we're doing it, not on someone else and what we think they're doing wrong.

Family

>CRS *I have a close relationship with my mom. My*
>   *mother and I didn't get along for many, many years,*
>   *and because of my recovery, I have started to see my*
>   *mother as a human being who really, really did the best*
>   *she could with what she had. So much of my early life*
>   *was about complaining and feeling like a victim, like,*
>   *"Poor me, my mother didn't give me this," "Poor me,*
>   *my mother burped me the wrong way." I just blamed her*
>   *for so much. It never dawned upon me that, while I was*
>   *saying she wasn't such a great mom, I was not a great*
>   *daughter. I was causing my mother all kinds of grief,*
>   *but now she and I are very close. I have really become*
>   *a good daughter. I've changed my thinking, and I've*
>   *changed my attitude.*
>
>   :: KRISTEN

Perhaps the relationships most affected by our addiction are those we have with our family members. They may be greatly affected by our recovery also. *Family* can be defined in a number of different ways, but in general, *family* refers to the people who know our private lives and who have lived with us for an extended period of time. Some of us have friends and relatives beyond our immediate biological family that we consider close family members. When we're in treatment, we create such strong bonds with the people we're in treatment with that they may feel like part of our family. We may become so close to certain people in our Twelve Step groups that they seem like family to us.

When we first get sober, our family members may experience a variety of emotions. They may be angry about our disease and behavior and just waiting for us to use again. They may be euphoric that we've stopped using. They may be scared and fearful that recovery won't work. Sometimes family members are jealous of our Twelve Step groups and friends because this new group of people has been able to help us when they couldn't. They may be uneasy about the changes going on. At least they knew what to expect when we were using, uncomfortable as that was. Now they're facing the unknown.

Whatever they're feeling, they need help during this time of change. In addiction, the disease has been in charge of the addict, and the family has been greatly affected. Love may have been dampened or destroyed. Just as we addicts violate our values in addiction, family members may violate their values. They may do things they never thought they'd do out of frustration and in their attempts to control our addiction. They need support and help also. They can benefit from learning about addiction and finding others who have been affected by it. As mentioned previously, Twelve Step groups are available for family members also.

Some family members may not be open to support or learning anything about addiction. That must not keep us from our own recovery. They don't *have* to do anything. We do. We're fighting for our lives. It's *our* recovery. Granted, it's helpful to both them and us if they get education and support, but we can't make it happen. All we can do is take care of ourselves, let them know what help is available, and continue on our recovery journey.

It will take time for our families to start to trust us again. Usually it's at least a year before they start to get some hope and trust that, this time, we may continue on the road to recovery. If we've had several relapses, it may take longer. Their trust has been shaken too many times. For them, the proof is in our actions. They're watching us. It's about what we do, not what we say we'll do. "Our behavior will convince them more than our words" (*Alcoholics Anonymous*, p. 83). For some reason, our families' lack of trust surprises us, even though our track records are full of trust-shattering behavior. It may hurt if, the first time we take a nap in recovery, they ask us if we've been using. It may hurt when we come home late after going out for coffee following a Twelve Step meeting and they smell our breath. We think they *should* trust us. We need to remember that they've been hurt too. Just as we're taking time to heal, so are they. No matter what our families do, we get to practice the principles we're learning in recovery. In particular, we get to practice our code of love and tolerance. With our families, some of us get lots of extra practice.

> A high point in my recovery was when I was about six months sober, and I found out that I was going to have a nephew. I was thinking, I get to be a sober aunt, and this child will hopefully not see his aunt drunk, and they'll trust me to take care of him, *whereas before I would not have been necessarily trustworthy with taking care of a baby.*
>
> :: BONNIE

Parenting

If we're parents, our children have been affected by our using. They may have been affected even before they were born. Some chemicals can damage the health of a fetus. We may also have eaten poorly or been in poor health because of our use, depriving our unborn child of some of the nutrients and other resources needed to develop into a healthy baby. Our children may have suffered physically and emotionally if we abused them, neglected them, or left them with unsafe people. We may have had to turn our children over to the care of social service agencies or to the other parent or another family member in custody battles. Some of us neglected our children in subtle ways that damaged them emotionally. This damage may not have been intentional, but they were hurt nonetheless. We may have been physically available for them and said we loved them, but our behavior said we didn't have time for them as we focused on other things, including our drugs. We didn't give them much emotionally or spiritually because we didn't have it inside ourselves to give.

One of the most painful things for many of us to do as we get sober is to look at the effect our using has had on our children. We may feel gut-wrenching pain. Fortunately, we can find other women in our program whom we can talk to about this and who will understand. Some of us are facing losing our children due to our addiction. We need others as we go through this pain. It may feel like our insides are being torn out. We are not meant to face this alone. It's way too painful. We practice the principle of fellowship and find others who can relate to us and support us through our parenting ordeals.

Being a mother can be one of the most defining roles in our lives. Most of us never had any training in how to be a mother and are basing our parenting on what we've seen others do. Being a mother can be stressful. We need support and encouragement. We may find parenting education classes to be helpful, or we can talk to a counselor or to women whose parenting skills we admire.

Kids are resilient. They're also loyal. It will take time for them to trust us again, but it will come. As we're consistent with our recovery and also with them, they start to feel safe. They see new evidence of boundaries in the family that provide safety. They notice that Mom is taking care of herself. If Mom is taking care of herself, she's also more likely to take care of them. As we practice self-care, our children learn that life is more predictable than in the past. The chaos of addiction is gone. Consistency provides a feeling of safety for children. They now know what to expect. Just as we work our program consistently and daily, we are there daily for our children. We're open to learning more about parenting and developing the qualities we need to be good parents. For help with our relationships, especially with our children, we can practice what we learn in the program about giving service and about being loving and tolerant. Caring for our children can give us lots of opportunities to practice what we learn in these areas. We also have many opportunities to practice setting boundaries. We also can be assured that, just as we have a loving Higher Power, so do our children.

> *Probably the highest point was when my daughter called me Mom. Another high point is now, when she says things to me like, "Mom, I love you." Because I don't get to have her every day, and I don't get to experience those little everyday things that kids do, I see them in a different light. I appreciate them maybe a little more than a lot of parents do.*
>
> :: KAREN

It's challenging to fit all our self-care and recovery activities into our schedule and still make time for our role as parents. While we put our recovery first, we need to be open to ways of working our program that also take our children into account. It's not always practical or loving for some of us to work full-time and also do all of the other things that are often recommended in recovery, such as "Go to ninety meetings in ninety days." It would be impossible to do *everything* that might help our recovery and still be there for our children.

We practice the principles of recovery and talk with others about how we can participate in the fellowship and still be there for our children. We can get creative. We can plan an outing with another mother in recovery and end up doing a meeting with her at the playground while our kids play. We can connect with group members by phone. We may be able to find meetings where child care is provided, or we may even start a meeting with that in mind. Some of us find that reading literature helps keep our focus on recovery while allowing us to be available to our children. We need to put our recovery first and practice the principles of connection yet be creative in how we do it as a parent. We ask for help. Our kids lost us to addiction. They don't need to lose us to something else now, such as meetings every day of the week.

Romantic Relationships

If we're not currently in a romantic relationship, we may strongly desire to be in one, or we might be hoping to find a way to get out of or "fix" the one we are in. Most of us desire to be loved in some way. That's a healthy desire. It becomes unhealthy when we make that the focus of our lives and our recovery. Being in a romantic relationship can be a mood-altering situation and can put us at risk for relapse. It has lots of ups and downs. While all relationships take ongoing work, a romantic relationship requires a lot of work. That said, it can also be one of the most satisfying relationships we enjoy in life. But we need to be extremely cautious as we get into a new one, especially in early recovery.

Early recovery is filled with lots of ups and downs. Big changes in emotions can come every twenty minutes or more often. The early stages of a romantic relationship are also filled with ups and downs. He loves me, he loves me not. She loves me, she loves me not. Mix the ups and downs of early recovery with the ups and downs of a new relationship, and we've got chaos. It's common to spend a lot of time thinking about the other person. This preoccupation with the person and the possibilities for the relationship can give us a sort of high. It's mood-altering. It can also put us at risk for relapse. We get so focused on the relationship and its ups and downs that we lose focus on our recovery. That's why it's generally recommended that we not get into a new relationship for the first year in recovery. It can be too distracting. Not that we shouldn't get into relationships at all. In fact, quite the opposite! Recovery is about relationships, but our recovery needs to be solid before we go down the path of romantic involvement.

Most romantic relationships have very intense feelings, both at the beginning and at the end of them. It's wise to avoid adding any intense feelings in early recovery. As mentioned in chapter 2, if we're in a safe and tolerable relationship, it's best to stay put and not make any rash decisions to leave it. If we're not in a romantic relationship, it's best to focus completely on our recovery. Holding off on getting into a relationship can be hard for some of us. As we work our program, everything in us starts to come alive. This includes our sexuality and our desire for intimacy.

> *The program has changed the way that I interact with men. Actually, I can be friends with men today, where before I didn't know how to be friends with them. I hate to say it, but I was very sexually active when I was out there in the throes of my addiction, and I am no longer like that. Today, I have morals. I kind of feel almost like I probably would have if I'd have stayed that sweet, innocent little six-year-old girl, before all the sexual abuse.*
>
> :: DENISE

A desire for intimacy is a good thing. Intimacy is not the same thing as sex. Intimacy is about getting to know someone deeply through sharing feelings, thoughts, and beliefs. We can have intimacy without sex. It's also possible to have sex without intimacy. Intimacy is a process. It's not an act. It deepens as we become closer and closer to someone, and at times it can be scary because, by revealing our deepest thoughts and feelings, we're making ourselves vulnerable. It can also leave us feeling more connected and alive than we've ever felt before.

Many of us begin learning how to have intimacy with others as we get into recovery. Intimacy is a process; it's active and it's constantly changing. As we share with others at a deep level, we connect emotionally. We may also feel sexually aroused. For some of us who struggle with boundaries, we may not know when and how to set the limit, so it's important to wait to pursue a romantic interest until our recovery is solid. We may end up thinking about the other person all the time or even end up in bed despite our best intentions. We need to have someone we can talk to about any romantic attraction before we act on it. We avoid talking about our feelings with the person we're attracted to until we've processed our feelings with a sponsor or another mentor in recovery. If we immediately tell the person that we are attracted to him or her, and the attraction is mutual, we're sure to be off and running with a full-blown relationship. Later in recovery, that may be great, but when we're new in recovery, we need some guidance around this potential relationship and how it will affect our recovery.

For most of us, getting into a romantic relationship can be scary. For some of us, it's terrifying. We may have had a history of abuse and have trouble trusting. Any kind of history of unhealthy past relationships may trigger some fear about re-creating them. We may be so scared that we start to have strong anxiety or even panic attacks.

Just like recovery, relationships are a process. They take time, and we need to be willing to give them time. It may be necessary to go extra slowly and to practice the principles of sharing and asking for help. We need to learn what a healthy and safe relationship looks like. Some of us seek outside therapy as we learn to be in relationships. Many other resources are available to help us learn, such as classes for women, books, support groups, and workshops on relationships. We work our program and practice the principles we've learned to use in other relationships. We ask our Higher Power for guidance each day to do the next right thing. We focus on our recovery and try to be kind and loving. We watch our expectations. We ask for help. We don't go it alone.

> ⟨∾ *In terms of men, it's harder for me to be selfish in relationships now. I used to use men to feel better about myself, or just to have someone—a warm body. Now I can't do that, because it would be selfish, and it would harm them in the long run. There have been a few relationships that I've had to end because I realized it wasn't what I was looking for. In the past, I might have stuck with it just to have somebody to call my boyfriend, but it's very different now. Also, I can't be throwing things across the room like I used to. I would bottle things up and then I would erupt, which I don't do as much of anymore. Now, I say, "This is how I'm feeling right now." Before, I didn't know how I was feeling, so I couldn't have voiced it. Now I can get in touch with it more and figure out: Are my motives in a good place? Am I using this person?*

:: BONNIE

Other Relationships

As our world widens in recovery, we get into relationships with many different people. That may happen through work, family, community, or place of worship. We may get involved with others through our children and their friends, our extended families, our support group, our interests or hobbies, and in other ways. We're bound to be in relationships with a wide variety of people. Addiction is about constriction; recovery is about expansion. This includes expansion in relationships.

Whatever types of relationships we enter, we practice the principles we're learning in recovery. We remain willing and open to support and guidance from others and our Higher Power. We learn to practice boundaries and self-restraint, to sidestep traps, to make amends, and to forgive. We often ask ourselves, *Am I doing to others as I would have them do to me?* We'll never arrive at perfection in our relationships, but we'll clearly make progress.

Developing healthy relationships is an ongoing process, and it's a lot of work. Some of us in early recovery wonder if we'll ever catch on and be able to have true friendships and partnerships. The good news is, we aren't alone. The program and the fellowship give us guidance and support. The Prayer of St. Francis of Assisi, which is found in *Twelve Steps and Twelve Traditions,* is another excellent guide for our relationships. Though this prayer or affirmation was created in the thirteenth century and its language is dated, its principles continue to be relevant for relationships today:

> Make me a channel of thy peace—that where there is hatred, I may bring love—that where there is wrong, I may bring the spirit of forgiveness—that where there is discord, I may bring harmony—that where there is error, I may bring truth—that where there is doubt, I may bring faith—that where there is despair, I may bring hope—that where there are shadows, I may bring light— that where there is sadness, I may bring joy (p. 99).

These are high ideals and may seem too lofty, but they can inspire us to create more loving attitudes in our day-to-day connections with the people we care about. To start with, we can pick one line from the prayer and focus on it, doing what we can to be more caring and supportive in our relationships in this one area. The more we work the program, the more this Prayer of St. Francis becomes the norm for the way we wish to treat other people. As we experience the freedom and happiness that come from being in true connection with others, we want to do everything we can to foster loving, respectful relationships in our lives.

As we get into recovery, put down the chemicals, clean up our messes, and live the Twelve Steps, over time we go from not being comfortable in our own skin to being connected and knowing we belong and are loved. What a miracle! We will experience this miracle. It's a promise if we do the program, one day at a time, one step at a time, as one among many.

KAREN'S STORY

When I was a teenager, I did a lot of experimenting with drugs. Most of it was more partying on the weekends. I started off smoking pot in junior high and went from there to acid and meth. I tried cocaine. I tried a lot of stuff in high school. In my early twenties, I became a full-blown meth addict. In those two years between high school and the whole meth thing, I had a pretty good job and a boyfriend, and I was going part time to junior college. I really wanted to be a nurse and help people. I just wanted to be happy. In the six months prior to my starting to use meth like I did, a few difficult things happened, and I started feeling really unhappy. I ran into some friends of mine from high school that I used to party with, and they're like, "Come over this weekend." I did and I got high, and I thought that I felt happy, and it totally snowballed from there.

As a result of the meth, I lost my job, I lost my apartment, and I ended a good relationship I was in. I ruined everything with my family. I have really great parents and I used to see them all the time, and they went from seeing me every week to not hearing from me for months at a time. When they would hear from me, often it would be a call from jail.

I ended up in jail many times—for everything from drug charges to forgery and possession of stolen property. My final big arrest was for making fake IDs. I went to federal prison. I was there for twenty-four months. That was the big one.

Every time I went to jail, it was horrible. Jail was not something that was in my family's history. I kept wondering, *What am I doing here?* Then I would get out, with good intentions, and I'd end up right back with those old people I used with.

A few years into my addiction, I ended up in a really bad, abusive relationship. The guy I was involved with was a heroin addict. He was abusive, and I just couldn't get away from him. It was like our addictions kind of fed off each other. He would beat me and I would leave, and he would come find me. It just got uglier and uglier. We were involved in a lot of crime together, and the addiction fed the crime. As our addictions got worse, the crimes would get bigger and uglier. The ultimate low point in my addiction was about four years into that relationship. I ended up pregnant, and I used during part of my pregnancy. He went to prison while I was pregnant, so I was all by myself.

When I was pregnant, they tested me for drugs, and it came up positive for meth. I ended up doing outpatient treatment at the end of my pregnancy and after my daughter was born, but honestly, I didn't embrace it at the time. I think it was because I had to do it and I wasn't ready for it. They told me I had to do it or they were going to take my baby, so I went through the motions of doing what they wanted me to do. I never really got anything out of it.

I cleaned up for a little while, but after my boyfriend got out, we relapsed. We were getting high, and we got back into the crime. The feds kicked in my door when my daughter was seven months old. They snatched my daughter out of my hands and took her into foster care. I was taken off to federal prison. It was horrible.

My daughter's dad tried to get her out of foster care, but they saw he'd just been in prison and he was using. They wouldn't give her back to him, so his dad came to the state we lived in to get our daughter. He thought he would be there for one week to go to court. He was there about five months. He eventually brought her back to the state they lived in. When I got out of prison, I moved to the state where she was living with her grandparents. By then, my daughter's dad and I had broken up.

In this new place, I had an opportunity to have a fresh start. It ended up being the best thing that ever happened to me. I got sent to a halfway house for women who had been in prison. The halfway house sent me to an organization that's supposed to help offenders find jobs. But as soon as they found out I had been in a federal prison, they were like, "Oh. I'm sorry. We can't help federal inmates." So they basically shut the door in my face. As I was leaving, this one lady that works there said to me, "You know, we can't really help you, but here's the number of a lady that works with federal people. You should give her a call." I gave her a call, and I ended up working for her. That started me off in the nonprofit community, and it paved the way for the job I have now, working for a nonprofit that helps inmates and ex-offenders. I had to work a lot of different jobs before getting this one, though. The whole employment part of it was really, really hard—having to talk to people about, "Yeah, I'm really qualified and I'm a great worker. But by the way, I have six felonies on my record, and I'm a recovering addict." It took a lot of perseverance.

Where I was incarcerated, there was a nine-month-long residential drug treatment program that you can take to get a year off your sentence. I didn't have enough time left to get a year off by the time I started the program. I actually think I ended up staying in prison an extra two weeks to finish it. But I remember at my sentencing, the judge said, "Do you have anything to say?" I got up and I said, "I'm a drug addict and I know I'm not eligible for all the requirements for the drug program, because of the year off and all that. But I really need help, and I just don't know what to do. I have absolutely no idea. Can you please let me in?" And they did. When I got out of prison, I already had a little over eighteen months clean.

My daughter, she's probably the greatest joy and the hardest part of everything. I saw her once the whole time I was locked up. After I got to the halfway house, I remember the first time her grandparents brought her up to meet me. I had last seen her when she was a year old, and now she was twenty-six months old. She was in the car seat, and I climbed in next to her. I was hoping I wouldn't be totally unfamiliar to her because I used to send pictures for her grandparents to show her when I was locked up. When I got in the car, I said, "Do you know who I am?" I said, "I'm your mom." And she goes, "You're not my mom. You're Karen." It was so hard. When you're locked up and you have all this time to think about what it's going to be like, you have all these dreams about how your kid's just going to run up and embrace you. I wanted to cry. She didn't know me. It took probably four or five months to get her to call me Mom.

A few months before I was released from prison, her dad convinced me to sign custody over to him because of some legal issues, saying I'd get her back a year after I was out. It's been four years, and he's never given me back custody. According to the court papers that I signed, I was given supervised visitation. At first I'd see her every Sunday, and then eventually it went to having her overnight maybe once a month. Now I have her every other weekend and one night during each week, but I don't have joint custody. I have absolutely no say in my child's life. On the bright side, I'm her mom, and she knows that, and she loves me, and she calls me all the time when I don't see her. For what it is, we have a wonderful, wonderful relationship. When I get down in the dumps about the whole situation, I realize I have so much more than I could have had.

When I first moved to be near her, it was a new city for me, and I didn't know anybody. I went to my first AA meeting when I was still in the halfway house. I remember I stood up and I got my eighteen-month medallion. They always ask, "How did you do it?" I told a little bit about what was going on, and I said, "I don't know anybody here. I have absolutely no friends, and I really need some help." A couple women gave me their phone numbers. One of them ended up being my sponsor for probably two years. She was awesome. She took me to speaker meetings. She connected me with the whole recovery community in the area. In the summertime, we went to different barbecues and camping trips with people in recovery. The other lady I met ran a sober house, and I ended up living there for the first year. She was very connected in the whole recovery community too, so I got a whole bunch of different people involved in my life. They helped to show me how I could do it and what I could hope for—the results I could get if I really put forth the effort and put my heart into working the Steps. They helped me learn to live a life of recovery.

One of the biggest changes I've made in recovery is to become honest. I lied so much when I was using—to everybody, including myself. Now I try to be honest about everything, even if it's not something that it's easy to be honest about. People respect what I say, because they know that I will tell them the truth. It feels good for me to know that I can be honest about any part of my life now, that I don't have to hide things.

I keep my program strong by going to meetings. I have a sponsor who's there for me. I also go to a therapist. I try to do yoga or Pilates or something to take care of the physical part of my well-being. I have a really good guy in my life who is really supportive, and I can talk to him about absolutely anything. He's in recovery too, and he's got a lot of sobriety. He and my daughter are probably the best thing about my life right now. They're wonderful.

CHAPTER 10

Relapse

WHO WANTS TO THINK ABOUT RELAPSE? IT'S A SCARY subject. Even the thought of reading this chapter can seem scary. What if all this talk about relapse "jinxes" our program and starts us using again?

Fear of talking about or hearing about relapse is normal. Most of us, when we're new in recovery, don't know much about recovery, and we know even less about relapse. What we do know is about using and the mess it makes. We're scared to even think about going back into that mess. Even after we've been in recovery for a while, we may worry about sliding back into active addiction. We've seen it happen in others who were clean and sober for a long time. Fear of relapse can be a healthy fear of, or better yet, a healthy respect for the disease of addiction. It can make us willing to do what we need to do to get in and stay in recovery. Reading or talking about relapse does not jinx us. Picking up chemicals again is not inevitable. Understanding the relapse process can help us maintain our *ongoing* recovery. Millions of women have found ongoing recovery and continue to live a sober life.

As addicts, we're *always* at risk for returning to chemical use. That's especially true in early recovery. If our bodies are going through withdrawal, our cravings tend to be more intense and frequent. Also, our lives are full of stress due to our addiction, and we haven't developed a strong recovery program yet. Though we're working on developing a support network of people in recovery, and we've started work on the Twelve Steps, we haven't had the time or experience to develop the coping skills we need for the ups and downs of life without chemicals. We need a great deal of structure and support in early recovery because we're so susceptible to returning to chemical use. We can also be quite vulnerable to returning to chemical use at other times in our recovery, depending on what is going on in our lives and how we respond to it. No matter where we are in our recovery process, our number one focus *must* be on recovery.

What Is Relapse?

Relapse is a medical term that refers to a return of the *signs and symptoms* of a disease after they had disappeared for a time. We can think we're over the flu, but then have a relapse. The same is true with our addiction sickness, but relapse to chemical use is usually much more serious. Both, however, have warning signs prior to becoming full-fledged relapses. In the case of the flu, we may feel a little more tired than usual, but we think we're done with the flu, and so we push ourselves to do our normal activities. It catches up with us, and the signs and symptoms of the flu return. With chemical use, many of us think we're doing fine because we're in recovery, and we fail to see the signs and symptoms of relapse before it's too late. Slowly or quickly, we may go back to old thoughts, emotions, or behaviors, and we eventually find ourselves picking up chemicals. We wonder how we got there, but in looking back, we recognize the signs and symptoms.

Red Flags: Warning Signs of Relapse

- minimizing or denying being chemically dependent
- avoiding others
- behaving defensively
- fantasizing about chemical use
- engaging in euphoric recall
- quitting needed medications
- being in a room with people but not connecting
- withdrawing from life's activities or responsibilities
- sleeping too much
- not getting enough rest
- practicing cross-addictions
- having the HALTS (being hungry, angry, lonely, tired or sick/stressed)
- indulging in magical thinking
- being intolerant of others
- behaving impulsively
- engaging in "stinkin' thinkin'"
- feeling confused
- exercising poor judgment
- playing mind games
- just complying
- daydreaming
- exhibiting grandiosity
- being exhausted
- being complacent
- lacking gratitude
- indulging in self-pity

- having dishonest or self-seeking motives
- being angry
- being resentful
- being selfish
- being fearful
- being indecisive
- having unrealistic expectations
- having sleep difficulties
- overreacting
- underreacting
- crisis building
- feeling shame
- getting restless
- letting go of structure in our lives
- thinking we're just fine
- thinking we don't need to go to meetings anymore
- cutting back on meetings without talking with people about taking back control in our lives
- behaving compulsively
- failing to talk about cravings
- thinking we're different from other addicts
- putting down recovery
- no longer working an active recovery program

Relapse Is a Process

Relapse doesn't start when we go back to chemical use. It starts way before we pick up the chemicals. It starts with the signs and symptoms. Addiction is a spiritual, emotional, mental, and physical disease. Just as addiction starts out by mangling us first spiritually, then emotionally, then mentally, and finally physically, so does relapse. The spiritual slide downward comes first, then the emotional and mental slippage. Once we pick up the chemicals, we've gotten to the physical part. Technically, at that point, we've gone beyond the relapse process into the active disease process. The physical allergy is activated, and we may or may not be able to stop using again. This realization can be horrifying. We're back into "can't use/can't quit." We need to learn about the relapse process, so we can make a plan to intervene *before* we pick up the chemicals. That may sound easy, but it's not.

We may start down the relapse path and not have any clue we're on the path. Our attitudes, thoughts, feelings, and behaviors may change quickly or slowly, but we're not likely to be aware of these changes early on. The good news is that, as we connect closely with other addicts and let them know us, they will see when we start to get into trouble. They can see the red flags before we can. Part of the relapse process is being in trouble and not seeing it. The denial that we had in our active addiction can also rear its ugly head in recovery. It blinds us to things that others can see. We need others in our lives who will see these concerns and care enough about us to tell us. Our part is to listen and take heed.

Any week I don't go to a meeting myself, it's pretty much on the rocks. It's a struggle. I'm blessed that my partner is in the program as well, and we're able to talk

*about stuff. And if I can't get to a meeting, then I know
I've got somebody that knows what's going on and will
keep me honest.*

:: TANYA

Recovery and Relapse

*I kept relapsing because I wasn't going to treatment
for the right reason. I was going to escape, to get some
rest, or because of somebody else. I wasn't going because
I wanted any recovery. I was going just to have a safety
net, just to have somewhere to be.*

:: GLORIA

Strange as it may sound, we can't relapse if we're not in recovery
in the first place. Once we sincerely enter into recovery, we make
major changes in many areas of our lives. The relapse process begins when we start to undo these changes or to drop some of them
and treat them as unnecessary. Without a turnabout in this process, we eventually pick up chemicals. However, if we never embrace the recovery process to start with, and we don't adjust our
thoughts, attitudes, and behaviors accordingly, we can hardly call
our return to using "relapse." We were "dry" and may have had a
"break" between our using times, but that was it.

*After treatment, I moved to supportive housing and
then got my kids back. But I had no recovery. I was just
clean. I stayed isolated. I didn't come out much, except
for paying bills or grocery shopping. I went to no meetings. I read no literature. I didn't have no network, no
sponsor, no nothing.*

:: GLORIA

Some of us find it helpful to define for ourselves just what recovery means for us personally and how we behave when we're in recovery. That way, when we start to let specific behaviors slip, we can more easily recognize that we're moving toward relapse. We make a list entitled "Recovery means . . ." If we aren't sure how to define our own recovery for ourselves, we can ask others what recovery means to them and borrow from their definitions. For instance, recovery may mean being kind, going to three Twelve Step meetings a week, reading program literature every morning, talking with our sponsor three times a week, keeping a daily journal, actively working the Twelve Steps, answering our phone and not isolating, exercising three times a week, and staying out of bars. When the activities on our list start slipping away, that can be a sign that we're heading down the relapse trail. Relapse is a process, and the process can start small.

A Question to Face

A good question to ask ourselves often is "Which way am I facing? Am I facing recovery or am I facing relapse?" We're always facing one way or the other, and it can change in the course of the day. Whenever we notice thoughts, attitudes, and behaviors that are negative for our recovery, we have a choice. We can decide to turn around and move toward recovery. It's the little things in life that sometimes decide which way we're facing. That's part of the "dailyness" of recovery. Daily, and sometimes several times a day, we choose which way we're facing.

> *Even sometimes being in recovery, my attitude, my behavior, was horrible. I would say, "Well, I'm only an alcoholic," as if that should excuse my bad behavior. I had to learn that my alcoholism was an explanation, not an excuse, for how I was acting.*
>
> :: FANNIE MAE

Myths about Relapse

Many myths have grown up around the topic of relapse. If we're new to recovery, learning about these myths will help us avoid being misled if we hear them. If we're more experienced in recovery, understanding these myths gives us a chance to reexamine our beliefs about relapse and perhaps change some of them.

Myth #1: Talking about relapse will make it happen.
REALITY: Just the opposite can be true. Not talking about it and not preparing for it can make it more likely. We need to talk about the cravings, thoughts, feelings, and behaviors that make us vulnerable for relapse. Talking about relapse does not jinx our recovery.

Myth #2: Relapse happens when we use. It's an event, not a process.
REALITY: Relapse starts long before we use. It *is* a process. When we use, technically the relapse process is over, and we're back in the disease.

Myth #3: Relapse is inevitable; it's part of the disease.
REALITY: Going back to using is not inevitable. Many people get sober and stay sober, one day at a time, for the rest of their lives. It's true that when we let up on the work and fail to maintain our spiritual condition, we start sliding down the relapse trail, but we *don't* have to keep going down that road.

Myth #4: I'll know when I'm going to relapse.
REALITY: Those of us who think we know when we're relapsing are really in trouble. In reality, it's possible we may get so far down the trail before we recognize we're slipping that we won't be able to get turned around on our own. That's why we need others. They

see us heading down a relapse trail and can point it out to us. It may be hard to hear, but we need to be open to what others who care about us tell us.

Myth #5: Knowledge about relapse will keep me from using again.

REALITY: Knowledge didn't keep us out of addiction, nor does it keep us immune to relapse. We have a disease that tells us we don't have it, and when we're headed down the relapse trail, our disease says we're not there. Knowledge can be helpful, but we don't base our recovery on it.

Myth #6: I must live in constant fear of relapse.

REALITY: While we need to be vigilant, we do not need to live in fear. Most of us find that eventually we get to the point where we're not craving alcohol or other drugs. That doesn't mean we can use again. We do need a healthy respect for our disease, as that keeps us doing what we need to do to live in recovery. We respect the disease, but we don't live in fear. The program is not about being in bondage; it's about freedom.

Myth #7: There will be no warning signs if I relapse; it will just come out of the blue.

REALITY: There are *always* warning signs before we pick up chemicals. We may not see them, but others will. Looking back, most of us who have gone back to chemical use can identify several key decision points where we could have intervened and not ultimately used. One story in the Big Book (pp. 35–36) talks about a man mixing whiskey with his milk even though he had no thoughts of drinking nor a plan to drink. In this case, it seems as if his using just came out of the blue. However, the rest of his story shows warning signs that he ignored: he was in a bar alone with no real reason to be there, he was hungry, he had done nothing to grow spiritually, and he was irritated at his boss. He might even have held resentments about working for a company he used to own. This story is an excellent example of the progression of a person going down the relapse trail without seeing it and without having others in his life who could warn him.

Myth #8: I'll know when I'm getting close to relapse, because I'll quit attending meetings.

REALITY: It may be too late by the time we've quit going to meetings. We usually don't quit attending meetings overnight. We've already gone a ways down the relapse trail in our thoughts, attitudes, and behaviors when we choose to quit meetings. We've started cutting corners in other ways first. Of course, we're in even deeper trouble when we quit going to meetings. We're leaving the people who could have noticed our red flags, and we're alone now with our own thinking. That spells trouble in a disease where part of the relapse process is that we don't see it.

Myth #9: If I work a spiritual program, I'll never have cravings or any signs of the relapse process.

REALITY: That statement itself can be a sign of relapse. It may signal grandiosity or imply that we think somehow we're different. We're all vulnerable to the relapse process and need others in recovery to provide their support and feedback, no matter how hard we work the Twelve Steps.

Myth #10: Relapse means I'm a failure.

REALITY: We can't use the excuse of being a failure to keep using. Using again means that something needs to get turned around in our recovery. It doesn't mean we're failures, but it does mean we will need to take some drastic actions quickly to strengthen our program.

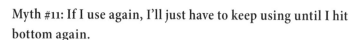

Myth #11: If I use again, I'll just have to keep using until I hit bottom again.

REALITY: Absolutely not! If we use again, it *does* mean we have to make urgent and sweeping changes to get turned around so we're facing recovery again. It doesn't mean we have to pursue using "into the gates of insanity or death" (*Alcoholics Anonymous,* p. 30) or that we need to pursue the belief that we have to bounce along the bottom for a while. We're told, "Bottom is when we quit digging." We put down the shovel and don't use our shame or guilt to keep us from turning around and facing recovery again. We need to make changes quickly, not wait for things to get worse.

High-Risk Situations

Some situations put us at higher risk for picking up chemicals than others. These are called high-risk situations. Anyplace where chemicals are is a very high-risk situation. Anyplace! In Twelve Step meetings, we're told, "If you don't want to slip, don't go to slippery places," and "If you don't want a haircut, don't go to the barber." High-risk situations also arise whenever we're around any person, place, or circumstance that has been connected with our using in the past. If we've used with someone previously, and we are with that person again, we're in a high-risk situation.

High-risk indicators can be very individual. What is a warning sign for one could mean nothing for another. We need to take time to identify which emotions, thoughts, situations, people, and places put us individually at high risk for relapsing. Once we identify these areas of concern, we need to make a plan around them. Some possible interventions are described later in this chapter.

Our feelings and thoughts can become high-risk situations if they have been associated with our using. For instance, if we used when we were bored, being bored can be a high-risk situation. If we used when we were feeling happy and on top of the world, having these feelings could become a high-risk situation. Of course, as addicts, we can use any feeling as an excuse to use. While our experience with feelings is highly individual, some feelings may be more dangerous for us than others, and we need to use the support of others and have a plan for when we experience them.

Some of us find ourselves in high-risk situations because of our thinking. We may be thinking we're doing well in recovery or thinking we're no good or having other thoughts that raise the risk level for us because they get us back into the spiritual, mental, or emotional state we were in while using. The point is that certain feelings and certain thoughts can be indicators that we're in trouble, and we need to have a plan for when we encounter them. Some common high-risk situations are described below.

Beginning or Ending a Romantic Relationship

The ups and downs of new relationships and also the pain of ending a relationship generate some intense feelings. Particularly in early recovery, this emotional distress is distracting. Relationships can create greater risk for relapse for women than men because women are generally more focused on connection and relationships. When relationships go sour, we generally feel more upset and may want to escape by using.

Physical Pain

The pain can be due to illness, surgery, high stress, fatigue, poor self-care, or a number of other reasons. Most of us, when we're in physical pain, want to escape the pain. To complicate matters, medication may sometimes be needed, and that medication may be addictive. The section on interventions later in this chapter tells how to handle the need to take mood-altering drugs. Pain medication is sometimes necessary, and there are measures we can set up to manage our intake carefully during those times.

Spending Time Alone

There is a saying that goes "Alone we use." The high risk of using when we're alone is one reason that living alone early in recovery isn't recommended. We think "nobody will know." It's easier to sneak and hide when we're alone. Living with others helps keep us accountable and less likely to isolate. Addiction is a disease of constriction. Our world gets smaller and smaller. Recovery is about expansion, opening up our world. We don't do this when we're alone. Alone we use.

Hormonal Changes

Changes in hormones take place at various times in our lives and can be associated with PMS, pregnancy, postpartum conditions, perimenopause, menopause, or other circumstances. During these changes, we may be uncomfortable physically, or we may have emotional distress. Some women say they're more likely to use drugs or crave sugar during certain times of the month. If we're in a high-risk situation because of hormonal changes, we need to ask for help, just as we do for other concerns. Each woman's body is different, and not all of us experience discomfort during hormonal changes. Those who do, however, must be vigilant about their recovery during these times, getting whatever help is needed to prevent relapse.

High Stress

Change is stressful, even when a change is for the better. Some people have what is called a "type A" personality, which puts them at increased risk for certain diseases such as heart disease and cancer. This type of personality is quite driven and thrives on stress. While someone with a type A personality usually accomplishes a lot, a side effect is increased stress in the body. Stress can make us more likely to relapse. Stress exacerbates some of the symptoms we may experience in early recovery, including difficulty concentrating, not thinking clearly, flat or out-of-control emotions, memory problems, sleep concerns, and poor physical coordination. There is enough stress in early recovery already without adding high-risk situations. We need to practice self-care and run ideas and concerns by others to minimize stress. Any huge changes (marriage, divorce, taking a promotion, moving), even good ones, should be delayed until later in recovery, if possible. If a change is necessary for our safety or our recovery, we make the change with the support of other women in recovery.

Milestones in Our Recovery Program

Some of us get anxious and stressed around our recovery anniversaries. We may experience what is sometimes called the "anniversary freakies" after being sober for three months or six months or a year. The reality is that each of these days is just another day, to be lived one day at a time, and while we need to celebrate and be grateful, it is just another day. Having one year of sobriety will not be much different from having one year and one day. Having six months of sobriety will not be totally different from having six months and one day. We all have today. That's it. Sure, we continue to grow and change, but we do that one day at a time. Talking with others and putting our anniversaries in perspective keep us grounded.

Complacency

Probably the highest risk of all comes from being complacent in our recovery program. We may get lazy and think we don't need to continue to do what we've been doing. We may think we've worked so hard that we can slow down a bit or rest for a while. This kind of thinking is a sign of trouble. We need to remember that we are literally fighting for our lives. We continue pursuing this solution one day at a time, even after the chaos of our using settles down. We keep going. Complacency is the number one enemy of the person in recovery. Complacency may come about slowly and look so harmless: "I'll just stop this one thing," or "I don't need to do that particular part anymore," or better yet, "I have such a full life, I don't have time for all this stuff." We are at a huge risk of using again when we're complacent and don't recognize that we are. Complacency is not glaringly obvious; it lulls us into a false sense of security. Staying connected with others in recovery in an ongoing manner is necessary to help us get back on track when we start to drift.

Cravings

Cravings are an intense physiological response that indicates a strong desire to use. Our bodies actually have physical symptoms. During a craving, we may salivate, have shortness of breath, and have an increase in our heart rate and blood pressure. Some of us who have used cocaine or certain other stimulants have reported vomiting or having diarrhea when we've thought about getting our drug. Sometimes when we're thinking about using a drug, the brain literally starts producing feel-good chemicals such as dopamine in anticipation of the drug. Sometimes the anticipation is part of the high. The body is flashing back to the euphoria the drug caused. Cravings are common for some people throughout early recovery and can be overwhelming.

Different triggers can induce cravings, and they vary for each person. For some of us, seeing white powder can induce a craving. Focusing on a pleasant memory about using can increase a craving. Heavy use of caffeine, nicotine, or sugar can increase our cravings. Having a dream about using can seem very real, and when we wake up, it can evoke total fear or induce a craving. Taking a drug, even if it's not our drug of choice, can easily induce cravings. At certain times of the month, some women crave more. At times, cravings can seemingly come out of nowhere.

Cravings are very real!

Cravings are powerful!

Cravings will pass!

Just because we're having a craving doesn't mean we're doing something wrong. What it does mean is that our addiction is alive and well, and we need to keep working on our recovery. We are not at the mercy of our cravings. We do not *need* to use just because we have a craving. While it may seem like an eternity, generally a craving lasts only five to fifteen minutes. The tools we use for other high-risk situations work for cravings too. Cravings will pass if we don't use.

There was one time I wanted to drink really bad, because I wasn't going to get money I'd been promised for my final semester to get my master's, and I was so angry. As I was approaching a bridge, I said to myself, That's it. Screw this. I'm going to go and have as many gin and tonics as I can. I've had it. I'm getting plastered. All this AA is just a bunch of crap. *At which time the bridge went up. And I had to stop. So I'm stopped there, and it was forever. I was sitting there for at least twenty minutes. And the first five minutes, it was like,* God damn it, stupid bridge, I want that drink now! *But then, I started thinking,* So when the bridge goes down, I'll go to XYZ bar and I'll have the gin and tonics—and then what? *And I started to think through what would happen if I did have the drink.* Okay, so now I go back to drinking, then what? So then what? What would my life be? *And then I thought to myself,* Okay, so if I don't drink, and I sit with this anger and frustration and I want to cry, then what? *I compared the two "then-whats," and as a Buddhist, I kept saying to myself,* Sit. Sit. Sit with the frustration. Sit with the anger. Sit with the upset. Cry. *I started crying. I put my head down on the*

*steering wheel, and I just cried. The bridge was still up,
so who cared? I was just crying. I wasn't holding up traf-
fic. After I let the tears flow, I realized that the reason I
was so angry and so frustrated was that I was so alone.
I said to myself,* Oh, my God, all it is that I'm feeling
here—this wanting to drink—is because I feel alone. *Then, as the bridge started to come down, this very still
little voice said, "Really, you'll only be ten minutes late to
go to the 5:30 meeting." And that's where I went.*

:: **KRISTEN**

Cravings will pass, and over time they get fewer and farther between. A sure way to increase cravings is to pick up again. Instead,
we can follow the interventions listed below.

Relapse Prevention

The *surest* way to prevent relapse is to work a strong program of
recovery, to make it a daily commitment, and to do it with the
help of others. Being accountable to a sponsor and other women
in recovery is necessary. Working a strong program is the essential
foundation for relapse prevention. In addition, we can do many
other practical things to help prevent return to chemical use.

Practical Interventions

Fortunately, many practical methods are available for preventing
relapse and intervening when we're at risk for entering into the relapse process and ultimately using. One of the most basic methods
is to avoid being around alcohol and other drugs, especially early
in recovery. Even in later recovery, we're better off keeping our distance from all these substances, especially in high-risk situations.
The Big Book says eventually it's okay to be around alcohol, pro-

vided we have a reason to be there, have worked a strong spiritual program, and have been in recovery for some time. Nowhere are we told it's okay to be around illegal drugs. We never have a reason to be near them, and even the most skilled addict in denial would have a hard time coming up with a good excuse for doing so. To be near any chemicals early on is courting disaster. To be in a bar just to be around alcohol in order to get vicarious pleasure from it is not a legitimate reason. To be in a restaurant that serves liquor so that we can go out with our family *may* be a legitimate reason, but only after we've worked a strong program for quite a while.

> *I didn't always medicate going directly to crack. It started off with alcohol socially, with me thinking,* I can do this. *But then every time I relapsed, it was worse and worse.*
>
> :: GLORIA

Here are more practical ways to reduce our chances of using again:

1. Get rid of all drugs and paraphernalia. This includes alcohol. Many of us have asked someone to go through our homes or cars or wherever we keep our stash to help us "clean house."
2. Immediately turn around and walk away from alcohol or other drugs we come across. Our greatest relapse prevention tools in this case are our feet or wheelchair or whatever gets us out of there. We don't need to stop and think. We get out of the kitchen where the white powder is. We leave the party. We get off the bus where someone just offered us a hit. More than one person has "thought" about what to do with the alcohol bottle she found in the holiday decorations, and during her thinking time started to drink. We don't "think." We move. "We recoil from it as from a hot flame" (*Alcoholics Anonymous*, p. 84). We move quickly away from it, and then

we ask for help. We ask for someone else to dispose of whatever we come across. We don't do it alone. "Alone we use."

3. If we're at a social event that we need to attend and where alcohol is served, we can use these refusal lines:
   - "No thanks."
   - "Not today."
   - "I don't do that anymore."
   - "I'm not drinking for health reasons."
   - "I've had my share."
   - "Doctor's orders."
   - "I'm in recovery; I don't use."
   - "I already said no. I really meant it."

   Many of us find that if we already have some beverage in our hand, such as water or soda, most people don't push it. They may not even ask if we want a drink containing alcohol.

4. If we *must* go to an event where alcohol is served (such as a wedding or business meeting), we first set up a plan. We may want to make sure we have our own transportation so we can leave when we need to. We may take someone in recovery with us or plan ahead to call someone in recovery during the event. Other options are to call for support before and after the event. We may even set up a planned time to call people so we know they're available and we hold ourselves accountable.

5. If we intend to go on a trip to events where alcohol will be served, we talk over our plans with someone well before leaving on the trip and not the day we're leaving. We call ahead to have the alcohol removed from the minibar in the hotel or wherever we're staying. These strategies provide accountability, which is a helpful part of relapse prevention planning. We have a plan *before* we go, and we set up the plan with support from another recovering person.

6. When we have a craving, we talk about it. Keeping it a secret is dangerous. However, we have to be careful about who we tell. If we talk about it to someone else who's also craving,

that person may say to us, "Let's go use." We need to talk about it with someone who's in a good spot in their recovery at that moment.

7. We take time to breathe, pray, meditate—anything to slow down. In the rush of life, sometimes we just need to get grounded. Even by just breathing deeply, we can feel our bodies and minds slow down. Some of us find that slowing down helps us think things through better.

8. We talk with someone about the using urge and our thoughts associated with it. We admit to our crazy thinking. We talk about the goofy thought we're having about the "need" to go to our crack dealer's house to visit his or her sick mother or to make amends. We talk with someone about our relapse-prone plan to go on vacation and *not* ask the hotel to take the alcohol out of the minibar ahead of time. We talk about planning to go to the doctor to get mood-altering anxiety or sleep medication "just for one month." We "tell on ourselves." Another addict can see though our excuses and can help us see how irrational they are. Some of us get offended at first when we tell people our thoughts, and they grin or even laugh out loud. Eventually, we are able to see the fallacy in our thoughts and can laugh at ourselves too.

9. We play out in our minds the whole using incident through to the end. We think about that one drink or drug we want to use and then move on to imagine what will happen after we use it, and then after that, and then later, and on to the next morning. Thinking past the first use of the chemical and playing out the inevitable disaster that will result will make that chemical much less appealing. However, some of us have such strong euphoric recall that we think it won't be all that bad this time. When our thinking is stuck there, we need to talk it out with someone who can remind us what the truth is: we "can't use/can't quit."

10. Some of us in early recovery take medications that decrease cravings. (Some of these same medications may also be

helpful following surgery, when pain medications have activated the physical allergy and the craving.) They're not recommended for all chemicals or all people. They're a tool that can be helpful, but they alone are not recovery. They're not a cure-all. We also need to work the Twelve Step program diligently.

11. We take care of ourselves physically and emotionally. Remember HALTS? If we become too hungry, angry, lonely, tired, sick, or stressed, we make sure we do what's necessary to relieve that condition. Ongoing self-care is important in our relapse prevention plan. We take it one day at a time and do what we need to do to face recovery for that day.

Pain Management

In the rare cases where we need mood-altering chemicals such as pain pills following surgery, we take precautions. Of course, the part of our brain that's affected by these drugs doesn't know that we just had surgery and we need these drugs. It just registers the possible feel-good reaction from them, and that reaction may cause a craving for more. When we're with medical staff, we tell them we're chemically dependent. We can ask someone else, such as a sponsor or partner or family member, to be in charge of giving us our medications. We may set up a plan with our health care professional to have a limited amount of medication on hand and schedule more frequent check-ins than people who are not addicted would schedule. We're less likely to abuse the medication if we only have a bottle of three pills than if we have a bottle of thirty. Not having a lot on hand buys us time to weigh the decision about whether we really need the pills. If we need them, we can ask for more. We may also consider an anti-craving medication to take while we are on narcotics and for a period following. Bottom line: We ask for help. We don't do it alone. We also increase our program activity during this time. We attend additional meetings, if possible, or ask friends in recovery to call or visit.

If we are diagnosed with chronic pain or have a terminal illness and need pain medication long term, we work closely with professionals and also people in recovery. We don't do it alone. While we may need to use pain medications in an ongoing manner, either intermittently or continuously, we still practice the principles of asking for help, connection, and accountability. There are resources written specifically for people in recovery with chronic pain.

What If We Use Again?

Relapse is not inevitable. It will not come out and grab us like the bogeyman. Relapse is a *process.* The relapse process starts small. It can start when we do one small thing that is not facing recovery, and if we don't get it turned around and face recovery, eventually it ends when we use. If we use, we aren't failures. We have, however, taken a huge gamble. Some women who pick up "just this once" never make it through the night. Others never make it back into recovery. There are no guarantees we'll have just one or get back in recovery.

We may have a onetime use, which is sometimes called a "slip" or a "lapse." Some of us call *any* use in recovery a relapse; others only use the word *relapse* to refer to repeated use. No matter what we call it when we go back to using, we're vulnerable to continuing using if we use even once. As soon as the chemicals are in our bodies, we're powerless. If we use again, we have activated the physical allergy, and we can end up craving just as much as we did when we were using. That's what happens. If we use, we need to get back to the basics. Safety first. We get medical attention or advice if detoxifying safely is a concern. From there we practice what we learned early on. We ask for help and get honest.

If we relapse, typically we feel shame. We don't want anyone to know. But all that secrecy does is keep us alone, and "alone we use."

We tend to go back into isolation, and the disease progresses fast. Our relapse started somewhere, with some sort of sneaking and hiding. We need to turn that around and get the truth out in the open. So we tell someone we've used. The power of recovery is that we get to talk about it. If we relapse, we need to know that there are other women in recovery who will understand. Immediately, when we share our using and practice humility, we're back in the solution. We've gotten willing, honest, and open-minded. It's a small but powerful step toward facing recovery again.

Picking up chemicals doesn't have to mean hitting a bottom or, worse yet, bouncing along the bottom for many years. It doesn't mean we need to be punished. It does mean that we need to do something different in our recovery, and we need to do it quickly. When we're coming out of using, we need to take radical actions, and fast. When we're coming back to recovery after using, "half measures [avail] us nothing" (*Alcoholics Anonymous*, p. 59). Absolutely nothing. It's time to take drastic measures. We reach out for help with more humility than ever. We need to be open to a different way, possibly a more radical way. Our way didn't work.

Relapse prevention is about doing what we need to do *before* the chemicals are in our bodies. Connection with others, working the program, and seeking help from our Higher Power are all forms of relapse prevention. Relapse is not inevitable. We do what we need to do just for today. One day at a time. One step at a time.

Which way are you facing?

DENISE'S STORY

I came from a drinking family, and I was six years old when I started drinking. I was abused physically and sexually, and the drinking was used to keep my mouth shut, so I wouldn't do a lot of screaming or whatever. I realized then that if I drank enough of what they were pouring down my throat, I wouldn't remember what they were doing to me.

I started having what they called "emotional seizures" when all of this was happening to me. I also had epilepsy. A lot of times I was taken out of school because of seizures.

When I was about fifteen, my father started beating me. He would take my clothing off me and throw me in a cold shower and beat me with a belt until I quit having those seizures. When I was going to school, I refused to undress in my gym classes and take showers with the other girls. I was getting straight As in everything else, but they flunked me out of PE because I would not take the showers with the girls. When I brought my report card home and showed my father, his boss was there, and my father was yelling and screaming at me, wanting me to say right in front of his boss why I flunked PE.

Something snapped in me that day. I looked at my dad, and I just told him point blank: "Because I'm full of bruises because you keep on beating the hell out of me." My dad punched me and almost knocked me down a flight of stairs, right in front of his boss. His boss had tears in his eyes, and he suggested that I go show my body to my PE teacher and tell her this is why I wasn't getting undressed in my PE class and why I refused to do those things.

I got taken away from my father when I did that and put in a mental institution for about a month. The court took me away from both of my parents. My parents were already divorced, but my mom couldn't seem to handle me, and my dad was too abusive. I got put into a foster home, and I was told then by doctors that I was a binge alcoholic. I thought they were crazy. The only thing I could think of an alcoholic being was like the bums that used to come through our town. And I was like, *I'm not like that. What in the world are they talking about?*

I started coming in to AA on my own when I was twenty-three. But it took me up until I was thirty-seven to open my eyes as to what the AA program really was about, what that First Step meant. I understood that I was an alcoholic and I was a drug addict. There was no doubt left in my mind. I had kept on being sent into mental institutions over those years, and I knew there had to be hope, there had to be some kind of help for that type of insanity. I also began to understand what that Third Step meant, about turning my will and my life over to the care of a Higher Power. Up to that point, I hated God. I really thought if there was a God, he had to be cruel. I had a lot of hatred and anger in me.

I can tell you what brought on the realization that caused me to do those first three Steps. I was always in a lot of trouble with the law. I got arrested one time right after my ex-husband had beat me up, and a few of the women that worked at the jail started calling me a martyr. They said I was going to die because of my beliefs. They thought I was going to end up getting beat up by my ex-husband and dying that way, or somebody would be killing me out there while I was drunk and half out of my head. I began to understand what they were talking about, and I was tired of people laughing at me and making fun of me because I couldn't seem to keep my life together. I certainly didn't want to go out of this world thinking that I was being a martyr for anybody. Not like that. It was a real eye-opening experience.

Right after I turned my life and my will over to God, I went into an alcoholic coma. I said, "Here I am, God. You help me." And a voice came through my head, and it told me, "Denise, if you mean what you're asking, you need to go tell your mother that you're intending to quit drinking and that she'd better call you an ambulance." I did what that voice that came through my head told me to do. Right then and there I passed out. My liver gave out and I went into an alcoholic coma. A month later, I came out of it. I woke up to my mother making my funeral arrangements. My mom was so excited, because I was on a life support machine. She hung up on the funeral people and she was like, "My gosh! I was supposed to be burying you. They were going to un-plug your life support machines today."

All the years I'd spent in AA, learning about AA and trying to change my life—all of that stuck with me throughout that coma. When I woke up, I told my mom, I know I'm an alcoholic and an addict, and I know what the AA program is, and I want to get back to AA and start working those Steps—working them properly, and being honest with other people. It took about a week, and my mom finally signed me out of the hospital and let me start going back to AA.

In the years before that, I wanted to change my life. But all that anger and resentment from my childhood—I kept on holding on to it. I did not know how to let it go. I was trying to work with sponsors, but they seemed to let me skip around from one Step to another. I kind of fishtailed through the Steps, and I never really did an honest Fourth and Fifth Step until I got out of the hospital.

My whole life changed that year. I found a sponsor who had come into the program while I was using. I had watched her change her life. I knew that she was working those Steps and that she understood those Steps much better than I did. At that point, the doctors gave me three months to live. So I was desperate to start working those Steps. That's when I first started learning to live one day at a time. I finally quit worrying about the past in any regard, except for trying to work those Steps and work them properly.

So, I asked the woman, "Would you help me?" And she started working with me. I did an honest Fourth Step and an honest Fifth Step with her. I was very honest about my anger and my resentment, and afterward she showed me how to look at it and to see my part in all of it. I quit blaming everybody else. It seemed like the weight of the world was starting to be taken away from me. Then she had me go do my Sixth and Seventh Steps, and then Steps Eight and Nine, those forgiveness Steps. I had what they call a spiritual experience. I guess you could say my spirit had already been awakened, but when I hit the forgiveness Steps, I had done so much throughout my lifetime that I couldn't figure how God could forgive me. I went for a walk one evening, trying to figure out how I was going to go to the people that I hurt and ask them for forgiveness, when I couldn't seem to find forgiveness for myself or anything else.

When I went for that walk and said that prayer, my Higher Power came to me. A spirit came to me and told me, "Denise, you have been forgiven a long time ago for anything that you have ever done wrong.

Your problem is that you don't know how to forgive yourself. And if you would learn how to forgive yourself, forgiveness from other people and to other people would come so much easier to you." I was crying, and I was told to quit crying, that I was not brought to this earth to be so miserable, and that I would be taught how to laugh and how to smile. I had about fifteen hundred dollars given to me that month in an inheritance, and I was told by that voice that I had just enough money in the bank to go get my teeth fixed. My last husband had knocked out all my front teeth. (I had kept on choosing men that seemed to be alcoholics, and as mean and controlling as my father.) I was told that if I would go get my teeth fixed, I would learn how to laugh and how to smile. That happened.

I do believe that was my Higher Power talking to me, and I knew that if he loved me that much—to forgive me, then . . . That night was one of the first times in my life I'd ever gone to bed not feeling full of shame and remorse or guilt, and it's one of the first times I've ever slept the whole night through. My whole life just started changing at that point.

I forgave my father. I realized my father came from a very sick family. He probably did to me what was done to him, and I do believe that had gone on for generations in my father's family. After learning how to look at it that way, it just doesn't seem to be all that bad anymore. All that anger and resentment, I kept asking God to take it from me. He took it, and I don't know where it is, and I don't want it back!

The people I hurt who are still alive, I didn't have any problem going back and telling them, "I'm sorry. I made a mistake. I did things wrong." My mom ended up being my best friend. She is one of the people I was the meanest to. I got two years sober with my mom before she died. I look at those as a gift, because my mom and I hardly knew each other before that. There were also people who had already passed on out of this life. But I learned that even if I did it with just my Higher Power, those people would know I was sorry if I had hurt them. I do believe that they forgive me, just as much as I was able to forgive them.

I'm coming up on my tenth-year anniversary. Ten years ago, the doctors only gave me three months. If I would have believed them and not what I felt in my heart when I woke up, I would have gone home and drank myself to death. But I didn't believe that. What I believed was what was in my heart, and I started throwing myself more into the AA program and volunteering my time with the AA people, trying to give back what has been given to me. I feel richer today than I probably have ever felt in my life.

When Hurricane Katrina hit in 2005, the town I lived in got totally wiped out. That was a frightening thing. All my clothes got lost during the storm. I had left a bunch of my money in my trailer, and my trailer got totally wiped out. I moved to the town where I live now, and the next day I got on the telephone and found another group here, and I threw myself into that group. It helped me because I had to mourn the loss. I lost everything materially that I had, and it was not an easy thing. But throwing myself into the program here, working with other alcoholics here, and sharing my life with them, I feel like I've gotten more back than I lost in the first place. The people here even gave me AA material because I lost all my AA books because of the hurricane.

I live on government support now, because I do have a few mental problems yet, and physically I pretty much destroyed my body. I cannot go out there and work. I broke my back during some of those bouts with my alcoholism. A couple of years ago, I was totally paralyzed, but after a surgery I now walk.

My mental health is a lot better. Since I began to remember my childhood and to face it and accept it, I quit having those "emotional seizures." The only medication I have to take is for my epileptic seizures. That all in itself seems like a miracle to me.

My worst day now is better than my best day when I was out there drinking and using. At least today, I can smile and I can laugh about those things. Some of those crazy thoughts still may come through my head. I find myself just sitting and even laughing at myself about some of it sometimes. But I have been able to find happiness.

CHAPTER 11

The Adventure of Recovery Continues

❧ *One of my kids asked me one time when I was teaching school, "What are you going to be when you grow up?" And I said, "Oh, about seventy-five." And I turned sixty this week.*

:: JULIA

ONCE THE EARLY MONTHS AND YEARS OF RECOVERY have passed, and the highs and lows are less dramatic, the adventure of recovering from addiction continues. We've put down the chemicals, settled into the routines of the fellowship and working the program, made some positive lifestyle adjustments, and experienced some of the promises of recovery. Yet, as much as our lives have improved, we may begin to wonder if we know how to make the program work for the long haul. *Will we have what it takes to continue working the program one day at a time every single day for the rest of our lives? Will we be able to get over the hurdles that remain? Will our lives get better over time, or will the routine of working the program wear on us after a while?* This chapter offers some guidance regarding these and other issues that may come up during the ongoing adventure called recovery. It offers hope and encouragement for the days and years ahead.

As tough as it is—and getting sober is tough—go through every moment of difficulty early on in sobriety because when you get to the other side, it is heaven. It is living heaven on Earth. You will know enlightenment. You will know the beauty and the awe, if you will, of sobriety. Whatever difficult moments come up in early sobriety—in year one, year two, year three, year four, year five—if you don't pick up that drink, all of a sudden, you'll start to know intuitively that things are good. Things will turn around. Once they start turning around, remain humble, because it's very easy to get arrogant and say, "Hey, I've got this thing licked," and go back out.

:: **KRISTEN**

Change Is a Constant

Life is about change. So is recovery. Early recovery is about making many changes rapidly. Eventually, the emotional roller coaster starts to level off. Changes continue over the years in recovery, but they don't tend to come as rapidly as in the early stages. If we continue to be abstinent and work on our recovery, we generally start to settle into a more stable lifestyle with a recovery support system and a good amount of structure in our life. This more "settled" state may leave us feeling bored because we're used to the high drama and the attention focused on us when we were in constant upheaval. Or we may be grateful that we're no longer in the middle of so much drama. Either way, we begin to adapt to a more stable, balanced lifestyle, continue working our program, and experience serenity more and more. For many of us, our worst sober day is better than our best using day.

I've been clean and sober for twenty-three years. In the middle of my sobriety, there was a group of us back home on the reservation, where we did a lot of things that were centered on sobriety. We held dances, and just groups of us would get together and go out. In the wintertime, we'd go Christmas tree hunting. Women would get together at somebody's house and bake cookies, and we found other ways of entertaining ourselves.

:: JOANNE

Living in recovery is about living life with all its joys and sorrows, excitement and boredom, peace and conflict, serenity and restlessness, and just about everything in between. Many of us have struggled in the past with living everyday life as it shows up. Lucky for all of us, the program of recovery is a plan for living. We can't outgrow this plan, and it's never finished.

I stuck to it. They say sometimes it happens quickly, sometimes it happens slowly. But I guess that goes back to perseverance and not letting the times you stumble or the times you hit a roadblock stop you. Some things end up taking a while, like the situation with my daughter, and custody is still in process. I guess sometimes it's just focusing on the day-to-day stuff, and sometimes it's focusing on the bigger picture.

:: TANYA

Most of us enjoy the periods of joy, happiness, peace, and serenity in our ongoing recovery, and we're grateful for them. We're not usually as fond of going through periods of struggle. Life is naturally filled with ups and downs, and we will, of course, experience ups and downs in recovery. What we need to know is that when we go through the "downs," we don't need to stay stuck there.

As addicts, we may think we should never have to feel uncomfortable, and when we do, we want to erase that feeling immediately. In the past, we thought using would erase it, but we're past that way of thinking now. Still, we may wonder, *What do we do when life's ups and downs come? How do normal people handle life? How do we go through emotional storms? What about times when our relationships seem strained or boring? How do we handle times of happiness? And what about the times that seem dull to us, when there are neither high highs nor low lows?* We may hesitate to talk about any of these concerns, thinking we're the only ones who have them.

> *Don't give up, no matter how hard things get. There's always somebody somewhere who's been there, who can help you. Talk to people. Call your sponsor. And when it gets to the point where it feels like you can't go on, turn around and look back at where you've been, and see how far you've come. Because when I get to those points, I can look back and say, "My gosh, look where I was and look where I'm at now." And it gives me hope.*
>
> :: TANYA

Some of the struggles we encounter are normal. Others are less common. But we're never alone or without help. By learning from other women who've gone before us and by being alert to possible pitfalls in ongoing recovery, we may avoid some struggles or get through them with reasonable ease. At times, we may have to accept that our only option is go through the struggle, even though it's hard. As we do, the tools of recovery that worked for others will work for us to help us get through it. Recovery is about living life "on life's terms" and not necessarily on our terms. The tools we use in recovery help us to do that.

I spent two and a half years in an unbelievably difficult job situation. It was really, really hard. There were many, many times when the thought of a drink crossed my mind, but that's all it did. I'd think, Hmmm, this would be a day, were I still a drinking person, that I would drink. But instead, I have an option today, I have a choice today. I can pick up the phone and talk to my sponsor. *And that's what I did. The other people in my office, who also were frustrated and had a horrible day, went out and drank. But I went to a meeting, or I called my sponsor and talked.*

:: **KRISTEN**

Possible Concerns in Ongoing Recovery

Periods of struggle, feeling a void, cross-addiction, becoming a dry drunk, character defects, self-sabotage, and complacency—these are all possible concerns in ongoing recovery. We have a choice about how we're going to face them. We can ask ourselves: *Am I facing recovery? Am I facing relapse? If I'm facing the wrong way, what do I need to do to get turned around?*

Periods of Struggle

I have lots of health problems that have stemmed from my abuse of drugs and alcohol and from cigarettes many years ago. I smoked three packs a day, and I have had respiratory problems over the years. I was an oral heroin user, so I consumed massive quantities of drugs through my nose, and even now the cilia has never grown back, you know, the hair inside of the nose. I suffer today still because of what I did to myself many years

*ago. Because of the accident I was in, my left leg is an
inch shorter than my right leg, and because of that, I
have had major back problems for the last twenty-seven
years. I have scoliosis.*

:: FANNIE MAE

Struggles come up whether we're in recovery or not. We may experience changes in our mental health or in our physical health and need to get extra help. We may face times of loss and grief, when we think our hearts will break. Memories from past traumatic events may surface, and we may wonder if we can bear going through them. At times, our physical or emotional pain may be so intense that we wonder if we can go on.

We can't predict what struggles we'll experience, or when, but we can learn not to live in fear of them. We live one day at a time, knowing that *if* unfortunate things come our way, we will be given what we need to deal with them. We will go through them with the help of others and our Higher Power. When we feel the most brokenhearted, we can lean in and let others and our Higher Power hold us. Just as in getting sober, we're not alone. We can let others carry us for a time.

*There was quite a period of time where there was a
lot of grief. I'd gotten divorced, and there were three or four
deaths in our family, and my stepmother had a massive
stroke, all within a two-and-a-half- or three-year period.
So I ended up going to treatment again, for ACOA [Adult
Children of Alcoholics] issues, for grief issues.*

:: JOANNE

Feeling a Void

At times we may feel a void inside. We're glad to be sober, but we wonder why we don't feel quite as "good" as we think we should. While many of us have had moments of happiness, we wonder how

to be truly happy and live in ongoing serenity. We think to ourselves, *What's next? Is this all there is? Why do I still feel empty at
times? I'm not using, and yet where are all the promises in my life?
Am I doing something wrong?*

Many of us feel guilty for even having such thoughts. We see
others who seem to be pretty content with life and think we should
be also. We may become frustrated if life feels like too much of a
routine or even like drudgery for us. We may even feel downright
miserable. Some of us might be closet white-knucklers, craving or
thinking about using but not telling others. We may be active in
other addictions, trying to fill the void and feeling shame and remorse about our behaviors. Knowing we can't stop, we continue to
hide and sneak.

Just as with other concerns in recovery, there is a solution. We
may be feeling a void because there *is* a void! We may need something to get our attention in order for us to change direction, and
it's that void that will get our attention. More than one woman has
said that "being sick and tired of being sick and tired" is what got
her to change. Not just to put down the chemicals, but to make
changes in other areas where change was needed.

We can choose to spiral downward, or we can start facing recovery in a new way. We can tighten up our program and work
it in a more structured and rigorous way than at other times. We
may increase the number of meetings we attend, do more reaching out to others, start dealing with a cross-addiction, find a support group for another concern, or take other measures suggested
by the program. Sometimes it's a good idea to slow down in what
we're *doing* and to focus more on *being*.

The bottom line is that feeling a void can get our attention. It
tells us that it's time to do something different. Many of us have
experienced this "moment of truth" and took action to make our
recovery even stronger because of it.

Miserable with Cross-Addiction

Cross-addiction is having more than one primary addiction. We may come into recovery with more than one addiction (gambling and alcohol, for example). However, it's not unusual for a new addiction to show up *while we're in recovery*. Without chemicals to fill the void, we become focused on food or sex or work or religion or love or something else that gives us a rush or relaxes or comforts us. We may become just as addicted to these other things or behaviors as we were to drugs. Chapter 7, on cross-addiction, talks in more depth about various cross-addictions such as food, gambling, sex, computer use, work, and relationships.

Some cross-addictions may actually show up *because* of recovery. In recovery, we may get so devoted to our work that it becomes our whole life. We want to make up for all the wasted time. Work becomes all-consuming. It becomes our identity. This addiction to work interferes with our recovery meetings, our family life, and our friendships.

Religion is another example of an all-absorbing addiction that may show up when we're in recovery. We may want very much to be good and to do the right things, so we turn to religion to find the path to goodness. That may be very helpful for some of us, but for others it becomes addictive. We may get so completely involved in religious activities that we neglect everything else, including our families and friends. We may do the same thing with Twelve Step meetings and our service work with other alcoholics. Our program activities may take *all* our attention, keeping us from living a balanced life.

Recovery is about living a balanced life. Addiction or preoccupation of any kind throws us off balance. Addiction is cunning, baffling, and powerful. Even in recovery, we can be vulnerable to falling into other addictions.

Each addiction needs to be treated separately. Our chemical addiction may be our primary addiction, and generally it's the one that will kill us the fastest. However, all addictions need to be dealt with as addictions. Some of us may think that we can treat our addiction to food, gambling, sex, or other nonchemical substances or activities as a character defect and work Steps Six and Seven around it, making it go away. The reality is that, just as we found with our addiction to chemicals, we need to be working on our recovery around people who have that same addiction and are living in the solution. We need people who will share with us the truth about their addiction and recovery—who will tell it like it is. Our Alcoholics Anonymous or Narcotics Anonymous sponsor may know nothing about gambling addiction, and she doesn't need to. We need to be around people who "get" our addiction, whatever it is. We need people we can identify with.

All addictions block us from our spirituality, disconnecting us from ourselves, others, and a Higher Power. If we want to be truly happy and "emotionally sober," we need to deal with all our addictions. During different periods in life, our emphasis may be on one recovery program more than another, but for each one, we practice the principles of fellowship, accountability, and working the program of the Twelve Steps. Just as we can recover from our addiction to alcohol and other drugs, we can recover from other addictions. The process of recovery may be somewhat different, but recovery is possible. We find people who know how to do it and listen to them.

Dry Drunk

Recovery is more than giving up chemicals. If we put the chemicals down, but our attitudes, feelings, thoughts, and behaviors are the same as when we were using, we become what is called a "dry drunk." A dry drunk is miserable despite no longer using chemicals—and miserable to be around!

Usually, when we're living as a dry drunk, we're not fully working the Steps. Chances are we're living with a lot of resentment, fear, and self-loathing. We become bitter, and people don't want to be around us. Bitterness and resentment can destroy us emotionally and spiritually, and they can lead us to using again.

If we're not working the Steps and living by the principles in the Steps, we may not be truly in recovery. We may be "dry," but we're not sober emotionally and spiritually. Nothing has changed inside. That's not recovery. Recovery is about change—ongoing change. Just as a body of water without an inlet or outlet becomes stagnant and smelly, so can our recovery. We need constant input and output to stay fresh.

We don't have to stay living as a dry drunk. We have a choice. We ask ourselves, *Which way am I facing? What do I need to do to face recovery?* We don't need to live in misery. Hard things in life may be inevitable at times, but suffering is optional. We can choose instead the solution of working the program of recovery and being part of the fellowship.

Self-Sabotage

Some of us struggle with self-sabotage in our recovery. We can be our own worst enemy. We may feel guilt or shame for all the wasted years and think we're not worthy of the freedom of ongoing recovery. We may do subtle acts that jeopardize our recovery, or we may deliberately and blatantly mess with our ongoing recovery. Some of us have a fear of success, thinking it's going to be too much ongoing work. Failing is something we're used to doing. If we can sabotage our recovery, we won't have to work at it, and we'll get the punishment we think we deserve for all our failures.

Whether we're fully aware that we're about to do something to sabotage our recovery, or whether we're feeling guilty about the successes we're having while living sober, we need to talk to others about it. Just as with relapse, others can help us see the signs before we do, and they can help us with the unrealistic and irrational thoughts we're having around the need to hurt our own recovery.

When we bring others into our self-sabotage, we're no longer in there alone. When we take the lonely "self" out of it, we can more easily recognize the sabotage for what it truly is and walk away from it.

Complacency

Some of us get to a point where we feel that we're sober, or "done." We've put down the chemicals, and now we're done! Since we're sober, we may think we don't need to do the rest of the Steps, or we think we've done everything in the program enough times that we're "recovered." We may have never done any of the Steps, or we may have done Step One through Step Nine, but we're not doing the "maintenance Steps"—Step Ten through Step Twelve—to maintain our recovery. We think we can cut back, take shortcuts, and minimize our spiritual work. We get back into attitudes, feeling and thinking patterns, and behaviors that are not pleasant for us or the people around us. We become complacent and don't work the program.

We start sliding backward. Chapter 10, on relapse, talks about how we won't notice that we're sliding down the relapse trail. We go down first spiritually and then emotionally. We become "restless, irritable and discontented" and eventually look for something to ease or comfort us. That's where we're vulnerable to isolation, other addictions, or even going back to our chemicals. The problem is, we may not see that we're headed for trouble. If we slip into complacency, some of our character defects may resurface or intensify. We may feel resentful and fearful. We may become judgmental, impatient, or controlling. We may lose some of the joy of early recovery.

Complacency is not inevitable, but it takes conscious effort to stay on the recovery trail. After working Steps One through Nine, we work Steps Ten through Twelve regularly in order to continue to stay on the trail. Staying the course brings fulfillment. We avoid complacency by "doing the dailies," those critically important every-day activities described in earlier chapters that we do every day to maintain our recovery. These dailies are the key for living a life of ongoing recovery—one day at a time. More is said about the dailies later in this chapter.

Character Defects

Character defects can have a huge impact on our life, interfering with our well-being and our relationships. We may be controlling, overprotective, resentful, jealous, gossipy, procrastinating, feeling entitled, addicted to our drama, rationalizing, people pleasing, grandiose, perfectionistic, fearful, always sure we're right, stubborn, full of false pride, impatient, unique, angry, rageful, sarcastic, a martyr—the list goes on. Some of us have lost our most important relationships due to character defects.

Just as with our drugs, with some character defects, a time may come when we have to surrender in a major way. Our character defects get so out of hand that they flatten us. We "kiss the concrete" because we've fallen on our face, and we really need to give up. Our character defects may get our attention and help prepare us for this "second surrender" at this new point of desperation, which is not unlike the point of desperation that initially brought us into recovery. We're prompted to deepen our relationship with our Higher Power, surrendering even further our will and our life to its care. Later in this chapter is a section on second surrender and the freedom it brings after we experience kissing the concrete.

In the ongoing adventure of recovery, we need to get very serious about working on our character defects. Steps Six and Seven are our tools for doing that. One woman in later recovery went so far as to say, "Steps Six and Seven *are* the Steps." Character defects get in the way of our emotional sobriety—of being "happy, joyous, and free" (*Alcoholics Anonymous*, p. 133). Character defects have been compared to the marrow in our bones. They are so much a part of us that they're likely to rear their ugly heads quite often, though we can do things to lessen their impact. The only way for them to be fully removed is through our Higher Power.

How Free Do You Want to Be?

> *Recovery has made a huge change in my life. I'm free. I don't have to hide behind chemicals to open up, or even to be able to go into a room and have a staff meeting.*
>
> :: TANYA

Recovery is about being "happy, joyous, and free." It's about experiencing the many promises of recovery. In recovery, many of us come to a place of healing acceptance where we know that life will have its ups and downs, but we'll be okay. We trust in a Power greater than ourselves to help us handle life during the pain and during the joy. We have an unshakable foundation that we stand on. We know that no matter what happens, we have a Power greater than ourselves that we can trust. We live one day or one moment at a time, and we connect with people around us in a loving way.

> *Just recently I was thinking about going back and looking at a Fourth Step, and it would look a lot different now. But I'm willing to dig deeper, because you're never finished. You're never through. And that's okay. And I guess that's a lot of what sobriety has given to me—the realization that all is okay and that peace does come from within. I'm so thankful for that. I can't get past the gratitude and the joy of being able to wake up without a hangover and thinking,* What the hell did I do last

night? *or* How much money did I spend? *or a gazillion other icky, nasty things.*

:: JOANNE

Peeling the Onion

As we grow in our recovery, we start to "peel the onion." Peeling the onion is a common analogy used to describe emotional growth. Just as we peel away one layer of an onion after another until eventually we get down to the center of it, so we strip away layers of emotional disturbance and dysfunction until we find the freedom at our center. We have an insight or awakening and make some changes (removing one layer), and then later some new information comes along and we go a little deeper. We take off more and more layers from the "onion" of emotional distress and eventually reach the center—our true self that our addiction has kept hidden.

Some of us think of peeling the onion as starting from the center, removing layers from the inside outward, opening up more space inside the onion for growth. Each time we pull a layer out, our world opens up and gets larger. We have more room to move, to be free, to expand, to be our true self.

Citizens of the World

As our world expands, we're able to connect with more people in a new way. We connect with others who aren't in Twelve Step rooms and become "citizens of the world," as Bill W. says (*As Bill Sees It,* p. 21). We find that the world we used to reject, and which used to reject us, isn't so bad. At first, we may feel scared about connecting with people outside of Twelve Step meetings, but we soon find out that humans are humans. What we started doing with people in recovery, we continue to do with others.

Before long, we begin to consider wider possibilities. Can we bring what we learn in Twelve Step meetings into our whole life?

What about our families, co-workers, neighbors, and others who don't always please us? Can we adopt an attitude of tolerance, understanding, and kindness toward them as we've done toward unpleasant people in Twelve Step rooms? Can we display the spirit of willingness, honesty, and open-mindedness in our work setting, families, school environment, or community activities? Can we meet sickness, loss, and other harsh realities of life with the Serenity Prayer on our lips and confidence in the help of our Higher Power?

Bottom line: can we live life on life's terms?

Yes! We say *yes* to life. Even when life isn't as we wish it to be, we say *yes*. We can live life on life's terms because we see others do it. We see the freedom they have, we've tasted some of that ourselves, and we want more of it.

A New Venture

Just because we've been in recovery for a while doesn't mean we have all the answers. In fact, it's unrealistic to think we'll ever have all the answers. What worked in early recovery continues to be helpful, but we also need to remain open to new learning. Remember the "put-aside" statement from page 87? That affirmation or prayer asks us to be open to set aside what we think we know so that we can learn new things. That same openness to learning needs to be part of our ongoing recovery. We open up our minds and hearts and become humble. Learning more can take us into a whole new venture, as we become even more open to experiencing and doing recovery in an expanded way. Ongoing recovery is about staying open to new learning.

Usually, we're willing to listen to others and learn from their experience when we go through big changes in our lives—moving, starting a new job, having our first child. However, that may not be the case when it comes to everyday events. For example, we may remember something we did while using that we feel shameful about and yet not talk that over with our sponsor. We may think that now that we've been in recovery for a while, we no longer need to talk about things that happened while we were using. Other distant memories may come up, or we may uncover some underlying anxiety or depression that we need to deal with, yet we may hesitate to talk about any of these things. They may seem shameful or insignificant.

In matters big and small, we need to remain open-minded, willing, and honest. When the Big Book says these three qualities are the essentials of recovery, it doesn't put a time limit on them. They remain the essentials throughout our recovery.

Second Surrender

Some of us experience a "second surrender" or a "second recovery." While it's called a second surrender, it may actually happen more than once. Just as with the chemicals, something painful gets our attention, and we become willing to do anything, absolutely anything, to get relief. This second surrender can come after we've been dry for years, yet aren't fully working the program and are feeling "restless, irritable and discontented." It can come following painful crises in our lives. It can come because of concerns or interventions by others. It can come because we're sick and tired of living like we're living. It can come just because we want more freedom. Usually, *something* gets our attention, and we become more willing. That can mean diving into recovery again, going deeper into the Twelve Steps, reaching out to others, getting outside help, or taking other measures. We become open-minded, willing, and honest at a deeper level than before. We make a huge internal change. We surrender; we give up the fight. We become open to information that we may not have been open to previously, and we don't argue about where it comes from. Even when it doesn't fit into our nice little belief system, we are open to it.

A second surrender allows a feeling of freedom. We quit resisting what we need to do to get beyond a character defect, another addiction, a dry drunk episode, problems with trying to do it *our* way, or something else that has us kissing the concrete. We quit fighting and we feel relief. One of the promises in the Big Book that is listed just after the well-known promises on pages 83–84 is "And we have ceased fighting anything or anyone—even alcohol." What a powerful promise, to know the joy of surrender and the peace that comes with giving up the fight. Serenity at last.

How free do you want to be?

Acceptance or Action

When we give up the fight, what do we do then? In general, the answer can be boiled down to two things—acceptance or action. Either we accept what's going on, or we take action to change it. That's the beauty of the Serenity Prayer:

God, grant me the serenity
To accept the things I cannot change,
The courage to change the things I can,
And the wisdom to know the difference.

It's that simple. We accept or we act. Sometimes we do both. A favorite passage from the Big Book for many of us is about acceptance: "And acceptance is the answer to *all* my problems today" (p. 417). Part of acceptance can include agreeing to do certain things we need to do to be in recovery. We go ahead and do these things, some of them daily. We accept *and* we act.

A Program for Life

Other people see me walk the walk. I don't have to talk about being clean. When people see me, they don't have to say, "Oh, you aren't getting high." They know *I'm not getting high. I don't just work the Steps, I live them.*

:: GLORIA

Just as we routinely make sure the clothes we put on each day are clean, we do certain routine things daily for our recovery to keep our program clean. They may vary for each of us, but the key is that we *do* them—and do them *daily*. We don't think that because we ate and drank or changed clothes two years, two months, or even two weeks ago that that should suffice for today. We routinely do those things. The same principle applies if we're going to live in ongoing recovery. What we did two years, two months, or even two days ago may have been helpful then, but we need to keep doing them day after day if we're planning to stay in recovery. One thing we do every single day is not pick up chemicals. In order to do that, though, we need to do a variety of other things to ensure that we don't pick up the chemicals. Just for today. Daily.

> *I've been sober more than half of my life. I am fifty-four years old, and I am twenty-seven years sober. That alone to me is a high point—the fact that consistently I have not picked up a drink or drug no matter what.*
>
> —FANNIE MAE

We consistently work our program, attend meetings, talk with our sponsors, and work with newcomers, even when we don't feel like it. We continue our daily reading or get some sort of input that helps us grow in our program. Some of us enjoy retreats, workshops, or CDs. They give us a needed shot in the arm at times, helping to refresh our recovery. We continue practicing accountability and work with our sponsors and other women who will support us but who will also tell us the hard things when we need to hear them. We have a home group where we commit to do some sort of service. We do evaluations of how our program is going through a daily Tenth Step. We pray and meditate daily, as the Eleventh Step tells us to do. We reach out to be helpful to others, and while we may do it most often in the Twelve Step fellowship, service also becomes a way of life. We ask ourselves, *What can I do to be of maximum service to God and others?* We practice humility and gratitude. We take care of ourselves physically and emotionally as well as spiritually. We schedule some fun into our lives and watch our diet and exercise. We celebrate the little things, like seeing a child smile, being kind to someone, or seeing a newcomer come to a meeting. Life takes on new meaning. We're fully present and fully alive, only because we do a little bit each day. Just for today. Daily.

Many stories from women in the Big Book talk about working the program daily. One young woman describes "willingness and action" as the two most important things in recovery (p. 317). The willingness to do the daily things we need for recovery comes one day at a time. We get the willingness to take the next step or do the next action, which leads to the willingness to take the next step and do the next action. It's a circular process that leads to a program for life. To live life with surprising vigor, we do the dailies. We're like athletes, training every day to keep in shape so we can accomplish our goals of recovery and live a worthwhile and satisfying life.

> *I learned that you can accomplish anything in your life that you put your mind to if you really train and you persevere. Your goal is not to make it to the top, but just to enjoy the journey. Like climbing out of addiction, it's the journey, and not the summit.*
>
> :: JULIA

We realize that we have to live a spiritual life, not just think about it or talk about it. Many of us exclaim with gratitude, "We *get* to live it." Yes, we do! The true adventure continues. One day at a time. One step at a time.

JULIA'S STORY

I was born and raised in Iowa, where basically drinking and bowling were considered fine arts. I started drinking at age fifteen with a fake ID. In college, I became social chairman of my sorority so I could order all the kegs of beer at the sorority and fraternity exchanges. After college, I got a teaching contract in northern California. I started experimenting with marijuana and then became involved with doing cocaine. When my mother passed away in the early eighties, I cross-addicted to methamphetamine.

I made the biggest mistake of my life in 1991. After teaching school in California for twenty-one years, in a moment of total insanity, I pawned a school district VCR to get money to buy a bag of cocaine. The pawn shop called the police department. After three years of fighting an unprofessional conduct charge against me in my file, I finally decided to resign my position, and they gave me a settlement check. I went through that money, then I pulled out my teacher retirement money and went through that, then went through all my tax shelter money and continued on the road to demise.

My parents started enabling me. They helped me pay my rent, keep my car running, keep the phone on, lights on, all those kinds of things, not realizing that I was a full-blown drug addict. As time went on, I was arrested for possession of a controlled substance, I had a DUI, I had a shoplifting charge, I had violations of probation. I went to jail three times. My enabling father bailed me out twice. The third time I went to jail was for shoplifting to buy cat food, a new low in my life. He didn't help this time, so I was in jail for a week.

Before my dad died, my brother had insisted that my father leave any money for me in trust to him. So when Dad died, the jig was up. I had to call my brother for money to keep me going. And he said, "Oh, we love you too much to enable you to kill yourself." That was the end. I had lost my teaching credentials and my living situation. My car had been stolen. I couldn't even keep my temporary job.

I finally made the hardest call of my life. I called my brother and asked for help. He had found a faith-based treatment program, so I headed there. It took them six months to get the drug culture out of me and six more months to pour recovery into me, because I was always in trouble for gossiping, manipulating, lying. Once I left there, I lived in a clean and sober house for almost two years. I had to start over. I was no longer able to be a schoolteacher. I had no other job skills, and I had to go to a job interview and tell them that I was in recovery. My first job was as a dishwasher at a school. I was in charge of the pots and pans, and I called myself a panhandler. Then I taught in their after-school day care for three years, and then I became the school librarian. During these five years, I was faithful, I was clean and sober, I did my program, I worked my Steps, and I was rewarded. I had to be willing to become humble every day, just taking those little tiny steps.

When I finally was broken, it was like breaking a horse. When you finally get a horse broken, you can start training it. I was so prideful. I was thinking that I had it made in the shade and I could do this. I could get sober my way. I finally said, "I can't do this." I finally humbled myself and said, "I need help, and I will submit to someone else's authority. I will do what my sponsor says. I will do what the program requires of me." Humility causes us to be teachable.

My brother let me have some of my dad's money to go back to school, and I now work as a CD counselor in a women's treatment program. For the first time in my life, I have passion for my job. I have become what God created me to be. I have regained my principles, and I have reconnected to my Higher Power, which is God.

One of the most thrilling things I've done is recovery to go on a climb up Mount Rainier with other women in recovery. We did the climb to raise money so people who couldn't afford treatment could go to treatment, and we wanted to eliminate the stigma of addiction for women.

I had been diagnosed with degenerative disc disease in my neck and my lower back. When they started talking about the climb in the recovery program where I work, I thought, *Well, I'm off the hook be-cause physically I can't do it*. But finally, I said, "Well, you know, I'm going to train for it, and then we'll see how I do." I loved the idea of equating the mountain climbing to the climb out of addiction, because after thirty-one years as a drug addict, I had a long, long climb out of my addiction. So I thought, *I'll just train like it's a one-day-at-a-time thing*.

We had meetings once a month to make sure we knew what we needed to bring on the climb, what we'd carry, and to get all our equip-ment. We had to listen to the person who was going to train us. He said, "I want you to do these exercises." At that time, I was fifty-nine, and though I had been exercising through running, I had to increase my strength. So I started working out at a gym three days a week. I had to build my muscles. I had to increase my stamina, my endurance. I worked out three days a week at the gym, I ran two days, and then I climbed hills around where I lived. I would put my pack on, and the first time I would carry ten pounds, and then the next two weeks I'd carry fifteen pounds, and I got up to forty pounds.

In terms of the climb itself, my goal wasn't to get to the top. My goal was to enjoy the journey. Just like in recovery. We started our climb at eight o'clock in the morning. We started walking, and our one guide got sick and couldn't go. Because of that, we knew that none of us were going to be able to summit, which was very disappointing, but my goal was to get to Camp Muir, which is 10,030 feet, and that was *my* sum-mit. We started hiking, and we had a mountain rescue gal who was in recovery who was our leader at that point.

It took me seven hours to get to Camp Muir. At times I would look up ahead of myself and I'd think, *Oh, my gosh, that's going to be a top right there and then it's going to level out*. And I would get to that top, and it wouldn't level out. I learned that I had to just do one step at a time. I could not continue to look ahead.

I also had to listen, to commit to the people in authority, and follow what they said: "This is the time you have this kind of snack." "This is the time that everyone has to drink water." "This is the time you put on this pair of pants." "This is the time you put on this jacket to avoid hypothermia." I learned you had to stay with the group; you couldn't get ahead. And if you're not feeling good, the first thing you do is to tell somebody: "I'm having stomach cramps." "I'm having a light head." You have to communicate at all times how you're feeling. Because if you don't do that, you could go down at any time. If you feel like you need rest, the whole group will stop and rest. We're a team here, and we're going to get there as a team. There's no race to get to the top. It's basically just doing it one step at a time. One day at a time. One step at a time.

They had told us that you get into a rhythm when you walk. But I kept stopping and resting and stopping and resting, and then I was more tired. It was just like in my relapse—I'd start recovery, I'd stop recovery, I'd start recovery, I'd stop recovery. If I slowed my pace down and got into a rhythm, I could keep my endurance up and keep my stamina up and keep making progress. But if I stopped, I would almost feel like I was going back. I had to remember it's progress, not perfection. And it's not a race to get there. It's the fact that I was taking it a little bit at a time.

There were times when I thought, *I cannot do this.* And I got so much encouragement from my team members. "You can do this, Julia. You can do this." It's the same when you get into a meeting and you're suffering, you're crying, and people say, "You can do this." I really could not have made it up to the top without those women saying, "You can do this." The last two hours, the person with me and the person behind me, they sang with me all the way up there to the top.

If I had had any knowledge of how hard it was going to be before I did it, I probably never would have done it. I was totally ignorant that this was a 50 percent or 40 percent grade all the way up. This was no hike around the park. This was hiking in twenty-pound snow boots. I think it was the greatest physical accomplishment of my life that I actually made it.

Once I got there, I felt like I was just delirious. It was the greatest feeling in my life that I accomplished a goal that I never thought I could do. I was the oldest one and I was the weakest link, but I actually persevered to the top because I had perseverance in my training, and I persevered in listening to people, and I persevered in my eating habits. Even though it took me an hour longer than anyone else, they waited, and I made it.

What recovery does is it opens up all these new options in your life. I couldn't climb out of my addiction, and yet now I climbed a mountain that is probably the toughest climb in the lower forty-eight states. It was a matter of being disciplined, and discipline is just being submissive in what people tell you to do. Just like in recovery. I wouldn't be having ten years of recovery on July 4 if I hadn't been willing to take a chance and say, "I can do this," and then listen to the people who knew more than I did and do what they said. The little engine that could.

CHAPTER 12

Living the Promises

 I no longer want to use or drink. God took that compulsion from me. That's one of the things that we get promised from the Big Book, and I don't know when he took that compulsion, but I no longer have it.

:: DENISE

RECOVERY LITERATURE, INCLUDING THIS BOOK, IS FILLED with promises—promises about how much better our life will be and how much better we will feel as we make progress in recovery. They speak not only of freedom from compulsion to use the chemicals that have nearly destroyed us, but also of the ability to live life joyfully and confidently, to have satisfying relationships, and much more. The promises in recovery are real. They're evident over and over in the stories of the women in this book as well as in other recovery literature and in the stories of untold numbers of women in recovery. What's most important is that they're available for every woman in recovery.

Promises of Radical Change

The most fundamental promise is on the title page of the Big Book: "The Story of How Many Thousands of Men and Women Have

Recovered from Alcoholism." *Recovered from alcoholism.* What a promise!

Beyond this basic promise, the best-known promises are listed in the Big Book beginning on the bottom of page 83. In the recovery community, these are often referred to as "the promises." They are worth reading over and over when we first enter recovery to inspire us and then later to keep us going and to remind us of what we have received through our diligent practice of the dailies. The promises of recovery are all about radical change. We turn into totally different people than we were when we were using. Sometimes the change is so radical, it's like one animal turning into a completely different one. Guinea pigs to giraffes, moose to panda bears, sheep to tigers, skunks to rabbits. Total change. Radical change! That's a promise!

While the promises in recovery literature are about changes inside ourselves, many of us experience outside benefits as well. We reap positive rewards due to the diligence in our personal affairs, which goes hand in hand with these inner changes. Some of the changes we experience and hear about from other women in recovery can seem almost miraculous. We see job promotions, career changes, reunions of moms with their children, renewal of trust within families and friendships, and many other inspiring results. As we change, the circumstances of our lives change.

> CD *I was promised, if I hung in there, that my children would come home. I was promised, if I hung in there, I would get another twenty-four hours. I was promised that if I hung in there, I was going to get a job and I would have a roof over my head, and I would be able to be self-sufficient. That's a big one for me, because I had a welfare mom, so I became a welfare mom. I was promised that I would be able to further my education. I start school in a few weeks. So a lot of promises were given to*

me, and I'm getting them. And they're not over, because my blessings are steadily coming.

:: GLORIA

While the program literature makes no promises or guarantees of these types of external changes in recovery, we are promised that *we* will change, that "our whole attitude and outlook upon life will change" (the Big Book, p. 84). And that changes everything.

❧ *The top of the climb was more than 10,000 feet. When my chiropractor and my doctor and my trainer all said, "Julia, we can get you to base camp," that was huge for me. I accomplished my goal. Even at fifty-nine years old, I could do that. We did it as a team. We got to say that in recovery any dream or goal is possible. I knew that if I even made it halfway up there, it was going to be an amazing experience.*

:: JULIA

Hear the Flutter?

❧ *If you trust enough—if you trust yourself, trust AA, trust the process—you can become very comfortable in your own skin.*

:: JOANNE

For many of us, recovery ultimately comes down to living a life "beyond our wildest dreams." Just like the butterfly, we start out alone in our cocoon of addiction (for us that's the bottle or our drugs). From our cocoon, we look up and see butterflies (women in recovery) and think we'll never be like that. We watch the butterflies fly, we listen for the flutter of their wings. We start to develop hope that if they can become beautiful butterflies, possibly we can too. As we gain hope, we go through the gooey process of coming out of our cocoons. At times it's messy. Other times, the light from the real world and the sky seems too much, and we want to retreat back into our cocoon. Gradually, we break out. We slowly unfurl our wings. Others teach us how and where to fly. At times, we fly on our own to places not yet explored. At other times, we stay around comfortable territory—our own gardens. Sometimes, the storms come, and we get wet or blown off course, but we dry off and get back on course. We learn from other butterflies what they do during the storms and follow their lead. We remember that there's a Power greater than ourselves, a master butterfly, if you will. Eventually, we're able to listen to the flutter of our own wings. We start to trust ourselves. Others start to trust us. We become the hope for others as they look up to us from their cocoons of addiction. We teach others how to fly. And the cycle of freedom continues.

How free do you want to be?
Can you hear the flutter?

Index

About the Author

BRENDA ILIFF, M.A., is a clinician, author, administrator, lecturer, and writer in the field of addiction. She is a licensed alcohol and drug counselor and has been involved in the addiction field for more than twenty years. She is currently the clinical director of the Women's Recovery Center at Hazelden Foundation in Center City, Minnesota.

HAZELDEN FOUNDATION, A NATIONAL NONPROFIT organization founded in 1949, helps people reclaim their lives from the disease of addiction. Built on decades of knowledge and experience, Hazelden offers a comprehensive approach to addiction that addresses the full range of patient, family, and professional needs, including addiction treatment and continuing care for youth and adults, research, higher learning, public education and advocacy, and publishing.

A life of recovery is lived "one day at a time." Hazelden publications, both educational and inspirational, support and strengthen lifelong recovery. In 1954, Hazelden published *Twenty-Four Hours a Day*, the first daily meditation book for recovering alcoholics, and Hazelden continues to publish works to inspire and guide individuals in treatment and recovery, and their loved ones. Professionals who work to prevent and treat addiction also turn to Hazelden for evidence-based curricula, informational materials, and videos for use in schools, treatment programs, and correctional programs.

Through published works, Hazelden extends the reach of hope, encouragement, help, and support to individuals, families, and communities affected by addiction and related issues.

For questions about Hazelden publications, please call **800-328-9000** or visit us online at **hazelden.org/bookstore**.

Other titles that may interest you:

A Place Called Self
Women, Sobriety, and Radical Transformation
Stephanie Brown, Ph.D.

With personal stories and gentle guidance, Brown points the way to true selfhood for recovering women. Softcover, 208 pp.
Order No. 2145

Each Day a New Beginning
Daily Meditations for Women
Karen Casey

This best-selling classic offers warm and wise counsel for women who are recovering—or simply pursuing personal growth. Softcover, 400 pp.
Order No. 1076

The Little Red Book for Women
annotated by Karen Casey

The definitive study guide to *Alcoholics Anonymous,* the classic *Little Red Book* is illuminated here for women readers. Hardcover, 156 pp.
Order No. 2311

A Woman's Way through the Twelve Steps
Stephanie S. Covington, Ph.D.

This guidebook has helped countless women make their own paths through the traditional, male-oriented Steps. A companion workbook is also available. Softcover, 264 pp.
Order No. 5019

Hazelden books are available at fine bookstores everywhere. To order directly from Hazelden, call 800-328-9000 or visit hazelden .org/bookstore.